REACHING A LOST WORLD

Cults and World Religions

VINNIE CARAFANO
with KIMBERLY ARNOLD

YWAM PUBLISHING

Seattle, Washington

YWAM Publishing is the publishing ministry of Youth With A Mission. Youth With A Mission (YWAM) is an international missionary organization of Christians from many denominations dedicated to presenting Jesus Christ to this generation. To this end, YWAM has focused its efforts in three main areas: (1) training and equipping believers for their part in fulfilling the Great Commission (Matthew 28:19), (2) personal evangelism, and (3) mercy ministry (medical and relief work).

For a free catalog of books and materials, call (425) 771-1153 or (800) 922-2143. Visit us online at www.ywampublishing.com.

Reaching a Lost World: Cults and World Religions
Copyright © 2010 by Vinnie Carafano
King's Kids El Paso, 936 W Sunset Rd., El Paso, TX 79922-2149
www.kkep.org

Published by YWAM Publishing
a ministry of Youth With A Mission
P.O. Box 55787, Seattle, WA 98155

15 14 13 12 11 10   1 2 3 4 5

ISBN 978-1-57658-499-6

Library of Congress Cataloging-in-Publication Data

Carafano, Vinnie.
    Reaching a lost world : cults and world religions / Vinnie Carafano with Kimberly Arnold.
        p. cm.
    Includes bibliographical references and index.
    ISBN 978-1-57658-499-6 (alk. paper)
    1. Christianity and other religions. 2. Religions. 3. Sects. I. Arnold, Kimberly. II. Title.
    BR127.C255 2009
    261.2—dc22   2009004606

Unless otherwise indicated, the Scripture quotations in this publication are from the New King James Version. Copyright © 1979, 1980, 1982, Thomas Nelson, Inc.

Names and details in the True Story boxes have been changed to protect privacy.

Printed in the United States of America

INTENSIVE DISCIPLESHIP COURSE

Developing Godly Character

Being Useful to God Now

Reaching a Lost World: Cults and World Religions

To the men and women of God who have invested so much in my life: missionaries Charles and Gloria Johnson, who took us to Mexico each Saturday and taught us to take the gospel to the poor, and pastors Fred Walker, Dale Walker, George "Buster" Russell, Ron Acton, and Warren Hoyt

"For a dream comes through much activity."
—Ecclesiastes 5:3

CONTENTS

Foreword

God has repeatedly called on teenagers throughout history to provide righteous, courageous leadership that has saved the people from destruction. The Intensive Discipleship Course materials provide a biblically based means to effectively equip the Davids and Esthers of our time, reinforcing their capacity to overcome today's giants and extend the kingdom of God throughout their communities and nations.

I deeply appreciate the diligence, wisdom, and sensitivity with which Vinnie and Jodie Carafano have faithfully invested in many young people for the past twenty-seven years in the context of local churches, mission outreaches, and communities at large. One of the main reasons for the Carafanos' effectiveness has been the strong biblical foundations they have been instrumental in nurturing within young lives. This, together with their understanding of how to help young people develop life disciplines that integrate these dynamic truths into all of life, provides an experience-rich backdrop, making the Intensive Discipleship Course series a particularly valuable training resource for any Christian youth worker, teacher, pastor, or parent.

May those who use these materials discover time-tested keys to unlocking the God-intended potential of their youth.

Dale Kauffman
Founder and President, King's Kids International

Preface

This book is the result of my thirty-two years of walking with the Lord, studying His Word, being fascinated by the differences between true and false doctrines, and observing a lost world. It is backed up by thousands of pages in stacks of books, countless hours of Internet research, and prayer to understand it all. Add to that firsthand observation of false religions in fifteen years of missionary work with Youth With A Mission (YWAM), plus many hours of interviews with pastors and missionaries in countries dominated by these religions, and you hold in your hands the result.

Discussing your faith with people from cults and other religions can be difficult, especially if you suggest their beliefs are wrong or cast their religious founders in a negative light. They may claim the facts in this book are wrong, the citations are incorrect, and the perspective is slanted and unfair. They may show you materials prepared from their own sources that deny or refute these points. Such materials may focus on small details that are in dispute, such as disagreements between translations of texts, events that took place hundreds of years ago, and quotations of leaders. However, fine points of dates and minutiae are less significant than the weight of evidence presented here.

In this work I have sought to be clear and objective. I have no motivation to write inflammatory rhetoric to insult people's cherished beliefs. My motivations are twofold: to help Christians reach people caught in the snare of false doctrines and to keep Christians from becoming victims of deception.

May the Lord Jesus Christ be honored by the billions of lost people for whom He came to give His life.

Vinnie Carafano

What Is the Intensive Discipleship Course?

How the Course Began

From 1980 to 1994 I was the youth pastor in a large nondenominational church. In 1986 I realized that it was impossible to give one message at our high-school and college-age group that would meet the needs of all the different kinds of people who came. We had totally devoted, radically sold-out, on-fire, holy, dynamic, soul-winning kids, but we also had unsaved, doing-drugs, criminal-record, topless-dancer, drive-by-shooting-gang-member, Satan-worshiping, lost kids. Then there were those kids in the middle. How in the world

could I present a message from the Word that could affect everyone there?

Most youth groups face the same dilemma. I developed this course to meet the needs of Christian students in high school and college who have a desire to grow in their relationship with the Lord and who need more in-depth discipling than we could do at youth group meetings. The foundational or evangelistic messages the rest of the group needed just weren't enough to challenge them. Since the first year we offered the Intensive Discipleship Course (referred to from here on as IDC), we saw a huge increase in the number of students who developed into leaders of their peers and became bold and dynamic examples of what a Christian student should be. Our goal is to produce disciples who are equipped with the power of God to fulfill His purposes throughout the world.

Who Should Do IDC?

Everybody who is hungry to know God more is invited to do IDC. Although the course is designed for young people age fifteen through college age, even adults (including pastors and youth leaders) who have taken the course say it has done a lot for their walk with the Lord. Setting aside time to focus on spiritual growth will benefit anyone who will stick to it.

How It Works

Learning God's Truth

IDC will increase your understanding of Scripture as you compare what God says in the Bible to other belief systems and worldviews. Sometimes slight deviations from truth can lead in dramatically different directions, so we must learn to read and study carefully to get the meaning of key doctrines. You'll find your Bible knowledge is stretched over the next twelve weeks as you study truth and error.

Be diligent to present yourself approved to God, a worker who does not need to be ashamed, rightly dividing the word of truth. (2 Timothy 2:15)

All Scripture is given by inspiration of God, and is profitable for doctrine, for reproof, for correction, for instruction in righteousness, that the man of God may be complete, thoroughly equipped for every good work. (2 Timothy 3:16–17)

The Need for a Mentor

The dictionary defines a mentor as a wise and trusted person. One of the major components of IDC is spending time with an older and more spiritually mature person who can help you grow in the Lord. In choosing your mentor, look for someone who has a relationship with the Lord that you admire, a person you could confide in, someone easy to get along with and not too busy to spend an hour or so with you each week. This could be one of your parents or a grandparent, your pastor or youth leader, or someone else in your church whom you respect. If you are a teenager, ask your parents whom they would suggest and don't choose a mentor they do not approve of. (Some parents may not be believers and may not support your spiritual growth. In this case, it's fine to choose a mentor with the help of church leadership.) We urge you not to try to do IDC by yourself—the accountability to another person will help you stick to the course and process the work the Holy Spirit is doing in your life. Guys need to choose a man, and girls should choose a woman if at all possible, but your parents may approve of someone of the opposite sex. All of us—even adults—need mentors. If you are an adult or a college student, obviously you don't need parental permission in choosing a mentor, but it's wise to choose prayerfully.

When you've found someone you would like to ask to be your mentor, make an appointment to see him or her and show the person your IDC book. Have the potential mentor read the section of this book called "Mentoring an Intensive Discipleship Course Student." You may want to leave the book with the potential mentor for a couple of days so that he or she really understands what IDC is. Make sure the mentor understands the commitment he or she is making to you and has the time to follow through with it. This is especially important with busy church staff members. If the person agrees, fill out the Course Commitment form on pages 23–24, sign it, and have your parents (if you are a teenager) and your mentor sign it.

Each week when you meet with your mentor, you'll show him or her the study you have done and talk about what you are learning. Make a commitment to be open and vulnerable about personal situations in your life. Since your mentor is a wise and trusted person, be honest about the victories and the needs in your life. If something comes up partway through IDC and your mentor can't follow through on his or her commitment, you can still complete the course and learn a lot from it. Don't give up!

COURSE REQUIREMENTS

Weekly teachings. During the twelve-week course, you'll complete one study each week. Don't wait until the last minute, but do a little each day and let the teaching sink in. Each of the twelve teachings focuses on the background knowledge you need to understand the major cults and world religions. The margins next to the teachings will allow you to write down thoughts and questions and anything the Lord shows you during your times of study.

Whenever you see Scripture references throughout the text (in weeks 1–4), look them up and write them *in your own words* on the lines provided. This will cause you to think through what each verse means and not simply copy a verse that you might not understand.

At the end of each teaching on a world religion or cult (weeks 5–7 and 9–11), you will see a Scripture Study section, where you will read through beliefs of the world religion or cult and write out Bible passages that counter those doctrines.

Daily Bible reading. In this third book of the IDC, you will continue reading the Old Testament where the second book, *Being Useful to God Now*, left off. (*Being Useful to God Now* ended after 1 Samuel 15, and this book begins at 2 Samuel 1. If you did *Being Useful to God Now* but didn't finish 1 Samuel 16–31 after the course ended, try to finish those chapters before you start 2 Samuel.) If you are doing this book without having completed the previous two books, we recommend that you do not use this schedule but begin reading three to four chapters of the New Testament daily. (An alternate Bible Reading Plan is provided for this on page 162).

If you read the Bible for about fifteen minutes each day, you can finish it in one year. Just keep at it. If you miss a day or get behind, try to catch up. Check off each day after you have read the chapters, and start where you left off the next day. Be sure to read a translation of the Bible that you can understand. The New King James Version and the New International Version are highly recommended. Each week you can mark passages that you find confusing and ask questions at the next meeting with your mentor.

If you have been reading somewhere else in the Old Testament or in the New Testament when the course begins, we suggest you put that study on hold for the duration of the course.

Scripture memory. Each week you'll memorize two verses or brief Bible passages. You don't have to get every word exactly. Have a clear grasp of the verse and memorize it as closely as you can. We suggest that you write out the verses on a piece of paper or 3 x 5 card and carry it with you. Read the verses throughout the week. It's not hard to memorize Scripture with enough repetition, but don't just memorize it as a parrot would, getting all the words right but having no idea what it means.

Prayer and fasting. Just as Jesus' disciples asked Him to teach them to pray, we need to learn to have an effective prayer life. The fifteen-minutes-per-morning requirement shown on the course commitment form is only about one percent of our daily lives, and yet many Christians don't spend that much time each day giving God their undivided attention. Once you begin at this level, it won't be long before you're thinking of more things to pray about and spending more time each day with the Lord.

Fasting builds spiritual discipline. You may have never fasted before except between meals, and then only if it was absolutely necessary. Believe it or not, you can actually survive for a day without food. Just look at the people in the Bible who fasted for forty days. Each month you'll pick a day to fast when your schedule isn't packed. Be sure to drink lots of liquids. You'll find that if you start feeling weak and hungry, your strength will come back if you'll pray. I always fast before important spiritual events, such as a youth camp or missions trip, and whenever I'm really burdened with a personal need or a problem in the life of someone I care about. God comes through when we seek Him with our whole heart. Your mentor will be able to explain more about fasting.

Caution: Not everyone should participate in fasting. People who have health conditions or are taking medication should consult their physician about whether they should fast. All teenage students should discuss fasting with a parent and make sure that that parent is aware of the days of a fast.

Evaluations. On the first day of the course you will evaluate your knowledge of cults and world religions by filling out the questionnaire on page

26. On the last day of the course you will fill out the questionnaire on page 159, evaluating each area you studied to discover what you learned. You will then be able to compare the two questionnaires so that you can chart your growth.

Mission report. Using *Operation World* by Patrick Johnstone and Jason Mandryk or another Christian missions resource, you will fill out the Mission Report page (during week 4) on a nation that interests you. Pray for the nation regularly, and don't be surprised if concern for its people grows in your heart to the extent that the Lord calls you to go there to serve Him. This is exactly what happened to me with the nation of India. Beginning in Bible school in the early 1980s, I prayed for India as part of a class assignment, and I've ended up there three times so far, with plans to return.

Book reports. During IDC you'll be reading two nonfiction books from the following list. You can read other books if you like, but these are some of the best. It's easy for people to let their minds wander during a teaching, but a good story keeps everyone's attention. Lots of students who hate reading have told me that they can't put these books down, and many parents have read the books because their students in IDC had said that the books were so powerful.

- Corrie ten Boom, *The Hiding Place*
- Elisabeth Elliot, *Through Gates of Splendor*
- Loren Cunningham, *Is That Really You, God?*
- Brother Andrew, *God's Smuggler*
- Bruce Olson, *Bruchko*
- Don Richardson, *Lords of the Earth*
- Don Richardson, *Peace Child*
- Sister Gulshan Esther, *The Torn Veil*
- Jackie Pullinger, *Chasing the Dragon*

The book report forms are included in the appropriate places in the twelve-week course. (Book one should be read by week 5, and book two should be read by week 9.) The book report is a time to tell what you learned through reading the book and how it affected your relationship with the Lord. The ways God has used the people in the books will amaze you and will challenge you to step out in faith for God to use you as well.

You can order these books through any Christian bookstore. To save money, you may want to see if you can borrow them from your pastor or the church library. After reading them you'll agree they are so inspiring that you'll want to have your own copies. You will find a list of useful books on cults and world religions at the end of the course. I encourage you to continue reading great Christian books.

You'll notice that most of the books listed above are missionary stories. Every Christian needs to know about missions. Even if you know that God has not called you to go to another country to preach the gospel, He has called you to participate in the Great Commission that Jesus gave to all Christians (Matthew 28:18–20). If you're interested in missions or have heard God's call to the mission field, be sure to read the fascinating book *Operation World* by Patrick Johnstone and Jason Mandryk. The book covers every country in the world and tells what God is doing there. Spend a little time looking through it and read about countries that interest you—places you'd like to go, the country your ancestors came from, or places you've gone on vacation. Then think about the needs there: What if you lived in China, where Christians are still martyred, or Mozambique, where the annual income is $140? Or Afghanistan, where there are 48,000 Muslim mosques but not one single Christian church? Take time to ask God to bring His kingdom to the ends of the earth.

TV and movie reports. Another goal in IDC is for you to examine your TV and movie viewing habits and find out what the Lord thinks about the things you watch. We don't believe that all TV and movies are evil or that it is a sin to watch movies and TV in general. The course commitment doesn't require students to avoid all TV or movies; it only asks students to write a brief report about what they do watch. Just the fact that you are accountable to your mentor and that you'll be writing reports might keep you from watching things you already know in your heart the Lord would not approve of. We want you to grow in discernment and not take for granted areas of your life that the Lord may want to change. Many Christians never stop to seek God's will in the areas of entertainment and recreation. You can watch anything you like, but if you do seek God's will about what you watch, you will be viewing it from the Lord's perspective. Then you will let *Him* decide whether it is something you should be spending your time and devotion on. (Please read "Changing Your Viewing Habits" beginning on page 14 for further discussion of this course requirement.)

Additional course requirements. In addition to completing the previous course requirements, you are encouraged to (1) attend church weekly, including Sunday morning services and any youth/college group, (2) spend at least fifteen minutes in prayer every morning, (3) tithe (give 10 percent of all your income to God's work), and (4) surrender to the lordship of Christ, which means being obedient to Him and not holding back any part of your life from Him.

Course evaluation. Please write us using the course evaluation form at the back of the book and tell us what you thought about IDC. Your opinions will help us improve future editions of the course. We also really want to hear how the Lord used IDC in your life.

Course duration. IDC is designed to be used for twelve consecutive weeks. A September–December or January–April session is best, as straddling the Christmas holidays might cause you to lose momentum.

Don't skip the prerequisite! The book you are holding is the third in the series. The first IDC volume, *Developing Godly Character,* deals with basic issues of personal discipleship and lays the foundation for the second volume, *Being Useful to God Now,* which teaches how to be the kind of person God can work through. Unless you have allowed the dealings of God in your life that come as a result of IDC 1, you will not be spiritually prepared for IDC 2 or 3. For example, there is no use trying to teach people how to witness for the Lord unless they have made a decision to yield their lives fully to the lordship of Jesus. They might listen politely to the teaching, but they won't take action, because being known as a Christian could be detrimental to their social life and popularity with peers. The decision to die to self is part of the foundation that will make ministry training effective and cause you to care about this lost world rather than just study about it in a purely academic sense. If you really are prepared to study world religions and cults, then by all mean, dive in!

THE CONTENT OF THIS VOLUME

Reaching a Lost World begins with four weeks of introductory teaching on true and false doctrines and sharing the gospel with members of world religions and cults. Weeks 5–7 are devoted to world religions, and weeks 9–11 are devoted to cults. During these weeks you will learn the major beliefs of each religion or cult along with current information and statistics about the religion or cult as it exists today.

The end of the teachings on world religions and cults contains a Scripture Study section that lists beliefs of the religion or cult in the left-hand column and provides blank lines for you to write on in the right-hand column. Here's where you will find out how much you know about your own faith. Read the beliefs in the left-hand column carefully. What do they say that's true? What is almost true? What is completely wrong? Then write scriptures in the right-hand column to agree with truth the members of the religion or cult believe or to correct their errors. Don't feel bad if you can't find enough biblical support

to answer their doctrines. When you meet with your mentor (or your class), you'll find out what verses others have found and you can fill in what you lack. This weekly assignment will allow you to gauge how well-equipped you are to be useful to God in evangelism and help strengthen your ability to communicate truth. A second goal of the assignment is to teach you to read and think carefully and critically. It's too easy to allow others to do your thinking for you or to accept whatever others say is true. If you learn to go to God's Word to find out the truth, you can stay out of error and lead others to the Lord.

During weeks 8 and 12 you will have an opportunity to practice using your knowledge in a role-playing scenario. Write out answers to the three questions to prepare for the conversation and then act out the scenarios with your mentor or group during your meeting.

This course can be used with supplemental reading. The best books for the purposes of this course are *The Compact Guide to World Religions* by Dean Halverson and *Truth and Error* by Alan Gomes.

CHANGING YOUR VIEWING HABITS

Do your viewing habits need to change? Maybe. If you recognize that sitting in front of a screen and passively absorbing endless hours of the world's values is having a negative effect on your relationship with the Lord, it's time for you to reevaluate your habits. When we click through the TV channels or go to the video rental store, we may not find anything that really appeals to us, but we've already planned to set aside time to watch something. We end up watching the least objectionable thing we can find, not necessarily something good. In this way, we squander a great deal of time. Have you ever finished watching a movie and then thought, *That was a total waste of two hours!* In the same way, the addictive nature of playing video games and surfing the Internet makes these activities an incredible time drain.

IDC might help you realize that you've been spending twenty to thirty hours (the U.S. average) in front of a TV or computer or at the theater each week, but you have "never had enough time" to read the Bible. Think of all the other things in addition to reading the Bible that you could do with the extra time:

- Reach out to someone who needs a friend
- Improve your grades
- Exercise
- Invest your life in discipling others
- Read a good book
- Learn the Bible
- Start a hobby
- Play sports
- Pray
- Help your mom or dad if you live at home
- Get more involved in church

Here are some helpful questions to evaluate TV shows, movies, video games, and Internet browsing:

1. Do you have aftereffects from things you have watched in the past that stir up temptations to sin? We've all had experiences of some recurring thought from the media: a gross or disgusting scene, a fear-producing image, a sensual or explicit picture. Different things will make different people stumble, depending on the weak areas in each person's life. The Lord already knows whether the movie that you'd like to see has elements that will tempt you to sin. Will you ask Him in advance if He wants you to see it? More important, will you obey what He tells you?

2. Have you ever regretted seeing a movie because of these effects? If so, will you ask God to help you stay away from anything that you'll regret later?

3. When we disobey the Lord, we disappoint Him. If God doesn't approve of your seeing a particular movie or TV show, how much of your fellowship and intimacy with God are you going to lose if you do so anyway? If you're ministering to others, how much of the anointing of God will you give up in exchange for that movie? Of course, we know that God will forgive us if we repent later, but aren't we abusing the grace of God to sin with the plan of asking forgiveness afterward?

4. God intends for us to remain in constant fellowship with Him. Will that movie or TV program cause you to live in a world without God for an hour or two?

5. Does the program ridicule God, people who believe in Him, the authority of parents, and the holiness of sex in marriage? Does it slowly whittle away the foundations of what you believe? Situation comedies are especially guilty of this. They make us take lightly the things God takes seriously. We laugh at evil, and it doesn't seem so evil anymore. Does the movie lie to you about the way God made the universe? Does it deny the law of reaping what we sow or the fact that this life is temporary and eternity never ends?

Fools mock at sin. (Proverbs 14:9)

Neither filthiness, nor foolish talking, nor coarse jesting, which are not fitting, but rather giving of thanks. (Ephesians 5:4)

6. Are we hiding behind the deception that since we are so strong in the Lord, the things that cause others to stumble won't affect us? There are some things that God simply doesn't want us to see or hear.

I will behave wisely in a perfect way. Oh, when will You come to me? I will walk within my house with a perfect heart. I will set nothing wicked before my eyes; I hate the work of those who fall away; it shall not cling to me. A perverse heart shall depart from me; I will not know wickedness. (Psalm 101:2–4)

Turn away my eyes from looking at worthless things, and revive me in Your way.
(Psalm 119:37)

These things that God wants us to avoid include the following:

- Horror movies that glorify evil, exalt the kingdom of darkness, and make God seem either powerless or completely absent. Horror movies are a fantasy about the world the way Satan would like it to be if it weren't for the restraining hand of God.
- Sensual and suggestive comments that create mental images of sexual sin.
- Explicit or implied sexual scenes, which filmmakers design to cause us to identify with one of the people involved. God didn't make beautiful girls or handsome guys for us to lust over. He designed sex to be a private act between a husband and wife. Viewing sexuality on screen is wrong.

7. How's the language? We know that God's name deserves respect. Is the language crude, offensive, disgusting? What does the Lord think about it? Hearing a lot of profanity makes it much easier for those words to come to mind when we stub our toe, drop something that breaks, or become frustrated. Are you conditioning your mind to react with impatience and anger rather than look to the Lord when things don't go smoothly?

8. The Bible contains lots of violence, but the media have a way of lingering on the gruesome results of violence rather than simply telling the story. Are you watching sensationalized, gory violence? Does it cheapen the value of human life in your eyes? Does it train your mind to think that violence is an appropriate response to others?

9. Will you be courageous enough to be the one among your Christian friends who says no to certain movies, who gets up and walks out of the theater, who insists on changing the channel?

This may be costly in terms of your immediate reputation, but it will gain you respect as one who takes following the Lord seriously and will bring conviction to those who aren't listening to their consciences. You see, the Holy Spirit is trying to bring to them the same sense of His disapproval over an ungodly movie or game.

"You shall not follow a crowd to do evil."
(Exodus 23:2)

The sinners in Zion are afraid; fearfulness has seized the hypocrites: "Who among us shall dwell with the devouring fire? Who among us shall dwell with everlasting burnings?" He who walks righteously and speaks uprightly…who stops his ears from hearing of bloodshed, and shuts his eyes from seeing evil: he will dwell on high; his place of defense will be the fortress of rocks; bread will be given him, his water will be sure. Your eyes will see the King in His beauty; they will see the land that is very far off. (Isaiah 33:14–17)

NOTE TO PARENTS ABOUT THE COURSE

may or may not choose to ask their parents to be their mentor. Don't feel rejected if your children ask someone else. This is a natural part of the maturing process for a student. Parents can still be involved through prayer and encouragement and by asking questions and reading the book-report books.

Important Note: Please be aware that one of the course commitments is for students to fast one day per month. Some people, because of health conditions or medication, should not participate in fasting. Please discuss fasting with your son or daughter and know specifically when he or she goes on a fast. If you have any questions or concerns about the appropriateness of fasting for your son or daughter, please contact your physician.

IDC is a proven method of spiritual growth. Previous versions of this course have gone across America and to every continent. The course is demanding, but it follows the necessary steps for producing strong disciples. We feel that the church needs to challenge today's youth. The requirements of the course will stretch young people spiritually and teach them responsibility, faithfulness, and ways to set and achieve goals.

We urge parents to be involved in IDC with their sons and daughters. One course requirement is for students to choose a mentor, and students

Mentoring

MENTORING AN INTENSIVE DISCIPLESHIP COURSE STUDENT

It is an honor when a young person interested in taking the Intensive Discipleship Course (IDC) chooses you to be his or her mentor. It shows that the person has a great deal of respect for you and sees in you a relationship with the Lord that is worthy of imitation. This intensive, twelve-week course focuses on the personal discipleship that takes place between a student and a mentor. IDC contains a solidly evangelical perspective and focuses on the Lord Jesus Christ and young people's relationship with Him.

IDC is a demanding course, but Christian young people need a radical challenge. Powerful results in the lives of hundreds of students over the past two decades show the value of this approach. Any young person who wants to play on a school sports team, perform in a band, or excel in any field must diligently apply effort to the endeavor. Unfortunately, in Christian circles all we usually ask of young people is consistent attendance at meetings. We, the creators of IDC, believe it is also necessary to call young people to diligence, faithfulness, self-discipline, and responsibility in their relationship with the Lord. We believe as well that young people will rise to the occasion if we encourage and support them.

We urge you to look through this material carefully and be sure that you have the time to fulfill the commitment you are making by agreeing to be a mentor. To disciple a young person in this way will undoubtedly take an effort on your part to free up time in your schedule, but the rewards will definitely be worth it.

YOUR ROLE AS A MENTOR

Your role as a mentor is different from that of a schoolteacher. You won't need to correct papers, read many reports, or give grades. Instead, your primary job will be to be available, to be open and honest with the student about your own walk with God, and to help him or her walk through a process of study and spiritual growth. You'll meet with your student each week for one to two hours.

Each week students work through a teaching designed to challenge their knowledge of Scripture and stimulate their walk with Jesus. They will be searching the Bible for truth to counter false doctrines. When you meet with your student, you will ask what he or she studied and discuss how the Lord is working in the student's life. Reading the student's answers to the false beliefs at the end of each chapter will help you see what the student has learned.

Each week your student will memorize two Scripture passages and will recite them to you. The student will also turn in two brief book reports during the course. Sometimes the student will have written TV or movie reports. You can briefly look at the student's Daily Bible Reading chart at the beginning of each teaching to make sure that the student is keeping up with the reading. Daily Bible reading should bring up questions that your student can write down on the chart and ask you to explain. Don't be afraid to say that you don't know the answer: Scripture contains plenty of passages that mystify all of us. You might suggest other Scriptures or recommend Christian books on a particular subject. You may want to present both sides of a controversial topic. Perhaps the best answer to a question you can't answer is, "Let's try to find out together."

Asking your student questions to stimulate his or her seeking the Lord to find the answer is preferable to handing out the answer. In discipling young people, we must be careful to avoid encouraging them to depend on us for answers. Our job as leaders is to be facilitators of learning rather than spiritual gurus. We don't have all the answers, and we must make this clear to the young people while pointing them to the One who does have all the answers. We are to let them find their own revelation from God's Word as we help them know the Holy Spirit as their teacher.

But the anointing which you have received from Him abides in you, and you do not need that anyone teach you; but as the same anointing teaches you concerning all things, and is true, and is not a lie, and just as it has taught you, you will abide in Him. (1 John 2:27)

"But the Helper, the Holy Spirit, whom the Father will send in My name, He will teach you all things, and bring to your remembrance all things that I said to you." (John 14:26)

You must be willing to help your student wrestle through difficulties and painful but necessary changes without allowing an unhealthy dependency on you. It is frequently the tendency of those with a shepherd's heart to try to make life easy for their flock, sometimes blunting the sharp edges of God's Word in the process. Yet you must allow the Lord to deal with your student and not abort the process of conviction in his or her life.

A mentor's message, though always spoken with compassion and love, must be "Here is truth—what are you and the Lord going to do about it?" Students will respond in one of three ways. One response is to feel miserable and condemned, which can lead some to hardening their hearts. We must steer them past this obstacle, giving hope that the grace of God will transform them. A second response is to try to improve, which results in legalism, performance orientation, and either spiritual pride or more condemnation. Again, we must steer students toward genuine heart change. A third response is the one we desire—lasting transformation by the work of the Holy Spirit.

You will not need to personally oversee some of the other parts of the student's commitment, such as tithing, church attendance, fasting, or daily prayer. The student is on the honor system for those aspects of the course.

THE PERSONAL TOUCH IN DISCIPLESHIP

Building a relationship in which your student feels comfortable in revealing personal thoughts, feelings, and needs is essential. Your interest and questions can draw the student into being open with you. Trust and confidentiality are part of the foundation for discipling a young person, who may entrust you with deep hurts, secrets, or confessions of sin. You'll need to use great care and wisdom to decide whether or not to disclose such matters and, if so, how to discuss them with the student's parents.

Don't be afraid to be honest with the young person you are discipling. If God could use only people who had everything worked out in their lives, I would certainly be disqualified, and probably you would be too. I've found that being vulnerable and open about my weaknesses allows students to feel confident in discussing their struggles. On the other hand, a leader who gives the appearance of having it all together can intimidate young people, causing them to fear being rejected, judged, or condemned if they confess sins or areas of weakness. Let's be careful to create an environment where openness and honesty prevail (Proverbs 28:13).

During the week, we urge you to pray for your student and listen for insights from the Lord to bring up the next time you meet with the student. Each week when you meet together, be sure to close in prayer to take before the Lord the specific needs of the student and the area of teaching the student is studying.

Either you or the student you are discipling may have an extra busy week or have to miss your meeting for another reason, such as vacation, illness, or final exams. As soon as possible, reschedule the meeting so that he or she doesn't lose momentum. If the student falls behind and hasn't completed the week's assignments by the day of your meeting, don't cancel the meeting. You can still talk and pray together. Encourage the student to catch up as soon as possible and follow up to see that the student does so. Many students need adult help in carrying through with their commitments.

We suggest a graduation ceremony or celebration of some kind for the student upon completion of the course. Include parents, family, and friends. Award a diploma to commend the student for the work done. This is a great way to recognize the student publicly when he or she has completed the course. Speak of the student's accomplishments in a way that will encourage others to take bold steps of spiritual growth. This can be a good witness to the church that some students are godly and dedicated to walking with the Lord. It may also be convicting for some of the church members, including other young people.

The Goal of Discipleship: Looking Beyond IDC

The result of the process of discipleship should be that disciples become disciplers. The following scripture outlines three phases in this process:

For Ezra had prepared his heart TO SEEK the Law of the LORD, and TO DO it, and TO TEACH statutes and ordinances in Israel. (Ezra 7:10)

The first step is seeking and learning God's ways. Next comes living out what we have learned. Finally, we teach others His ways. The order here is crucial, and all three steps are necessary for discipleship to be complete. Some people try to live the Christian life without a genuine understanding of it and end up inventing their own versions of Christianity. Others try to teach what they haven't worked out in their own lives and sometimes bring reproach on the Lord and the church. Still others seek and do but never teach, and the chain of events from the patriarchs through the cross and the church finds a dead end in their lives: they never pass the gospel on to others. As leaders of young people, we need to aim their spiritual lives in such a way that the truth we pass on to them continues to affect the world for generations to come.

And the things that you have heard from me among many witnesses, commit these to faithful men who will be able to teach others also. (2 Timothy 2:2)

PASTORS AND YOUTH LEADERS WITH MULTIPLE STUDENTS

One option for a pastor or youth leader is to have several students take the course at the same time and meet for discipleship and mentoring in a small group. Be sure not to let this group become too large, or the personal nature of it will be lost. We recommend no more than five young people at a time in a small group. If you have many young people you would like to have take the course, either raise up other qualified small-group leaders or teach the course in a large group with smaller discussion groups. Follow the same course guidelines as for mentors with one student.

STUDENT PROGRESS CHART

Here is a chart to help you keep track of your student's progress through the course. Check the appropriate box when the student has completed each assignment.

Week	Scriptures Memorized	Daily Bible Reading	Teaching and Study Questions Completed	Assignments Due
1				Evaluation 1
2				
3				
4				Mission Report
5				Book Report 1
6				
7				
8				
9				Book Report 2
10				
11				
12				Evaluation 2 & Course Evaluation

Mentor's Course Evaluation

We value your input! When the student has completed the course, please take a few minutes to give us your suggestions and comments.

Name:

Address:

Phone: E-mail:

Name of student(s):   Age of student(s):

Dates of course:

1. Please rate the following on a scale of 1 to 10, with 10 as the best rating:

	1	2	3	4	5	6	7	8	9	10
Quality of content and presentation	1	2	3	4	5	6	7	8	9	10
Ease of use	1	2	3	4	5	6	7	8	9	10
Practical value of teachings	1	2	3	4	5	6	7	8	9	10
Effect of the course on the student	1	2	3	4	5	6	7	8	9	10
Format of the book	1	2	3	4	5	6	7	8	9	10

2. What were the strongest points of the course?

3. What were the weakest points?

4. What part of the course or experience was most encouraging?

5. What, if any, other topics would you like to have seen covered?

6. Other suggestions for improvement?

Thanks for your help!
Please photocopy and mail to
Vinnie Carafano, 936 W Sunset Rd., El Paso, TX 79922

COURSE COMMITMENT FORM

Carefully read and fill out this course commitment after discussing the course with your parents (if you are a teenager) and your mentor, and after receiving their approval to go ahead.

Name: Age:

Mentor's Name:

Please answer the following three questions on another sheet of paper:
1. How did you become a Christian, and how is your relationship with the Lord now?
2. Why do you want to participate in the Intensive Discipleship Course?
3. What are your goals in your relationship with Jesus?

You are about to enter a time of great spiritual growth. This statement of commitment will show your decision to the Lord, your parents, your mentor, and yourself that you have set aside the next three months to focus on seeking God, doing those things that will help you grow in Him, and being accountable to spiritual leadership.

I commit to do the following:
1. Complete all twelve sessions of the course.
2. Read a portion of the Old Testament.
3. Read two of the recommended books and write a one-page report on each book.
4. Attend church weekly—Sunday morning and youth/college group.
5. Memorize twenty-four assigned Scripture verses.
6. Fast one designated day each month.
7. Spend at least fifteen minutes in prayer every morning.
8. Tithe (give 10 percent of all my income to God's work).
9. Surrender to the lordship of Christ, which means being obedient to Him and not holding back any part of my life from Him.
10. Research and write a one-page missions report on the nation of my choice.

I will be accountable to do the following:
1. Keep up, or improve, the school grades I am earning now.
2. Put ungodly influences out of my life:
   - For the next twelve weeks I will listen only to Christian music.
   - For any movie or TV show I watch (other than the news, sports, or documentaries) I will write a brief summary of the plot and comments on the movie or show from God's perspective.
3. Keep Jesus as my first love (Revelation 2:4). This includes putting aside dating relationships and romances for the next twelve weeks and setting the time apart to seek the Lord without being

Continued on next page…

distracted. Parents of a teenager and the mentor can make an exception to this commitment for a student dating another committed Christian before the course begins.

No one will be looking over your shoulder to see whether you are fulfilling these three commitments. The purpose of the commitments is to help you grow, and you will benefit from IDC according to the degree you are willing to enter into the spirit of it.

Don't overload your schedule. If you have a difficult semester load of classes or a job and take IDC, you won't be able to do your best in any of these areas. Prayerfully decide whether this is the right time for you to make this commitment and, if so, how you will rearrange your schedule.

Parent's Commitment (for teenagers)

I have read the course requirements and believe this is a valuable experience for my son or daughter. I will encourage my student in spiritual growth and pray for him or her daily.

_____

Mentor's Commitment

I have read the course requirements and believe this is a valuable experience for a Christian young person. I will encourage him or her in spiritual growth, meet each week for twelve weeks, and pray for him or her daily.

_____

Student's Commitment

I have read the requirements and know it will be tough, but I'm going to give the course my very best and become a man or woman of God. I'm ready for the challenge!

_____

SCRIPTURE MEMORY

1 Peter 3:15
But sanctify the Lord God in your hearts, and always be ready to give a defense to everyone who asks you a reason for the hope that is in you, with meekness and fear.

1 John 5:19
We know that we are of God, and the whole world lies under the sway of the wicked one.

FILL OUT EVALUATION 1 ON THE NEXT PAGE.

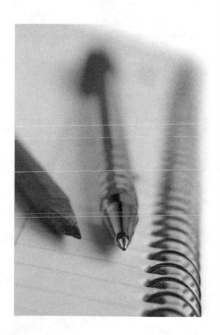

DAILY BIBLE READING

✓ Check when completed		
Sunday	2 Samuel 1–4	_____
Monday	2 Samuel 5–7	_____
Tuesday	2 Samuel 8–10	_____
Wednesday	2 Samuel 11–14	_____
Thursday	2 Samuel 15–18	_____
Friday	2 Samuel 19–20	_____
Saturday	2 Samuel 21–24	_____

See the Daily Bible Reading section on page 11 about this and alternative Bible reading schedules.

BIBLE READING QUESTIONS/THOUGHTS

_____
_____
_____
_____
_____
_____
_____
_____
_____
_____

PRAYER NEEDS THIS WEEK

_____
_____
_____
_____
_____
_____
_____
_____
_____

1

EVALUATION 1: *Evaluate Your Knowledge of Cults and World Religions*

Use the following questions to evaluate your knowledge of cults and world religions. At the end of the course you will fill out a second evaluation and be able to see how much you have learned.

1. Have you ever seen someone come to the Lord through your witness?

2. Have you felt inadequate to speak about your faith? Why or why not?

3. Briefly write what you know about the following:

   • Islam:

   • Hinduism:

   • Buddhism:

   • Mormonism:

   • Jehovah's Witness:

   • The New Age Movement:

   • Other cults and religions:

4. Have you ever witnessed to

   • a Muslim?
   • a Hindu?
   • a Buddhist?
   • a Mormon?
   • a Jehovah's Witness?
   • a New Age follower?
   • someone from other cults and religions?

   How effective were these witnessing encounters?

5. Are you willing to spend the time and energy and do the work to be prepared to reach a lost world?

6. What do you need to be equipped to deal with false doctrine and opposing beliefs?

Lesson one

REACHING A LOST WORLD

Jesus told the parable of the man with one lost sheep to describe the heart of God and His own mission to the world. Although the man had another ninety-nine sheep, he left the safety and comfort of home to search the mountains for the missing one. He knew that, alone in the wilderness, the sheep would become easy prey for predators and be lost to him forever. He felt a sense of urgency to get to the lost sheep before predators destroyed it.

Matthew 18:11–14 (Write out this verse and all subsequent verses *in your own words.*)

_____

_____

_____

In the same way, Jesus came from heaven with a clear purpose: to save that which was lost. Something valuable to Him was in imminent danger and could be lost to Him forever. Jesus came to the earth with full knowledge that this pursuit would cost Him His life, and with the intent to make the greatest personal sacrifice in history to retrieve that which was lost. The Lamb pursues the lost sheep. By extension, His story becomes our story. Christians respond to the Great Commission and work together with Him to find lost souls throughout the world before they die without the salvation that Jesus came to provide.

Matthew 28:18–20

_____

_____

_____

Spiritual wolves are on a quest to find the same people Christ sends us to look for. In many cases, the wolves have begun the process of eternal destruction in the lives of the lost through false teaching that blinds the sheep to the Shepherd who is looking for them. There's a sense of urgency among Christians who understand that the eternal souls of men and women are at stake as they blindly rush toward destruction. Motivated by the Father's love and a desire to see others find the mercy we are so grateful to have received, we go out to look for the lost sheep.

2 Corinthians 5:14

_____

_____

TELLING THE WORLD ABOUT JESUS CHRIST

More than God's love is in action as we look at a lost world. Also, the greatest injustice of history is taking place as God's love is daily ignored and rejected. God has a rightful claim to the whole earth by creation and redemption. He formed the world and owns it as His handiwork and made it His again through Christ, redeeming fallen humanity.

Psalm 24:1

_____

_____

It's not right that God should be dishonored by over a billion Muslims calling on the name of Allah, nearly a billion Hindus worshiping countless gods, or Buddhists seeking perfection apart from the cross. His covenant people, the Jews, are ignorant of true righteousness, New Agers find false peace, occultists seek demonic power, and millions of sincere cultists follow the broad road to destruction. My motivation in writing _Reaching a Lost World_ is that the Lamb deserves the reward of His sufferings, as early Moravian missionaries said so clearly. The right thing is that all the nations would worship the Lord Jesus Christ. Traveling and ministering in many nations has convinced me of the lostness of most of mankind and the church's need to fulfill the Great Commission.

To achieve this goal, the church needs to be equipped. Many Christians don't know _why_ they believe what they believe. As a result of a low emphasis on Bible study in many churches, Christians can easily be led astray by cultists who are more certain of their beliefs than Christians are of theirs. Because many Christians can't adequately explain their faith, and thus are not equipped to tell about Christ when the opportunity arises, they tend to avoid confrontations with people who believe differently. By the end of this course, you will be able to do the following:

- Give a defense of major Christian doctrines such as the deity of Christ, the existence of the Trinity, the need for atonement, and the reliability of God's Word
- Discuss the major beliefs of cults and other religions with their members, comparing and contrasting these beliefs with biblical doctrines
- Help friends and relatives stay out of cults and find the truth in Jesus

WHY CHRISTIANS SHOULD STUDY CULTS AND WORLD RELIGIONS

Since our world is no longer divided into isolated parts, you need to know what this book teaches. A century ago most North Americans would not have known a Hindu, a Buddhist, or a Muslim. Mormonism and Jehovah's Witness were small fringe groups, and the New Age movement as we know it today had not officially begun. Now we have people of every major world religion nearby, living in our neighborhoods, sitting next to us in class, and working together. Our careers may take us to branch offices and factories overseas, and we should thank the Lord for the opportunity to interact with people whose ancestors were separated from ours by oceans. Now we can bring the light of the gospel to people from every world religion, as long as we've prepared ourselves through study and prayer. We must be able to recognize deception and false doctrine when we encounter them, and be prepared to respond with biblical answers.

2 John 7–11

_____

_____

_____

Romans 16:17–18

_____

_____

_____

_____

2 Timothy 2:14–19

_____

_____

_____

_____

_____

We need to have the knowledge of our own faith to stay out of deception. A strong foundation in the Bible is the basis for identifying and being able to answer false beliefs. This will protect Christians from error, as long as they are humble. The Bible shows a clear link between deception and pride. Deception easily takes root in a proud heart, but humility is a safeguard against error.

Obadiah 1:3

_____

_____

_____

Proverbs 1:17

_____

_____

_____

_____

1 Timothy 6:3–10

_____

_____

_____

_____

TRUE STORY

The men walking down the street dressed in white bed sheets drew plenty of attention. As we drove by, I thought, *Maybe I should stop to witness to them.* Since we had other plans, I kept driving until my wife, Jodie, asked, "Aren't you going to witness to them?" Oops! I turned around and pulled up beside them. We sat on the side of a busy street, and the men introduced themselves as Brother Bartholomew and Brother Nicodemus.

The men were from an obscure cult that taught that Jesus had returned and was living in California. Their "Jesus" traveled in a converted school bus with a harem of women. I had read about the cult in a magazine and knew what the members believed. Brother N was clearly a burned-out ex-hippie, while Brother B was as high as a kite. The sacrament in their cult was smoking marijuana. They confirmed their belief that Jesus had already returned, and I said I didn't believe it, because when He returns, He will come in the clouds and every eye will see Him (Matthew 24:30; Revelation 1:7). From his drug-induced haze, Brother B piped up, "No, man, the clouds are in your mind." I had news for him: the clouds weren't in *my* mind. Persisting in trying to show the men their deception, I replied that when Jesus returns, He will be riding a white horse and the armies of heaven will be with Him (Revelation 19:11–14). Brother B countered by saying, "No, man, *we're* the horse!"

Brother N had been arguing more steadily than his stoned partner, and I felt sorry for him. He seemed to be the kind of person who had tried everything in his search for reality and truth, but his heart was still closed to the gospel. He rebuked me sharply for wearing leather shoes, probably coming from the Eastern religious perspective that one of the most basic levels of spirituality is vegetarianism and respect for all living things. While I was processing that, Brother B reached into his backpack and came out with a small tin can and rolling papers. Recognizing the drug paraphernalia and that a police car could come at any time, I exclaimed, "No! Not here!" He replied, "It's okay, man. I don't have any more herb. It's just tobacco."

Eventually, we all realized that the conversation was futile. These men were convinced that they should follow a false Messiah, and I wasn't interested in their doctrines. Many cultists are just as closed-minded, but we still need to reach out to them.

THEOLOGY 101: An Explanation of the Gospel for Non-Christian Readers

If you are reading this book as a member of another faith, please know that my purpose in writing it is not to insult you or anyone else who believes differently than I do. Through the years I have had respectful conversations with people from every religion explained in this book and many others. You are most likely an honorable person with sincere faith and a concern that a book like this will attack the most cherished beliefs of your family and culture. My intent is to help people understand what a genuine faith in the Lord Jesus Christ is and to communicate that faith to others.

I do not believe in Jesus simply because this is what I have been taught. Instead, I have discovered by personal experience that God's revelation to man in the Bible is reasonable, practical, life changing, and true. Christianity can withstand the scrutiny of science, philosophy, and debate.

If you can put aside for a moment the cultural baggage associated with Christianity—including the historical failures of professing Christians to live like their Savior, present-day hypocrisy among others who claim to be genuine Christians, and the immoral Western culture, which is falsely believed to be a Christian society—then we can deal with the foundational issues. I grieve over Christians' failures and hypocrisy and over the false examples of Western Christianity portrayed to the world as the truth, such as the prosperity gospel and bizarre offshoots of the true church.

Let's get to the root of this discussion. On the basis of the teachings of the Bible, I assert that a loving God created the universe and all that is in it so that He could have a relationship with mankind. The first humans disobeyed the only command that God gave them, and all their descendants followed in rebellion. God would be entirely justified in destroying all of us, including you and me, for our continual failures to obey the clear teachings of right and wrong found in the Bible and echoed in most cultures around the world. In His kindness, He made a way of escape by providing a blood sacrifice for our sins through His Son. The Lord Jesus Christ died but remained dead for only three days. By faith in Him as the sinless Savior who was the only Person capable of paying our enormous debt to God, we can receive forgiveness as a gift from a merciful God and receive the undeserved blessing of an eternity with our Creator in a perfect place known as heaven.

You may agree with some, little, or none of the preceding statements, so let's make it more personal. Allow me to ask you two questions.

First, what will you do with your sins? Your conscience echoes the laws of God found in the Bible when they tell you that it is wrong to tell a lie, steal anything regardless of its value, hate another human being, look lustfully at an attractive person, dishonor your parents, or greedily desire something that does not belong to you. Every time you have broken one of these laws, from your childhood until now, you have been accruing God's righteous judgment. Do not confuse God's mercy with leniency. All of those who are outside of the forgiveness He provides for us in Christ will face His wrath. Your conscience motivates you to become right with God, although a conscience can be ignored and eventually silenced.

It may be that your religion or personal code of ethics requires you to perform religious duties, sacrifices, or good deeds to balance out your failures. But deep inside, your conscience will tell you that these aren't enough. Human efforts are insufficient to cancel even the smallest sin and inadequate to make us right with God.

Let me give you an illustration. Suppose you, your friend, and I stood on the beach facing the Pacific Ocean and decided to swim across it. I am a terrible swimmer and would get only a short distance from shore before I drowned. Your friend may be a good swimmer, and he may go a fair distance before his strength runs out and he, too, drowns. Let's say you are an Olympic swimmer and can go for a very long distance. Will you make it across the ocean? Obviously, you will eventually drown also. It's just too far. This illustrates the danger of trusting in human goodness. We compare ourselves with others, and one seems much better than another. What we fail to realize is that none of us can please God or make it to heaven on the basis of our own works. It's just not possible. Now consider a swimmer who has done his best, realizes he falls short, and sees a boat nearby. Wouldn't he call with all his might for the boat to save him, knowing it is his only hope of being rescued and avoiding death? This is how Christians look at Jesus Christ, who alone can take us across the gap that separates us from God.

So the second question is, what will you do with Jesus? You can receive or reject the knowledge of God,

---

but you can ignore Him only temporarily. Eventually the day will come when you and I will stand before Him. We will face Him either as our Savior or as our Judge, but we *will* face Him. We must individually choose to repent (turn from our sins) and believe the gospel (the good news of God's forgiveness in Christ).

Here's my challenge to you. Begin by reading the New Testament of the Bible. Beware of the preconditioning your religious background has given you, which would cause you to see the Bible through the eyes of your leaders. You can do your own thinking, and the Bible is easy enough for even a child to understand. Look carefully at the person of Jesus Christ and His teachings in the four Gospels (Matthew, Mark, Luke, and John). Come to terms with Jesus' claim that He would rise from the dead and with the testimonies of many people that He actually did so. Continue reading the rest of the New Testament (the book of Acts and the epistles) to see the way the early believers in Christ lived, and finish with the book of Revelation, with its description of Jesus returning to the earth as the Judge of all mankind.

Isaiah 55:6–7: Seek the LORD while He may be found, call upon Him while He is near. Let the wicked forsake his way, and the unrighteous man his thoughts; let him return to the LORD, and He will have mercy on him; and to our God, for He will abundantly pardon.

John 6:37b: The one who comes to Me I will by no means cast out.

My hope is that you will find what I have found in Christ: a clear perspective on myself by seeing my own sinful life through His eyes as I understand the truth of the Bible, my humility as I recognize my inability to save myself, and my confidence in what the Lord Jesus Christ did for me and for all repentant sinners by dying on the cross. This perspective has resulted in my having had thirty years of peace of mind as I view my own death and eternal destination with hope, and daily assurance that a loving God is with me as I face the difficulties life presents to all of us. May He reveal His goodness to you.

---

1 John 2:26–27

We need to gain a more complete understanding of salvation and how to live the Christian life. Sometimes we understand more fully when we can contrast one thing with another. When we invest time studying truth from the Bible (as you will do while completing this course), we become more spiritually attuned to error, even when it is not part of an organization or from another alleged scripture. Many people, regardless of religious affiliation, have invented their own views of spiritual truth. For most, it will be a comforting deception that tells them they are already right with a passive and tolerant god who smiles benignly and allows everyone to live as he or she pleases and still get into heaven. All of us live under the influence of the spiritual climate around us, yet truth is never derived from majority opinion. As Christians, we must be on our guard not to succumb to the popular perspectives on spiritual truth and lifestyle choices.

1 Corinthians 11:19 (note that the KJV uses the word *heresies* instead of *factions* [NKJV] or *differences* [NIV])

1 John 5:19

_____

_____

1 Corinthians 2:12

_____

_____

We need to develop love and compassion for the lost, whose souls are hungry for the truth. The reason they follow false teaching and destructive practices is that they don't yet know their Creator, who is the only one that can satisfy the emptiness within.

TRUE STORY

While I was reading my Bible during a six-hour layover at Los Angeles International Airport, two men came up to me and asked me if I was a Christian. As a fairly new Christian, I was eager to talk to who I assumed were fellow believers. After a few minutes of small talk, one of the men asked me if I still sinned. Thinking they were very naive, I replied, "Of course. We all still sin, but we can go to the Lord for forgiveness and He will cleanse us. Why do you ask? Don't you sin?"

"No," the man replied with deadly seriousness. "I haven't sinned since I became a Christian. If you still sin, you aren't a real Christian."

I was shocked as the two men proceeded to demolish my faith with a dazzling attack of half-truths, Scripture taken out of context, and skilled arguments. One man was much more aggressive than the other, and my limited Bible knowledge at the time was just not equal to the onslaught. The man overwhelmed my every reply. I had a strong impression of homosexuality from one of the men, and then a group of men who were in the background waiting for my two spiritual assailants began calling them to get on their flight. During the final boarding call, the men ran off, shouting, "Read First John."

Shaken to the core, I sat back with my Bible and tried to pray. Immediately the Lord brought to mind the eighth verse of First John: "If we say that we have no sin, we deceive ourselves, and the truth is not in us."

That should have been enough to comfort me, but condemnation, confusion, and fear were roaring through my mind. I was trying to be a good Christian, obedient to God and living in the fear of the Lord, but I knew I failed Him in many areas. Could these men be right?

After returning home, still unable to shake a sense of dread, I met with our senior pastor. The pastor had heard this kind of teaching before and told me that it was a matter of terminology. Some people redefine _sin_ so that their own sins are labeled shortcomings and flaws, but this denial is exactly what the verse the Lord had reminded me of is talking about. Thus, these people are able to excuse sin while living in the sins of spiritual elitism and pride, among others. Unfortunately, we all still sin (James 3:2; 1 Timothy 1:15, note the present tense; 1 John 2:1). Now, many years later, I can balance the verses those men used with a more complete understanding of grace, knowing the difference between sin as an occasional fall and sin as a lifestyle, and between a biblical view of the whole counsel of God and hand-picked verses (Acts 20:27).

Proverbs 27:7

_____

_____

Psalm 107:9

_____

_____

We need to fulfill the scriptural commands to be ready to share the gospel with everyone.

1 Peter 3:15

_____

_____

_____

2 Timothy 4:1–5

_____

_____

_____

_____

We need to settle in our hearts and minds that sincerity doesn't equal truth. We can place sincere belief in, fervent devotion to, and deep faith in the wrong object, which is any religious system outside of faith in the Lord Jesus Christ. It doesn't matter how heartfelt a person's beliefs are if these beliefs are not based on truth. Billions around the world unknowingly follow after lies.

Joshua 24:14

_____

_____

SCRIPTURE MEMORY

Psalm 43:3
Oh, send out Your light and Your truth! Let them lead me; let them bring me to Your holy hill and to Your tabernacle.

1 John 4:1
Beloved, do not believe every spirit, but test the spirits, whether they are of God; because many false prophets have gone out into the world.

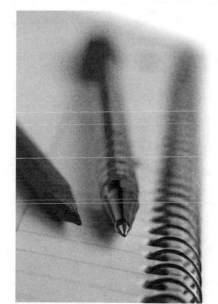

DAILY BIBLE READING

✓ Check when completed		
Sunday	1 Kings 1–4	_____
Monday	1 Kings 5–8	_____
Tuesday	1 Kings 9–11	_____
Wednesday	1 Kings 12–16	_____
Thursday	1 Kings 17–19	_____
Friday	1 Kings 20–22	_____
Saturday	2 Kings 1–3	_____

BIBLE READING QUESTIONS/THOUGHTS

_____
_____
_____
_____
_____
_____
_____
_____
_____
_____

PRAYER NEEDS THIS WEEK

_____
_____
_____
_____
_____
_____
_____
_____
_____

Lesson two

THE DIFFERENCES BETWEEN TRUE AND FALSE DOCTRINE

Doctrine simply means teaching, and it comes in many varieties. Some doctrines are closer to the truth found in the Bible, and some are much farther from it. False doctrine is nothing new. Moses stood against the priests of the Egyptian gods, the Israelites confronted the pagan religions of the Canaanites, and the early church battled false teachers. Throughout history, new religions have developed, each claiming to have the truth others before them lacked. A major part of the battle between the kingdoms of light and darkness takes place in the arena of words and ideas, which shape conduct and lifestyles.

God loves every person regardless of his or her belief system, yet He hates false doctrine. We, too, should love the people and hate the deception for several reasons. First, false teaching dishonors God by portraying Him as He is not. An inaccurate perspective on who God is and what He is like is the foundation of all false teaching and keeps people away from Him. Misrepresenting the nature and character of God is more than a minor mistake but is the invention of another god. Enticing another person to serve a different god is such a serious matter that it carried the death penalty in the Old Testament.

Deuteronomy 13:6–9

_____
_____
_____
_____

Second, false doctrine invariably harms the people God created, loves, and sent Christ to redeem. This takes place in an eternal sense by functioning as a substitute for truth, allegedly filling the spiritual hunger of a lost person but with something that harms rather than helps that person. It obscures the narrow way that leads to life and points people toward the broad path that leads to destruction. False doctrine also harms people during their lifetimes because it is not rooted in God's order and plan for how people should live. It excuses and promotes many abuses, such as authoritarian control of others, devaluation of women, and distortion of marriage and family relationships. It causes violent clashes with people who hold other beliefs, encouraging pride and leaving its victims spiritually empty. Millions of people with hungry souls eagerly take in doctrines that lead to spiritual ruin. Despite

Terms & Concepts

prophet: one who speaks on behalf of God. A true prophet's words will draw people close to God, warn them about straying from Him, confront sin, and comfort believers. Some prophets in Scripture also foretold future events. A false prophet claims to speak on behalf of God but distorts the truth and leads others astray. Being a false prophet does not always mean speaking from a demonic influence but can include speaking human thoughts and presenting them as though they were the Lord's words.

heresy: a teaching that contradicts established beliefs. For example, saying there is no Trinity is a heresy, as is denying the divinity of Jesus.

blasphemy: cursing God, failing to act with due respect toward holy things, or claiming to be God.

orthodox: conforming to biblical truth.

heterodox: failing to conform to biblical truth.

orthopraxy: correct action or practice.

Now we'll put this all together. False religions are often founded and encouraged by false prophets. They teach heresies, which may include blasphemy. Since they have left orthodox Christianity, they are heterodox. The outcome of their beliefs will be visible in the behavior of the leaders and followers, whose lifestyles will not show orthopraxy.

its destructive results, the nature of deception is that a deceived person is unaware of his or her error. Deception is believing a lie to be true. Its victims can be sincere and dedicated, certain and committed, but the object in which they have put their trust will let them down in the end.

Think of doctrine and the truth of Scripture as the two rails of a train track. As long as they remain exactly parallel, the train is safe, but when one rail veers off just a little, that angle results in a wider and wider difference farther down the track, and will eventually cause the train to derail. A slight variation will grow larger, and unless the variation is corrected, a wreck becomes inevitable. The rail of Scripture always heads directly toward a relationship with God through Christ, but if the rail of doctrine veers away from it, trouble results. When a train derails, much destruction occurs all around it. You may have seen pictures of a train accident leaving chemical spills, crushing homes, or starting fires that take many lives. In the same way, false teachers sometimes start off with the truth of Scripture and then slowly move away from it. Untold numbers of people in the history of mankind have suffered because of these spiritual lies, and the one the Bible calls the father of lies rejoices in the ruin of individual lives, families, and nations. We who know the truth have a commission from the Lord to stand up for it and seek to rescue people from error.

John 8:44

_____

_____

_____

_____

Jude 3–4

_____

_____

_____

_____

TRUE STORY

Shawna came to youth group with a story about the two handymen her mom had hired to make repairs at her house. She told me they were dedicated Christians who knew a lot about the Bible, and she and her mom enjoyed talking to them. I didn't pay too much attention at first, but these men kept coming up in Shawna's conversations over the next few weeks. Shawna and her mom seemed to be captivated by the handymen's faith, but at the same time, I heard a disturbing tone in Shawna's reports. She was becoming more and more critical of the church and Christianity in general as it is practiced in the United States. She seemed suspicious and distrustful, even though she was one of our key youth and had always been enthusiastically involved in the group. She developed a growing prideful tone, indicating that she knew much more than the rest of us about God, and she was clearly closing her heart to us. It was time to take action.

I asked Shawna to tell me more about the handymen, realizing that these developments must be related. Shawna came back with some answers, including the name of the group the men came from in Montana. I called a cult-watching ministry and discovered that this small and obscure cult had many unscriptural beliefs, including beating demons out of women and children. A five-year-old boy had died in one of these deliverance sessions. I immediately went to Shawna and her mother, who were horrified that they had been duped. The rest of what the handymen had taught them sounded so good and right that they didn't realize the spirit behind it was wrong and they were slowly being indoctrinated into the cult. Obviously, the handymen had been careful not to tell them any of the more bizarre teachings since that would have scared them off. Shawna and her mom immediately broke all ties with the men, stayed in our church, and were probably much more careful in the future.

TRUE STORY

The youth group kids were all excited about the missionaries who had been hanging around their high school campus all week before heading into Mexico. They were inspired by these missionaries' zeal and asked if they could bring them to youth group on Wednesday night. I agreed, and several French-Canadian college students showed up at church. I asked them what the name of their group was, and they replied with a name I'd never heard of. That wasn't a problem, since there are many small mission organizations, and I invited them to give a testimony about what they were doing.

The girl who was their spokesperson was very enthusiastic. English was her second language, and her intriguing accent added to the group's interest as she spoke. "We are sairving ze Lord and taking ze gospel to evairy nation. Ze Lord sends us out to tell all ze people zat He is coming soon and we must, how do you say, follow Heem."

The girl continued, to the delight of our group, but my spirit became more and more uncomfortable. Something was wrong, but I couldn't put my finger on it. Everything she said was true, but still. . . . Then I realized that I hadn't heard the name of Jesus the entire time, only mention of God and the Lord. When the girl finished and the kids applauded, I led the rest of the meeting and went to the girl's group afterward, asking for more information. She told me the name of their founder and gave me a short book he had written. I went home and read the entire book that night. My suspicions were confirmed when I read that they didn't believe Jesus was God. The book was riddled with false teachings about the end of the world, and it exalted the group's leader.

The French-speaking group was long gone by the next youth meeting, and the kids were shocked when I told them what I had found. This was a lesson to all of us to be careful and wise when we come in contact with an unknown group or person purporting to tell us spiritual truth. It was encouraging to me to see that even before I had a clear reason for the mistrust I felt in my heart, the Holy Spirit was doing His job of leading me to all truth by showing me that the group's message was false.

We can trust the inner witness of the Holy Spirit to show us what is true and what isn't, and we can also use study and wisdom to be careful of spiritual input we receive. This event took place before the Internet made it easy to search for the name of a group or leader. Today we should all take advantage of our easy access to information so we won't be led astray.

CHARACTERISTICS OF FALSE DOCTRINE

Since avoiding false doctrine and reaching those snared in it are so crucial, how can we recognize false teaching? Watch for the following.

Wrong perspective of Jesus. If the teachers' understanding of Jesus is wrong, they do not know God the Father.

John 14:9

_____

1 John 5:11–12

_____

1 John 2:23

_____

2 John 9

_____

Contradictions to the Bible. God won't contradict Himself. Refuse to listen to convoluted reasoning that tells you that God's Word in Scripture is somehow different from God's direction to the leader, and do not accept new revelations of supposed truth that disagree with the Bible, regardless of how dramatic or appealing the package that contains them may be.

1 Thessalonians 5:21

_____

_____

1 John 4:1

_____

_____

Redefinition of Christian doctrines. Anyone seeking to redefine the core doctrines of Christianity is in error. Hearing or reading that Jesus isn't God and didn't live a sinless life, die for our sins, or rise from the grave is all the warning you need to know that the source is false, despite the good deeds of those who teach this or the friendliness of their members.

Galatians 1:6–9

_____

_____

_____

2 Peter 3:16–17

_____

_____

_____

Inclusion of pagan doctrines. If the foundation of a spiritual practice is pagan, it can't be incorporated into the worship of the true and living God. Many elements of modern society—including the names of days of the week and months of the year, many Christmas and Easter traditions, and even such things as birthstones and superstitions—hearken back to pagan religions. We can't avoid all contact with heathen roots of our culture, but it is a different thing altogether to claim that a practice that has come from those sources and not from Scripture has any spiritual value. Let us clearly state that nothing from a false religion (meaning those practices, rituals, and approaches to God not found in Scripture) has any value in seeking and knowing the true and living God—ever. God has given us *all* we need for life and godliness. Sometimes Christians who are bored with their current knowledge of God ignorantly open themselves to dangerous sources, or they want to start a new trend out of a desire for acclaim and they find a pagan practice and bring it into the church. Examples of this are repetitive breathing prayers, yoga, meditation that produces an altered state of mind, and the writings of ancient mystics. Let's note that the teachings of orthodox early Christian leaders are very different from the writings of those who dabbled in occultism and searched for hidden knowledge.

2 Peter 1:3

_____

_____

"New truths." Sometimes in Christian circles we hear arguments for new truth. Watch out! While there may be certain points that the Holy Spirit emphasizes in a particular season as God works in the church (2 Peter 1:12), these are simply the unfolding of *existing* revelation found in Scripture. No new spiritual interfaces will take place with God. Segments of the church have become captivated with alleged signs not found in Scripture: stigmata (the appearance of Jesus' wounds from His crucifixion on an individual), gold dust, angel feathers, gemstones, and oil appearing in their meetings, but these serve to distract people's attention from the One who deserves it. Strange occurrences become the focus and goal, so even more unusual things need to happen to keep up the excitement level. We don't need

---

THEOLOGY 101: God's Nature and Character

One of the major differences between a biblical understanding of God and the views of cults and world religions is the question of what God is like. This includes His eternal attributes (His nature) and the way He acts in a given situation (His character). On the basis of what we know about God as we study the Bible and grow in personal knowledge of Him through our relationship with Christ, we can look at the way others portray Him and say either, "That seems like God" or "That doesn't sound like God to me." This is more than a subjective decision on what we would like God to be like. We must always go back to His Word, which is the revelation of what He wants us to know about Him, and to the person of Jesus Christ, who is "the fullness of the Godhead bodily" (Colossians 2:9).

Here are some of the qualities of God's nature. He is
- Real (Hebrews 11:6)
- Alive (Psalms 84:2; 115:3–11; Luke 24:6–7; Romans 6:23; Galatians 2:20; Ephesians 2:4–7)
- Powerful (Psalm 29:4; Matthew 28:18; Romans 1:20; 1 Corinthians 1:18, 24; 4:20)
- All knowing (Psalm 139:1–6; Isaiah 55:8–9; Romans 8:29; Ephesians 2:10; 2 Peter 1:19–21)
- Holy (Psalm 99:9; Isaiah 5:16; 6:3; 57:15; James 1:13; 1 Peter 1:15–16; Revelation 4:8)
- Unchanging (Numbers 23:19; 1 Samuel 15:29; Malachi 3:6; Hebrews 13:8; James 1:17)

Here are some of the qualities of God's character. He is
- Good (2 Chronicles 5:13; Psalms 34:8; 73:1; Matthew 19:17; Mark 10:18)
- Faithful (Numbers 23:19; Deuteronomy 7:9; 32:4; Psalm 117:2; 1 Corinthians 10:13; 1 John 1:9)
- Compassionate (Exodus 34:6; Psalms 78:38; 116:5; Romans 9:15)
- Forgiving (Psalms 86:5; 103:12; Jeremiah 31:34; Luke 23:34; Acts 13:38; Ephesians 1:7)
- Trustworthy (2 Samuel 22:31; Psalm 9:9–10; Proverbs 30:5; Isaiah 26:3–4; 2 Corinthians 1:9–10)
- Loving (Isaiah 63:8–9; Jeremiah 31:3; John 3:16–17; Romans 5:8; 1 John 4:9–10)
- Merciful (Psalms 103:8–11; 136; Joel 2:13; Matthew 18:14; Luke 6:36; Hebrews 8:12)
- Gentle (2 Samuel 22:36; 1 Kings 19:11–12; Isaiah 40:11; Hosea 11:4; Matthew 11:29)
- Kind (Psalms 36:7; 63:3; 117:2; Isaiah 54:8, 10; Ephesians 2:7; Titus 3:4–5)
- Patient (Exodus 34:6; Numbers 14:18; Romans 15:5; 2 Peter 3:9, 15)
- Righteous (Deuteronomy 32:4; Psalms 11:7; 116:5; Isaiah 41:10; 2 Timothy 4:8; 1 John 2:1)
- Jealous (Exodus 20:5; 34:14; Deuteronomy 4:24; 32:16; Joel 2:18; Zechariah 8:2)
- Just (Deuteronomy 10:18; 32:4; Proverbs 29:26; John 5:30; 1 John 1:9)
- Passionate (Judges 10:16; Ezekiel 6:9)
- Creative (Genesis 1:1; Psalms 104; 139:13–16; Isaiah 40:26; Colossians 1:16; Revelation 4:11)
- Joyful (Nehemiah 8:10; Zephaniah 3:17; Matthew 25:21; Luke 15:7; John 15:11; 17:13)
- Wise (Job 28:12–28; Isaiah 31:2; Romans 11:33; 16:27; James 3:17)
- Friendly (Proverbs 18:24; Matthew 11:19; James 2:23)
- Caring (Psalm 121; Isaiah 25:4; 40:11; Jeremiah 29:11; Matthew 6:25–32; 1 Peter 5:7)
- Generous (Jeremiah 33:6; Luke 9:10–17; Romans 5:15; 1 Timothy 2:3–4; James 1:17)
- Slow to anger (Exodus 34:6–7; Numbers 14:18; Nehemiah 9:17; Psalm 103:8; Joel 2:13)
- Impartial (Matthew 22:16; Acts 10:34)

questionable manifestations to prop up our faith. Run from spiritual fads and stick to the Word of God and the New Testament works of the Holy Spirit.

Ephesians 4:13–15

_____

_____

_____

1 Timothy 1:3–7

_____

_____

_____

Reasons Why Christians Sometimes Fall into False Doctrine

It's a sad fact that genuine believers can fall prey to cults and error. Here are some of the root causes for this.

Pride. In a religious sense, this is the desire to have or the belief that one already has greater spiritual experiences or understanding of truth than other believers. Many still search for hidden knowledge, just as when the Gnostic heresy clashed with the early church. The Gnostics claimed to have understanding of secrets that only a select group had obtained. This error repeats itself in many cults today, although the specifics of the alleged hidden truths will vary.

Proverbs 16:18

_____

_____

2 Timothy 4:3–4

_____

_____

Biblical illiteracy. In many cases, Christians get their knowledge of the Lord secondhand. That's fine for baby Christians, but as we grow, God expects us to take responsibility for finding our own food. Many Christians don't read the Bible consistently. Few have finished even the New Testament, let alone the Old Testament. Cultists can often run circles around Christians by misusing the Bible or using corrupted editions of the Bible to teach error. If believers are not well-grounded in the truth, they can easily be deceived.

Hosea 4:6

_____

_____

2 Timothy 3:15–17

_____

_____

Psalm 119:160

_____

_____

Psalm 43:3

_____

_____

Deceiving spirits. Deceiving spirits, demonic beings with the intent of luring people away from the truth, will be more active in the last days before Jesus returns. There are many groups whose practices display both actual supernatural involvement that is not of God and the deceptive power of confusion and lies.

1 Timothy 4:1–3

_____

_____

_____

Matthew 24:3–5

_____

_____

_____

2 Thessalonians 2:1–4

_____

_____

_____

Openness to sin. False teaching that permits us to do things that God's Word condemns can be very appealing. By twisting Scripture to support desires such as greed and immorality, cults snare many people who don't want to walk on the narrow path.

Titus 1:10–11

_____

_____

1 Timothy 6:5

_____

_____

1 Timothy 1:18–20

_____

_____

SCRIPTURE MEMORY

2 Corinthians 11:3–4
But I fear, lest somehow, as the serpent deceived Eve by his craftiness, so your minds may be corrupted from the simplicity that is in Christ. For if he who comes preaches another Jesus whom we have not preached, or if you receive a different spirit which you have not received, or a different gospel which you have not accepted—you may well put up with it!

Acts 20:29–31
For I know this, that after my departure savage wolves will come in among you, not sparing the flock. Also from among yourselves men will rise up, speaking perverse things, to draw away the disciples after themselves. Therefore watch, and remember that for three years I did not cease to warn everyone night and day with tears.

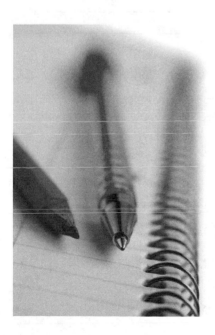

DAILY BIBLE READING

✓ Check when completed		
Sunday	2 Kings 4–8	_____
Monday	2 Kings 9–12	_____
Tuesday	2 Kings 13–17	_____
Wednesday	2 Kings 18–21	_____
Thursday	2 Kings 22–25	_____
Friday	1 Chronicles 1–5	_____
Saturday	1 Chronicles 6–9	_____

BIBLE READING QUESTIONS/THOUGHTS

_____
_____
_____
_____
_____
_____
_____
_____
_____
_____
_____

PRAYER NEEDS THIS WEEK

_____
_____
_____
_____
_____
_____
_____
_____
_____

3

Lesson three
HOW TO AVOID FALSE DOCTRINE

Some basic principles of walking with the Lord can help you stay on track. Without developing an overly suspicious attitude, we must still compare what we read, hear, and see with the objective standards of God's Word and learn to be sensitive to the Holy Spirit's voice as He points us to the truth.

John 16:13

_____
_____

Acts 17:10–11

_____
_____
_____

Hebrews 13:9

_____
_____

TIPS TO AVOID FALSE DOCTRINES

Love the truth, even when it hurts, when it denies your flesh the opportunity to express your fallen nature, and when you feel like you're the only one who believes it.

Proverbs 23:23

_____
_____

Psalm 25:5

_____
_____

Psalm 119:30

_____
_____

Watch out for spiritual trends followed by popular culture. Celebrity endorsement has caused many gullible people to investigate new religious beliefs. Examples of this are Madonna and the Jewish Kabbalah, John Travolta's and Tom Cruise's involvement in Scientology, Michael Jackson's conversion to Islam, the Beatles' support of Transcendental Meditation, and numerous Hollywood Buddhists.

1 Timothy 6:20–21

_____

_____

_____

Realize that we live in an age that's trying to rid itself of truth as fast as possible. Western society says there are no objective standards, so anything goes. We hear that it's all good. People believe that there is no universal truth. Our culture proclaims tolerance of everything except biblical Christianity. Even though cultural standards deteriorate and change, God hasn't changed. He wrote the laws on tablets of stone with His own finger, not with chalk on a board. A world that's lost its way still needs to hear the Ten Commandments, not the Ten Suggestions.

Hosea 4:1

_____

_____

Isaiah 59:14

_____

_____

Watch out for lawlessness. A lawless spirit has invaded some parts of the church, saying that grace permits us to do whatever we want, as long as we say a quick prayer asking for forgiveness afterward. This is contrary to the biblical definition of grace and the place of the law of God.

1 Corinthians 9:21

_____

_____

Galatians 6:2

_____

_____

Romans 3:31

_____

_____

Matthew 5:17–19

_____

_____

_____

Be careful to avoid the "it's all about me" mentality of life in the Western world. Even in the church, messages focusing on my happiness, my fulfillment, my security, my comfort, my goals, my things, my life are proclaiming the opposite of biblical Christianity. False teachers are adept at bringing the kind of self-exalting messages that people want to hear: messages that boost the hearers' self-esteem, coddle their sinful appetites, tell them that God is the means to achieve their goals, and make them comfortable in lukewarmness.

Matthew 16:24–26

_____

_____

_____

1 Samuel 12:24

_____

_____

TRUE STORY

Sara was a sweet girl and a dedicated Christian. She had taken the Intensive Discipleship Course with me and had a good basic understanding of Scripture. A few months after she went off to college, her mom came to talk to me. She had a sense of uneasiness about a campus ministry that Sara had become involved with. Most of their teaching seemed right, but there were a few odd things. The more I heard, the more I became concerned. Cults often look for vulnerable Christian college students who are away from home, are lonely, and don't have the nearby spiritual support of their church or families.

Two cults seemed to fit the facts her mom told me, and I contacted Sara right away. It was one of the groups I suspected. Sara was very receptive to the things I told her and decided immediately to leave the group, even though they were the only friends she had made so far on campus.

Here's how this applies to all of us: no one is beyond deception. Cults look for unmet needs, vulnerabilities, and doors that are open through sin or pride. Sara's need to make friends as a new student was the cult's opportunity.

We need to investigate teachings we hear, groups we may think of joining, and teachings of any new church we start to attend. Do the same thing when a friend or co-worker tells you about his or her involvement in a religious group. The best ways to do this include finding out the name of the founder of the group and authors who are respected and quoted by the leaders, then researching them online or calling a trusted spiritual leader for his or her counsel.

Trust your judgment if you have an uneasy feeling, even though you may not be able to identify exactly what's wrong. This is the Holy Spirit directing you into truth and away from error. He will also remind you of Scripture that shows the error of the beliefs you are hearing. Search the Scriptures with His help to find answers.

1 John 2:26–27: These things I have written to you concerning those who try to deceive you. But the anointing which you have received from Him abides in you, and you do not need that anyone teach you; but as the same anointing teaches you concerning all things, and is true, and is not a lie, and just as it has taught you, you will abide in Him.

Acts 17:11: These were more fair-minded than those in Thessalonica, in that they received the word with all readiness, and searched the Scriptures daily to find out whether these things were so.

Strive for a pure heart. False teachers can easily ensnare those who love sin more than righteousness. A lukewarm Christian looking for an excuse to sin may find it in a doctrinal aberration (deviation from the truth) that permits or even makes a virtue out of things that a plain reading of God's Word clearly condemns. Numerous Christian leaders have excused immorality in their lives, often by believing and telling others that they have reached a spiritual level in which God has different rules for them. Gullible followers, dazzled by the leader's exalted status, are ready-made partners for these wolves in sheep's clothing.

Matthew 7:13–14

_____

_____

2 Peter 2:18

_____

_____

Beware the error of becoming a heresy hunter. Many people are so intent on finding false teaching that they read into every sermon and book, looking between the lines until they find something wrong. Sometimes they distort the intentions of the leader out of a motive of suspicion and mistrust. Their critical spirit makes it easy for them to attack anyone with even the slightest difference of opinion, and they use sharp judgments, negative labels, and vicious sarcasm. This goes completely against the biblical approach to dealing with error and shows a stronghold of pride in the critic's life.

2 Timothy 2:24–26

_____

_____

_____

2 Thessalonians 3:14–15

_____

_____

WHICH SPIRITUAL LEADERS OR GROUPS CAN YOU TRUST?

In a world full of false teaching, and with strange beliefs branching off in every direction, it's important to know some basic principles so that you can be sure you are going in the right direction and not being led astray. It's easy for this to happen when college students move away from home and are too far away to continue attending the church where they have been worshiping. How will you know whether a particular Bible study group, campus fellowship, or church will lead you closer to Christ?

The leader. Look at the character of the leader. All leaders are flawed and fallen human beings, and none of us has fully reached Christlike character, but you'll see humility and fear of the Lord in genuinely godly leaders. Such leaders will be willing to acknowledge their sins, ask forgiveness of those whom they have offended, and take correction and heed counsel from others. They will be very cautious about the slightest hint of immorality, aware of the need to keep a good reputation before the

THEOLOGY 101: God's Revelation

God has many testimonies to the fact that He exists, to the qualities of His nature and character, and to His relationship with mankind. General revelation, through which we gain a general knowledge or awareness of God, comes to all of mankind: creation shows that there is a Creator and reveals His power and faithfulness (Psalm 19:1–4; Romans 1:19–20), and each person's conscience shows that one's actions bring either God's approval or His disapproval (Romans 2:15). These are foundations for understanding God.

God has also given more specific, or special, revelation of Himself through His mighty acts throughout history, which culminated in the coming of Jesus, the earthly representation of the Father. God has provided a written record of His nature and work in history—the Bible. Without this special revelation of God recorded in the Bible, mankind wouldn't have enough knowledge of God to be saved. From this basis, the church proclaims the gospel, and changed lives show God's mercy and power.

The canon, that is, the collection of sixty-six books that make up the Bible, is closed. No new books are needed or will be added, no books written in ancient times that aren't currently included belong in the Bible, and no other scriptures from other religions carry divine authority as truth. These are bold statements and would offend Muslims, Mormons, and many others. Here's why we as Christians believe these statements are true:

- 2 Timothy 3:16–17 says, "All Scripture is given by inspiration of God, and is profitable for doctrine, for reproof, for correction, for instruction in righteousness, that the man of God may be complete, thoroughly equipped for every good work."
- Jesus treated the Hebrew Scriptures (the Old Testament) as authoritative (Matthew 4:4, 7, 10; 21:42; Luke 4:17–21).
- The apostles' teaching in the New Testament reveals the truth of God in Christ and, like the Old Testament, is authoritative Scripture given by the Spirit (1 Corinthians 2:12–13; 2 Peter 3:15–16).
- God preserves His words, which are pure and to which no other words can be added (Proverbs 30:5–6; Psalm 12:6–7; Revelation 22:18).

God reveals Himself through the Bible, warns of severe punishment for adding to His words, and promises to keep His words from corruption—which makes sense because there would be no point in inspiration without preservation. The early church, guided by the Holy Spirit, had an established, wise, and documented procedure for determining which of the large number of books and letters in circulation at the time were divinely inspired. The past two thousand years have been a testimony to the early church's careful and prayerful compilation of the sixty-six books of the Bible in that no other inspired writings have been discovered. Plus, it wouldn't be logical for God to inspire Scripture and allow it to be lost for centuries.

What about ongoing revelation? Does God speak to us directly today? Christians are divided on this issue. The term *revelation* may be an obstacle for some people, since it is the name of a book of the Bible and since it seems to put individual leading on the same level as the Bible. It is true that some Christians display their pride by making it seem that God talks to them in a way that's far beyond the experience of most believers. Perhaps for these reasons, some Christians believe that after the books of the Bible were written, God ceased speaking to mankind in any way other than through the Bible. These believers refuse to acknowledge that God could give a person a dream or vision or speak profoundly and personally in modern times. This perspective developed partly out of a concern that people could be deceived by following after subjective revelations rather than the sure foundation of Scripture.

Most Christians do, however, make room for God's leading in subjective ways. For example, the Bible can't direct a missionary in a definitive way to choose between serving in Bolivia or Botswana, since it doesn't mention either country, but God can lead that individual through subjective means. Likewise, direction regarding which college to attend or whom to marry can be found through principles of Scripture but not in explicit verses describing every possible combination of choices we may face. The wisdom God gives us as we pray and read the Word is a subjective source of direction.

God uses prophecy to warn His servants of dangers or trials to come (Acts 11:28; 21:4, 11) and to build up believers, call for righteous living, and comfort the suffering (1 Corinthians 14:3). Some Christians believe that in modern times God speaks only through the Bible. They rightly label as prophetic the words of preachers who call the church and society to repentance, or who frequently warn about dangers of the occult and Satanic activity today. Here is a problem: do we really believe that God has abandoned the entire supernatural realm and that only the devil is active there now? With demonic signs and wonders in false religions, would it make sense for God to back out of the arena and not confront the false with His genuine power, as in the days of Elijah (1 Kings 18:19–40)? Let's leave room for God to step into human life as powerfully and clearly in modern times as He has done in the past.

Here's where we draw the line: subjective revelations are not to be used as a source of developing Christian doctrine or teaching. They are not on par with Scripture and must always be tested against it. If there is any discrepancy, the subjective revelation must be discarded as false. Revelation from any source that contradicts the Bible is not from God; it may be from the mind of the speaker or author or from a seducing spirit. There will be no new truth; subjective revelation does not replace or update but only applies biblical truth. If subjective revelations are in line with the written Word and are understood as a release of God's wisdom, we are on safe ground. We should confirm any subjective direction with confirmation from Scripture and godly leaders in the church, with prayer for clarity before we act, and with a sense of peace and assurance in our hearts (which, according to Philippians 4:7, is in itself subjective but valid).

world, and not be greedy and materialistic. They will grieve over the thought of misrepresenting the Lord by their own failures, lay down their lives in service to the body of Christ, love the people they serve, and are careful not to hurt or offend others. Godly leaders will show evidence of a personal devotional life and walk with the Lord, while ungodly leaders will show a professional front, displaying charisma and personality instead of character.

Titus 1:5–9

_____

_____

_____

_____

1 Timothy 3:1–13 (summarize)

_____

_____

_____

_____

Beware of leaders who refuse to change course even when confronted by wise advisors, won't place themselves under accountability, and show unscriptural sexual standards in their actions or comments. Such leaders may frequently boast about their accomplishments and possessions, display arrogance by trampling on the feelings of others, and use people for their own benefit. Steer clear of those who exalt subjective personal experience and minimize the Word of God, seek to draw attention to themselves rather than to the Lord Jesus, make sure everyone knows who they are, and act like a celebrity. In short, if you can't picture the Lord acting the way a supposed man or woman of God consistently acts, that person is probably not genuine.

Realize that false teachers can arise from within the church. Some may have been false converts who had the appearance of being believers but never personally came to the Lord. The fact that leaders once held to the truth or were part of a respected denomination or ministry is no guarantee that they won't fall into pride and error. Examples of this include Jim Jones, whose followers were victims in the greatest mass-enforced suicide in history, and William Branham, who adopted bizarre doctrines and whose followers exalted him as the return of Elijah.

Acts 20:29–31

_____

_____

_____

TRUE STORY

"Hi, Brother Vinnie!" a familiar voice said as I walked through the psychiatric ward at the hospital. We frequently got calls to visit teenagers who had attempted suicide and were hospitalized for their own protection. The young man calling my name was not one of them, and I was shocked at the sight when I entered his room. Ray had disappeared for several years, and his story was a strange one. He had been a hard drug user in high school and was well known for his partying, but Ray had been dramatically converted and became even better known for the change in his lifestyle. The whole school community witnessed the difference Jesus had made, and Ray preached to anyone who would listen. He came faithfully to our Friday night chapel meetings for months until he took a turn for the worse.

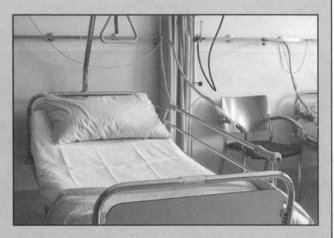

We noticed that Ray seemed to lose the joy of the Lord and became withdrawn. He carried a big stack of Greek reference books and told us he had begun going to a place called The Temple for Bible study. The Temple turned out to be a house where a budding cult had informed Ray that he couldn't be saved until he was baptized, that only their baptism was valid, and that they wouldn't baptize him until he became sinless. All our efforts to show Ray from Scripture that this was entirely wrong were in vain, and soon he attended only The Temple's meetings. Fear dominated him as he tried his best to become sinless so he could be baptized and truly saved. Soon, as he walked away from grace and into self-righteousness, Ray had alienated everyone from school who had seen his conversion to Christ and had been favorably impressed by the transforming grace of God in his life.

Now, about three years later, Ray lay in a hospital bed with his leg in traction and a huge cast with metal pins and other medical apparatus attached to it. He told me in a strangely detached way that he had been doing missionary work in Mexico when he was hit by a car, which shattered his leg. Ray was convinced that God had sent this car as a punishment for his sins, and he had refused medical attention so as to accept God's discipline. Somehow his family found out and forcibly took Ray across the border, where the hospital determined that his injury wasn't the only thing wrong with him.

"I used to wear glasses," Ray rambled, "but then I saw that Jesus never wore glasses. And I don't brush my teeth anymore. Jesus never brushed His teeth, so why would we think it's okay to brush our teeth? It's all evil, brother." Ray gestured toward a painting of a mountain scene on the wall, a serene view probably there to help calm the patients who stayed in that room. Ray told me it, too, was evil. He warned me that he was there because he followed Jesus, and that if I followed Jesus, they would get me, too. It was both pathetic and frightening to see that Ray had suffered a complete mental breakdown, beginning with the deception and fear induced by the people at The Temple, then encouraged by their brainwashing and the devil's plan to steal, kill, and destroy a naive young believer.

1 John 2:18–19

_____

_____

_____

2 Peter 2:1

_____

_____

The message. Watch out for a complicated message. False teachers are skilled in complicating the simple message of the gospel to the point of convincing people that only the leader can really understand God and they should just blindly follow the leader.

2 Corinthians 11:3–4

_____

_____

_____

Miracles. Working miracles, even in Jesus' name, is not necessarily an indication that a person is under God's power. Test to see whether the glory points to Jesus Christ or to somewhere or someone else. It is possible for genuinely supernatural events to have their source in demonic powers and to be part of a deceptive religious system, using the miracles to lead people into following false doctrine.

We must also be aware that there are many ways to fake the appearance of a miracle, including having an associate planted in the audience who works in cooperation with a supposed healer, making exaggerated or unverifiable claims of an alleged gift of healing, putting words in the mouth of a person called on to testify to a healing, and performing in a general circus atmosphere of hype and hysteria. Some Hindu holy men are skilled in deception, and fraudulent miracle workers in North America have also deceived many.

Genuine miracles are the work of the Holy Spirit, not the laws of faith or some anointing that resides in an individual and can be used at his or her discretion. The Holy Spirit came to glorify Jesus, and His work will always point to Christ alone and will never glorify man. We can still expect that God will confirm His Word with signs and wonders, and we should be careful to avoid an attitude of skepticism toward all supernatural events, but we should be wise and discerning about their source.

Mark 16:16–20

_____

_____

_____

_____

John 15:26

_____

_____

2 Thessalonians 2:9–12

_____

_____

_____

2 Corinthians 11:13–15

_____

_____

_____

Matthew 7:22–23

_____

_____

_____

Matthew 24:23–27

_____

_____

_____

The Bible. Examine the message of the leader by comparing it with your own Bible. Don't believe that you need a leader or organization to interpret the Bible for you. God sent the Bible not for scholars and religious leaders but for common people to read and understand. If you have a nagging sense that the leader or group is misusing Scripture, trust your instinct because it is the Holy Spirit who is ultimately our teacher. Be bold enough to leave a spiritual system that is misusing the Bible. Confront a leader who is straying from the truth or jumping to conclusions not evident in the passages he or she quotes or pulling verses out of their context. Beware of a leader building his or her messages on personal thoughts rather than on a genuine biblical foundation, constantly emphasizing favorite themes, or quoting from the writings of any person in a way that gives that person the same authority as the Bible.

1 John 2:26–27

_____

_____

_____

Isaiah 35:8

_____

_____

SCRIPTURE MEMORY

Galatians 5:22–23
But the fruit of the Spirit is love, joy, peace, longsuffering, kindness, goodness, faithfulness, gentleness, self-control. Against such there is no law.

2 Timothy 2:24–26
And a servant of the Lord must not quarrel but be gentle to all, able to teach, patient, in humility correcting those who are in opposition, if God perhaps will grant them repentance, so that they may know the truth, and that they may come to their senses and escape the snare of the devil, having been taken captive by him to do his will.

COMPLETE THE MISSION REPORT ON THE NEXT PAGE.

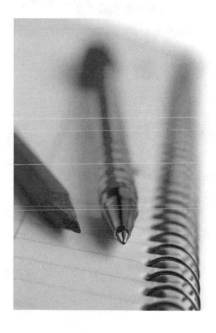

DAILY BIBLE READING

✓ Check when completed		
Sunday	1 Chronicles 10–16	_____
Monday	1 Chronicles 17–21	_____
Tuesday	1 Chronicles 22–27	_____
Wednesday	1 Chronicles 28–29	_____
Thursday	2 Chronicles 1–5	_____
Friday	2 Chronicles 6–9	_____
Saturday	2 Chronicles 10–12	_____

BIBLE READING QUESTIONS/THOUGHTS

_____
_____
_____
_____
_____
_____
_____
_____
_____

PRAYER NEEDS THIS WEEK

_____
_____
_____
_____
_____
_____
_____
_____

4

MISSION REPORT

We recommend using *Operation World* (21st Century Edition) by Patrick Johnstone and Jason Mandryk as a reference. See page 12 for details.

Country name:

Capital:

Population:

Ethnic groups:

Official language(s):

Literacy rate:

Average income (or GDP per capita):

Major religions:

Percentage of evangelical Christians:

Number of missionaries to the country:

Prayer needs:

1.

2.

3.

4.

Lesson four
KEYS TO SHARING THE GOSPEL WITH PEOPLE FROM CULTS AND WORLD RELIGIONS

It's important to balance several aspects of our witness to a lost world. Having rational answers to theological issues is only one part. We must understand and communicate doctrinal truth, but it's also crucial to know how to establish relationships with others, live a godly lifestyle, and demonstrate Christianity as well as discuss it. In this lesson we will look at some keys to sharing the gospel with people from cults and world religions. These keys will be important to keep in mind as you study cults and world religions in the coming weeks.

1. Live an honorable life, keep your word, and show Christlike character. People from other belief systems are often highly moral, try to live out their ethical standards, and will watch to see if you do the same.

Galatians 5:22–23

_____

_____

_____

2. Show respect for God, the Bible, and His laws. Mention God throughout your regular conversations. We must demonstrate that faith in God is not just a small compartment in our lives but the underlying reason for our existence.

Proverbs 28:14

_____

_____

3. Show an emphasis on family ties in your own life. Many other beliefs point to the decline in the family in Western life and put a high value on relationships at home. The Bible stresses the importance of love, respect, and honoring family members.

Ephesians 5:22–32; 6:1–4

_____

_____

_____

_____

4. Find ways to respect and serve the person you are witnessing to. Because servanthood shows Christ's character, help people with homework, with transportation, on the job, etc. Because courtesy honors others, hold doors open and let them go first, show appreciation for things they do, and look for opportunities to demonstrate the way your faith governs and guides your lifestyle.

Matthew 5:16

_____

_____

5. Don't debate or argue. Your goal is not to conquer others' beliefs and show your superior knowledge, but to speak the truth in love (Ephesians 4:15). The main point is not to destroy their religion by showing its contradictions, flawed leadership, and embarrassing history but rather to introduce them to Jesus. What good have you done if you leave their faith destroyed but have not given them a replacement belief in Christ?

TRUE STORY

The strange young man approached me in the post office parking lot with an offering bucket and a magazine. He seemed somewhat mentally scrambled as he talked about the Holy Spirit Foundation and getting kids off drugs. I asked to see the magazine he was holding, and he kept mumbling while I flipped through it in search of a name to identify what group he was affiliated with. The last page told of the great achievements of the Reverend Sun Myung Moon and the Unification Church. Bingo!

"I see you are from the Unification Church," I said, "and I can tell you that Reverend Moon is definitely not the second coming of Christ, because I know the first coming of Christ!"

The man's eyes widened with terror, and he bolted across the parking lot. At the time, I didn't know that the thoroughly brainwashed disciples of this false messiah are taught that if anyone confronts their beliefs, it is actually Satan in disguise. So, not knowing that he thought I was literally the devil incarnate, I chased him and caught him as he approached another postal patron.

Never taking his fearful eyes off me and not saying a word, he kept backing up slowly as I tried in vain to tell him about the real Jesus. After a while, I gave up and left him. Another victim of end-times deception.

2 Timothy 2:24–26

_____

_____

_____

_____

_____

_____

James 1:20

_____

_____

_____

_____

6. Have fun together. Build relationships and become friends. The best illustration of the value of friendship in evangelism comes from Laurence Singlehurst's excellent book _Sowing, Reaping, and Keeping._ Singlehurst compares the gospel to a five-ton truck that has to go over a bridge with a one-ton weight limit. The truck symbolizes the gospel message, and the bridge is the relationship with the lost person. The weight of the five-ton truck would collapse the bridge and destroy the relationship. It's better to break the load down to five trucks, each carrying only one ton, and drive them across one at a time.[1]

Proverbs 18:24

_____

_____

_____

_____

7. Make friends with foreign students. Far from home and in a foreign culture, many foreign students experience loneliness and desire friendship. Show them hospitality and include them in activities with godly friends.

Leviticus 19:33

_____

_____

8. Listen to people. Find out what they think and how they feel. Are they convinced that they have the truth, or are they still searching?

James 1:19

_____

_____

9. Beware of individuals trying to convert you to their beliefs. All cults and religions have their apologists—people who have studied and have answers for Christian evangelists. This course is not detailed enough to answer every argument. Refer to the recommended resources on pages 172–174 for more in-depth study. Beware of less knowledgeable cult members or members of another religion who find themselves stumped when talking to you and come back with an expert in their faith. If they want to meet with you, be sure to bring reinforcements who are more knowledgeable than you are. Study, pray, and fast before the meeting, and have reference materials with you as well as literature to leave with them.

Jeremiah 10:2

_____

_____

10. Be familiar with current beliefs and thoughts. Jesus and the apostles were aware of Greek poets and contemporary issues. Christians today should have something to say about the topics under discussion in the world around them and use these topics as opportunities for sharing the gospel. Ignorance is not a sign of spirituality.

Luke 13:1–5

_____

_____

_____

Titus 1:12

_____

_____

Acts 17:28

_____

_____

11. Don't read the scriptures of cults and other religions. These scriptures contain more than different ideas and are demonically inspired and have the power to deceive. Powerful spiritual forces are behind Mormon books, New Age books, and the Koran.

Hebrews 13:9

_____

_____

1 Timothy 4:1

_____

_____

12. Don't go to non-Christian religious meetings. You'll come under the influence of the spirits behind their beliefs. Taking off your shoes to enter a mosque or temple is a sign of reverence for the deity within, as with Moses before the burning bush (Exodus 3:5), so don't do it! Remember that Ephesians 6:15 tells us to keep our feet shod in a spiritual sense with the gospel of peace.

Hebrews 13:9

_____

_____

13. Use your personal testimony. Doing this will help people know that you're not just repeating theology your leaders have taught you or that Christianity is not just a part of your culture or family background. A story of God's intervention, protection, provision, change in your lifestyle, peace in your heart, or other results of a living relationship with a living Savior will take your discussion out of the realm of comparing religions and make your doctrine come alive.

Mark 5:19

_____

_____

Acts 4:20

_____

_____

14. Avoid belittling, insulting comments. Such comments make people feel as though you think they are primitive or uneducated. Also avoid critical remarks about the Christian church, disputes about denominations, and discussion on the flaws of Christian leaders.

2 Timothy 2:24

_____

_____

THEOLOGY 101: The Differences between Cults and World Religions

Frequently people mix the terms *religion, cult,* and *occult* as though they mean the same thing, but there are important distinctions between them.

A religion, broadly defined, is a system of faith and worship. World religions are not based on a Christian foundation but are developed from ancient idolatry as described throughout the Old Testament. They generally recognize Jesus as a good man, a teacher of truth, or a prophet while denying His claims to be the only begotten Son of God. World religions rely on holy books reflecting an entirely different view of creation, the nature of God, man's role and future, sin, and the afterlife. The one religion that is an exception to this description is Judaism, which follows Old Testament truth while missing the Messiah it points toward.

Cults are religious groups that distort the doctrines or practices of established religions. Some branches of world religions function as cults by taking some of the fundamental teachings of the original religion and modifying them. Examples are Sikhism, Jainism, and Baha'i.

"Christian" cults hold false doctrines based on a generally biblical framework. Although they may use the Bible and Christian terminology, they deny one or more fundamental truths, such as the Trinity, the deity of Christ, and the blood atonement of Jesus as being sufficient to save us. Most cults rely on teachings or writings of strong leaders who claim to have revelations of a restored Christian faith or a better faith that supersedes Christianity. Cults often teach doctrines that appeal to a lost person, such as denying the existence of hell, allowing immorality, and gaining salvation by human effort. Cult policies generally try to shield their members from the truth of God's Word and often train them in arguments against a true Christian witness.

The variety of "Christian" cults is endless, but generally they repeat false doctrines that developed in the days of the early church and were refuted by the church fathers. Often cults exalt humans to the status of a god or present God as just a few steps above humanity. Cults emphasize converting outsiders and have a persecution mentality, believing that all rejection of their beliefs reinforces the truth of their doctrine. Manipulation, fear, and authoritarian control are tools used to gain members and keep them in a cult.

New cults develop all the time. Some are offshoots of older, more established cults, and spiritually bankrupt places like the Western world are the prime breeding ground for new doctrines to develop.

Occult means hidden, and occultism is the use of hidden or secret practices to gain knowledge and power. This includes magic, witchcraft, fortune-telling, and a wide range of supernatural practices designed to give the user an advantage over others through calling upon mystical and paranormal forces to intervene in the natural realm. By bringing in the element of the supernatural, these approaches to harnessing and using spiritual power set the false belief systems of cults and world religions apart from philosophies and theories. Occult practices can be found in many world religions and cults.

15. Recognize the reasons people join cults or are members of other religions. These include spiritual hunger, the desire to belong, ignorance of God's Word, cultural faiths expected in their nation, the need for direction in their lives, concerns about guilt and the condition of their souls, family influences, and demonic deception.

Proverbs 27:7

_____

_____

16. Expect a time of reasoning rather than instant conversion. This is particularly the case for those who come from a non-Christian-based culture. Although we in the Western world have forsaken our spiritual roots, we still have a culture based upon a biblical framework. This includes basics of a

Christian worldview such as believing in objective truth, a legal system based on biblical ethics, general belief in the God of the Bible, and acceptance of many of the issues that Scripture delineates as right or wrong. The presence of these qualities in Western culture, although they are diminishing, still means that we are starting from a similar foundation in discussing faith with most people in our nations. This is a springboard from which we call people to faith in Jesus.

One of the greatest surprises to me when I first went to India and preached in villages where no Christians had ever been before was that the people weren't ready to see the light and immediately surrender their lives to Jesus. When I prayed about this, the Lord reminded me of the many places in Scripture that refer to reasoning, which means to discuss something logically. This helped me to have realistic rather than idealistic expectations for the results of my preaching.

Acts 18:4

_____

_____

Acts 24:25

_____

_____

It is unreasonable to think that in an hour or two a person is likely to discard centuries of cultural, family, and religious background to believe in something he or she has never heard of before. This is not meant to say that God couldn't reveal Himself in a convincing way in an instant and that the person receiving such a great revelation couldn't sincerely turn to Him. Both history and people's testimonies show that this happens, but often Scripture shows a slower progression of faith. Keep in mind that Jesus warned us about converts whose faith springs up immediately but doesn't have roots. Instant conversions are a special concern with people who are coming from a polytheistic (believing in many gods) background, such as Hinduism, because they may just add Jesus to the list of gods they already worship. A true conversion comes when Jesus takes His place of supreme lordship over all the false gods in a person's life, and this kind of decision may take time.

Matthew 13:20–21

_____

_____

_____

In the case of a cultist who is familiar with basic Christian doctrine but has been taught false beliefs, sorting out the true from the false is also a process. Don't give up in frustration if the results come slowly. And don't draw back from the person and make him or her feel that Christians love others only in order to convert them but stop loving them if they don't immediately respond.

Isaiah 1:18

_____

_____

17. Realize that people have to count the cost. The person you are trying to reach has the added dilemma of counting the cost to believe in Christ. This may mean being ostracized by family members, losing a job, or even suffering violent persecution. Understanding this will keep you in an attitude of compassion, but you must still firmly present the claims of Christ on your friend's life.

Matthew 16:24–26

_____

_____

_____

18. Be sure your knowledge of the Bible is up to the task. Your study of Scripture is an essential foundation and preparation that the Lord can supplement with supernatural wisdom at the time you need it.

2 Timothy 3:16–17

_____

_____

_____

Titus 1:9

_____

_____

Know how to use Scripture in evangelism. Many religions and cults don't recognize the authority of Scripture. They will claim that anything which contradicts their beliefs is an incorrect translation of the original message of the Bible, or they may replace the Bible with their own books, although they would claim to recognize the Bible as the truth. New Agers may say that the Bible is your truth, not their truth, since they don't believe in an objective source of reality. Instead of trying only rational arguments, recognize the power of God's Word and its ability to cut through their defenses and deceptions.

Hebrews 4:12

_____

_____

Isaiah 55:10–11

_____

_____

_____

Don't mislead the person into thinking you see his or her holy book as an authoritative source of truth. Since books from other religions and cults present a false picture of Jesus, they are useful only as a starting point for evangelism. Your use of that book is only to find a common ground of shared belief, similar to Paul's use of Athenian thought in Acts 17:22–31.

Galatians 1:6–9

_____

_____

_____

19. Pray and fast. Intercede for the person you're trying to reach, asking the Lord to break through their defenses, to open his or her heart and mind, to bind the work of deceptive spirits, and to send other Christians to reinforce the message you're sharing. Pray for the person to be overcome by the truth, and pray against the influence of family and friends who would keep the person in the false belief. Pray for life circumstances to point the person toward his or her need for Jesus. Pray for wisdom and patience for yourself, and ask the Lord to protect you from deception and spiritual attacks.

2 Corinthians 4:4

_____

_____

James 5:16

_____

_____

20. Be accountable to a spiritual authority. This includes your pastor, youth leader, or parent who knows that you are sharing the gospel with someone living by false doctrine. He or she can pray for you and with you and also make sure you're not falling into error.

Hebrews 13:17

_____

_____

Introduction

INTRODUCTION TO STUDYING WORLD RELIGIONS AND CULTS

In the following lessons you'll find some very negative information about the religion or cult under discussion. There are two directions you can go with this. The first is to use it as a weapon against people in that faith, embarrassing them publicly or privately with sarcasm, mockery, and haughtiness, knowing that the facts are on your side and that history shows these points are accurate and valid. You may silence your opponents and win arguments but forever close their hearts to Christians, the Bible, and the true God. Approaching a lost person as an opponent is not God's way. This book is written with the hope that you will go the second direction—that you will react to the dark secrets of these religions and cults in a Christlike manner and that you'll be mature and wise with the sometimes sordid history you'll read. These points were put here not for shock value but for the following reasons:

- To make absolutely clear that these other belief systems cannot be from God, when their founders taught and practiced lifestyles so obviously contrasting not only Christian doctrines but also commonly accepted standards for behavior, even among the lost world.
- To strengthen your resolve not to be lured into these religions, not to date or marry someone who is part of them, and not to accept them as valid belief systems, as our world's perspective on diversity and tolerance pressures us to do.
- To instill in you a burden to win people from these false teachings to the truth found in Jesus.

If there is ever a reason to bring up the darkest points in history and practice to people from one of these faiths, it would be the following. Speaking in humility and earnestness to openhearted people who are torn between their background and a growing knowledge of the truth, we appeal to their awakened conscience with points that show their beliefs are not founded on the solid ground of truth. In a gentle rather than attacking spirit, we show that their leaders violate the people's own view of decent conduct and that their religion has made absurd statements that prove it cannot be valid. This is completely different from bludgeoning others with superior knowledge and dazzling facts and ridiculing them in public. On the basis that you are committed to a godly approach to evangelism, let's move forward. But if you plan to use this book as a weapon, please mail it back to me for a refund!

The final section of each teaching lists beliefs of the cult or religion on the left and contains a column of lines on the right. Here's where you will find out how much you know about your own faith. Before meeting with your mentor or class, carefully read the beliefs in the left-hand column. What do they say that's true? What is almost true? What is completely wrong? Then write Scripture in the right-hand column to agree with truths that the cultists or members of other religions believe, or to correct their errors. Don't feel bad if you try but can't find enough biblical support to answer their doctrines. During your meeting with your mentor or your class, you'll find out what verses others have found and you can fill in what you lack. One goal of this weekly assignment is to help you gauge how well-equipped you are to be useful to God in evangelism. You'll repeat this for each chapter.

A second goal of completing the two-column assignment is to teach you to read and think carefully and critically. It's too easy to allow others to do your thinking for you or just accept whatever others say is right. If you learn to go back to God's Word to find out the truth, you can stay out of error and lead others to the truth. Once you get the idea of this, you'll be excited to see your discernment of truth and error and your knowledge of the Bible growing. Are you ready? Let's go!

WORLD RELIGIONS

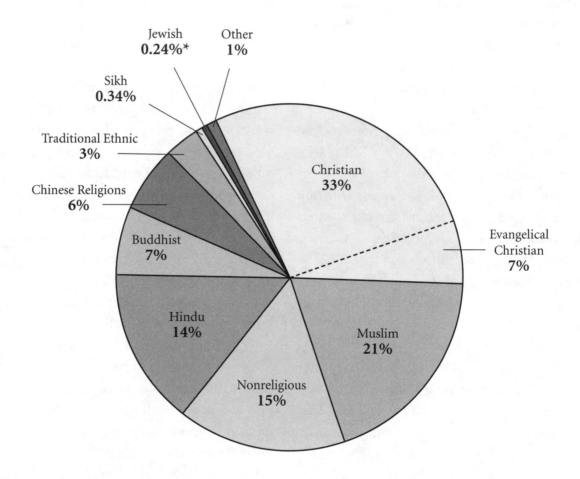

Then He said to His disciples, "The harvest truly is plentiful, but the laborers are few. Therefore pray the Lord of the harvest to send out laborers into His harvest."
—*Matthew 9:37–38*

* Religion percentages are from Patrick Johnstone and Jason Mandryk, *Operation World: 21st Century Edition,* updated and revised ed. (Tyrone, Ga.: Authentic Media, 2005), 2.

SCRIPTURE MEMORY

Romans 5:8
But God demonstrates His own love toward us, in that while we were still sinners, Christ died for us.

Isaiah 53:6
All we like sheep have gone astray; we have turned, every one, to his own way; and the LORD has laid on Him the iniquity of us all.

FINISH READING YOUR BOOK AND COMPLETE BOOK REPORT 1 ON THE NEXT PAGE.

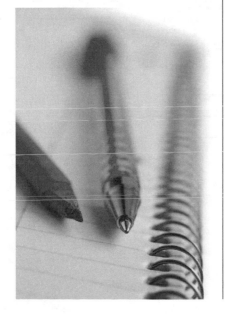

DAILY BIBLE READING

✓ Check when completed	
Sunday	2 Chronicles 13–16 ____
Monday	2 Chronicles 17–20 ____
Tuesday	2 Chronicles 21–25 ____
Wednesday	2 Chronicles 26–28 ____
Thursday	2 Chronicles 29–32 ____
Friday	2 Chronicles 33–36 ____
Saturday	Ezra 1–3 ____

BIBLE READING QUESTIONS/THOUGHTS

_____
_____
_____
_____
_____
_____
_____
_____
_____
_____

PRAYER NEEDS THIS WEEK

_____
_____
_____
_____
_____
_____
_____
_____

5

BOOK REPORT 1

Book title: _____

Author: _____

What did you like about it?

_____
_____
_____
_____

Would you recommend it to others?

_____
_____

What impressed you most about this book?

_____
_____
_____
_____

How did God use the book to speak to you?

_____
_____
_____
_____

Other comments or thoughts about the book:

_____
_____
_____
_____
_____

Lesson five

ISLAM

Islam is the name of the religion that began in Mecca, Saudi Arabia, about AD 610, and Muslims are the followers of Islam. The "prophet" Muhammad claimed to receive divine revelations from the angel Gabriel. These revelations became the content of the Muslim holy book, the Koran (or Qur'an, abbreviated as Q). (These events are very similar to the way that Mormonism began. See page 115.) Gabriel allegedly choked Muhammad into submission and ordered him to proclaim these teachings. Muhammad stated that he didn't know whether these experiences originated from God or from the devil, but his wife convinced him they were from God.

Muhammad began with the already accepted teaching of a supreme god named Allah and emphasized to the idol worshipers in his region that there is only one true god. Although Muhammad had contact with Christians, he misunderstood the concept of the Trinity and believed that Christians worshiped three gods—God the Father, Jesus, and Mary (Q 5:116). His teachings spread rapidly, usually because his armies forced the people they conquered to convert to Islam. Since Muhammad was illiterate, others wrote his teachings, which formed the Koran. Muslims also follow the *hadith,* sayings attributed to Muhammad and leading Muslim clerics.

ISLAM TODAY

Islam is the fastest growing religion in the world because of the high birthrate in Muslim countries. (Christianity is growing much faster in terms of conversions.) Now about 1.4 billion people—more than one-fifth of the world's population—are Muslim. About fifty nations follow Islam as their primary religion, including 97 percent of the Middle East, 50 percent of West Africa, and 40 percent of Southeast Asia. Increasing numbers of Muslim immigrants and their large families are affecting the religious makeup of Europe; there are twelve Muslims for every born-again (evangelical) Christian in France.[1]

Muslims don't all live in the Middle East. The largest Muslim country in the world is Indonesia, with 205 million followers of Muhammad. You might be surprised at the Muslim population in the following countries:[2]

China, 25 million	Russia, 15 million
France, 6 million	Thailand, 3 million
India, 127 million	USA, 4 million

Terms and Concepts

sharia: strict Islamic law based on the Koran.

hadiths: sayings attributed to Muhammad and leading Muslim clerics that outline the basics for living.

mosque: an Islamic place of worship.

The Five Pillars of Islam:
1. Reciting the creed "There is no God but Allah and Muhammad is his Prophet."
2. Prayer bowing towards Mecca five times each day.
3. Giving alms to the poor.
4. Fasting, especially until sunset each day during the month of Ramadan, during which Muhammad said he received the Koran from Gabriel.
5. Making a pilgrimage to Mecca at least once in their lifetime.

jihad: holy war against non-Muslims. Many Muslims consider it to be the sixth pillar. Moderate Muslims believe jihad is an internal struggle, while fundamentalists believe it is divine approval for violent conquest of the enemies of Islam.

Islam is a missionary religion with a focus on spreading Muhammad's message throughout the earth. Its goal is to dominate the entire world, bringing it into submission to Allah and Islamic law. Oil-rich Middle Eastern nations pay for the spread of Islam into new areas. Saudi Arabia has committed $87 billion to convert the United States to Islam.[3]

Countries that follow strict *sharia* (Islamic law) are the most radical and violent against those who disobey the Koran. Islamic fundamentalist groups try to bring moderate Muslim countries under *sharia*. Many Muslim nations won't allow open Christian evangelism. The most effective ways for Westerners to enter and live in a closed nation are through business contacts there, by attending a university, or by teaching English. Medical and relief workers also are able to enter closed nations.

BELIEFS AND PRACTICES

Muslims believe that Allah is the one supreme god and that they must submit to his will on all matters. This perspective traces back to the meaning of *Islam*—submission to whatever Allah wants. Because Islam is a religion of submission, Muslims generally don't ask Allah to bless them. Both happy events and disasters are the will of Allah; therefore Muslims accept whatever he wills, without trying to change circumstances or expected outcomes through prayer. This is called fatalism, and differs from Christian belief that God hears fervent petitions yet has the final authority to override prayer. Our faith in God's nature and character causes us to trust Him, regardless of how circumstances turn out.

The Allah of Islam is vastly different in nature from the God of the Bible, and Muslims relate to Allah in an entirely different way from how Christians relate to the Lord. Allah is an absolute and incomprehensible god who cannot really be known and does not intimately care for his people. A point of possible confusion is that Christians in Arabic-speaking nations use the common word *Allah* for God but define His nature according to the Bible rather than the Koran. Because of their common language, Christian and Muslim Arabs use the same title for differing deities.

Some Muslims use a rosary to recite the ninety-nine known names of Allah in order to remember his attributes. Some of the ninety-nine known names acknowledge characteristics that correlate to the God of the Bible, but others show the fundamental differences in the natures of Allah and Yahweh. There is no name for Allah meaning "god is love," and he is called by names that Christians would recognize as attributes of Satan, including the following:

Al-Darr—The Harmer
Al-Mumit—The Bringer of Death, The Destroyer
Al-Mutakabbir—The Most Proud One[4]

The concept of God as Father is offensive to Muslims, who believe this means physical parenting, which is blasphemy. This affects their understanding of Jesus as the Son of God.

Allah is described in the Koran as willing to send people to hell based on his personal decision on judgment day and not on the life of the individual. Muslims don't believe in the need for forgiveness because of their belief that man is essentially good, but they still devotedly attempt to fulfill all of the Koran's requirements so that their good deeds will outweigh their bad deeds. Good and bad angels sit on the shoulders of each Muslim and record his or her deeds, but even the record of a "good" life isn't enough to guarantee entrance to paradise—this depends on Allah's decision.[5]

The only certain way of attaining paradise is to die as a martyr in *jihad* against the enemies of Islam (Q 47:4–6). A Muslim can be martyred in the commonly understood sense of being killed for one's faith, as has happened frequently in India at the hands of Hindu nationalists. Radical Muslims, however, interpret *jihad* to include both traditional warfare and terrorist acts. The motivation of a guaranteed entrance to paradise is why an endless pool of *jihadi* warriors and suicide bombers is available to terrorist organizations.

Paradise is viewed not as a place of eternal fellowship with god but as a place of eternal eating, drinking, and sex. Islamic tradition teaches that seventy-two virgins await each Muslim man who enters paradise. Traditions of some Muslim clerics have increased this to five hundred prostitutes, four thousand virgins, and eight thousand divorced women.[6] Interviews with young men training as suicide bombers show that the expectation of sensual delights in paradise is their primary motivation, not love of their country or religion.[7]

Islam has various divisions, with a history of hatred and war between them. *Shiites* (10 percent, mostly found in Iran) and *Sunnis* (90 percent) disagree on who should have followed Muhammad as leader of the Muslim faith when he died. *Sufis* are a small, mystical group who meditate on Allah for deeper understanding. *Wahhabis* are the most radical group. They believe in the strictest interpretation of the Koran, including violent *jihad* and strict *sharia*. Secular Muslim nations such as Turkey have majority populations who practice Islam but don't rule their nation based

TRUE STORY

We spent five life-changing weeks in Ethiopia in 2004. Hearing the voice of the *muezzin* through loudspeakers near our base shouting, "Allahu Akhbar" (God is great), the wailing call to prayer from the mosques five times each day, was a regular reminder of the billion-plus Muslims living in darkness.

A meeting with a pastor in one of the largest churches there shed some interesting light on understanding Islam. He said that Muslims already consider Ethiopia to be an Islamic nation and that over half the elected officials in the country are Muslims. This is due to their strategic approach to take complete control of the country.

Pastor Girum told me that Muslims are taking over through numerous means, including population growth. The Koran allows men four wives and unlimited slave girls. Though slavery is illegal in Ethiopia, multiple Muslim wives are common, and many Muslim men have up to thirty children. Ethiopia has the second highest population in all of Africa and is the poorest nation in the world. I asked Pastor Girum how the men can support such large families, and he said that Muslims are very aggressive and successful in business. He added that because they often have no scruples about dealing dishonestly in business and cheating others, they make a lot of money. In a country with low life expectancy and lots of AIDS and starvation, Christian women are often widowed at a young age. Muslim men offer to marry them, provide for them, and give their children an education. Faced with the alternatives of starvation and prostitution, they agree. Then their husbands rename the children Mohammed, Hussein, etc., put them in Islamic schools, and force their wives to convert to Islam.

Oil money from Saudi Arabia and other nations is flowing into Africa to promote radical Islam, and Ethiopia is one of the places this is happening. I heard about villages with traditional mud and stick huts in which the only nice buildings are the mosque and the Koranic schools. On Muslim holidays, the mosques bring in Muslim villagers from far outside the capital of Addis Ababa to parade through the streets in a show of force, thus intimidating Christians into believing that Islam has already taken over. As we ministered in churches that consisted of leaky tents, it was sad to see the construction of large and modern mosques nearby.

on the Koran. A majority of the world's Muslims follow what is called folk Islam, in which they replace or supplement traditional Islamic beliefs with superstitions, angels, demons, charms and spells, genies, the evil eye, saints, and holy men and their tombs.

Only about 15 to 20 percent of Muslims are fundamentalists, who believe in following Allah's orders to conquer the world for Islam.[8] However, this amounts to 200 million Muslims worldwide. From followers of this perspective come a smaller number of radical terrorists.

The majority of Muslims are not terrorists and place a high value on close family ties, honorable living, hospitality, loyalty, and prayer.

The Nation of Islam, or Black Muslims, are an entirely different branch of Islam, not accepted by most Muslims as genuine followers of Allah. Their beliefs include angry racism, reincarnation, and the existence of UFOs.[9] Followers make up a small percentage of the Muslims in the United States.

Despite differences and offshoots of Islam, the major branches hold most beliefs and practices in common. For example, many devoted Muslims known as Qurras memorize the entire Koran (containing 78,000 words in 114 chapters or Suras—about 80 percent of the New Testament's length) and recite it on a special Muslim holy day known as the Night of Power toward the end of the holy month of Ramadan. To avoid idolatry, Muslim art consists only of intricate geometric patterns and plant life, without statues or representations of any animal. The strictest interpretation of this causes Muslims to believe that even photography of people is idolatry. Muslims are not allowed to drink alcohol, eat pork, or gamble.

ISLAM AND CURRENT EVENTS

Islam is at the forefront of world news, and not just because of oil prices and terrorism. Other significant social issues and the impact of the large number of Muslims in the world make Islam a focal point of global attention. For example, slavery is going on today in Sudan, Pakistan, and Mauritania.[10] Christian adults and children are major targets of Muslim slave traders.[11] Upheavals in Muslim nations are the reason that nearly one half of the refugees in the world are Muslim.[12]

Islam often makes the news because of the violent behavior of some of its followers. Note the following headlines and news stories about Islamic violence from respected news sources from 2005 to 2008:

- "Indonesians Jailed for Beheadings" tells that "An Indonesian court has sentenced three Muslim militants to jail for beheading three Christian schoolgirls in Central Sulawesi in 2005."[13]
- "Sudan arrests UK teacher for teddy bear blasphemy." In Sudan, British schoolteacher Gillian Gibbons was formally charged with blasphemy after allowing her students to name a teddy bear Muhammad. A blasphemy charge is punishable by 40 lashes, but a later international outcry lessened the sentence to 15 days in jail.[14]
- "The rise of the female suicide bomber: Number of Iraq attacks involving women has doubled this year."[15]
- "Muslim cartoon fury claims lives." When a cartoonist in Denmark drew a picture of Muhammad with a bomb in his turban, riots around the world claimed many lives. Muslim protestors throughout Europe carried signs saying, "Europe you will pay—your 9/11 is on its way!" and "Massacre those who insult Islam." *Behead, slay, butcher,* and *exterminate* were also words used on the signs carried by representatives of Islam.[16]

TRUE STORY

The Indian shopkeeper was the last person I would have expected to be the most aggressive, skilled, and knowledgeable Muslim "evangelist" I've ever met. After I had looked around his store, Ali asked in flawless English where I was from. Hearing that I was from the United States, he smiled broadly and said, "I love the United States and its people, because they are responding more rapidly to the message of Islam than anywhere else in the world."

This statement threw down a challenge I couldn't ignore. "Have you read in the Koran that Muslims should study the Injil to learn about the life of Jesus?" I asked.

Ali's eyes grew wide. "For seven years I have talked with many Christians and many missionaries, yet you are the first one to quote the Koran to me!"

From there, the battle was on. Only one customer entered the store the entire time, and Ali ignored her completely. I told him I am a follower of Isa al-Masih according to the way of the Injil (a follower of Jesus the Messiah according to the New Testament). For an hour and a half we covered every angle on the topic of Christianity and Islam. We left out politics and jihad, and I avoided the offensive but true issues of bloody Muslim conquests, mistreatment of women, and Muhammad's pedophilic sexual relationship with his nine-year-old wife.

Ali charged that Christians have different Bibles, but there is only one Koran. I countered that the Catholic Church inserted additional historical books into the Old Testament in much the same way that Muslims value the hadiths of Muhammad's sayings. Ali brushed aside my answers, telling me that he had studied all the world's religions before converting to Islam.

I pushed hard on the fact that the Koran teaches that Muhammad never did a single miracle (although they consider his dictation of the Koran to be miraculous), while it says that Jesus did many miracles. I pointed out that the Koran shows that Muhammad had to ask for forgiveness, proving he was a flawed and sinful man, while it says that Jesus was sinless. Why should anyone follow Muhammad when Jesus was clearly superior to him? Ali couldn't answer why Jesus is only the second highest prophet in Islam when His life was greater than Muhammad's. I explained that the concept of Jesus as the Son of God, which is called *shirk* in Islam and is the greatest blasphemy, does not at all imply sexual relations between God and Mary, as Muslims believe. Ali quoted Koranic verses on the wrath of Allah and the eternal torment of unbelievers and claimed that he loved Jesus more than I did because he believed in Him according to the Koran's teaching.

As members of our mission team walked by the door, they saw the intense conversation and kept going without entering. I found myself hoping they would pray for me to have God's wisdom, and I stretched to remember everything I had learned about Islam. It was a huge challenge for me, even though I am the one who wrote this book! (You'll notice that the points I made in this encounter sound a lot like this chapter. That's because my research for this book is where I learned them.)

Each time I hit a nerve, Ali changed the subject. He was forceful and insistent all the way through the conversation. I found that waiting for him to pause so I could speak was pointless, since he never ran out of breath. I had to just jump in and start to reply to his charges against Christianity.

Ali pulled a worn and bookmarked Bible from behind the counter. He could quote Scripture better than most Christians, but his eyes were blinded to the truth. He relied on obscure scientific claims for the Koran being God's final and greatest revelation to mankind, while I homed in on his need for salvation. "Ali," I asked, "what about your sins? You know that there are many things you have done wrong, just as I have. Everything you stole as a boy, lies you have told, women you have lustfully desired…how will these sins be forgiven?"

I stated that even our bodies produce continual uncleanness, which is a reminder to Muslims, who carefully follow procedures of washing before prayer, that we can never be completely clean. The uncleanness of our sins also comes from within. Ali didn't have an answer. Finally, appearing frustrated and agitated, he asked me if I ate pork. Hearing a yes, he lit up and triumphantly accused me of not living out my own religion. It backfired as I explained the reason for the laws of the Old Testament and how, under the new covenant, we don't obey the laws as a source of righteousness. He looked with interest as I showed him Acts 10:10–16 in his own Bible.

By this time, we were both mentally exhausted, and my team was waiting for me. Ali asked for my e-mail address, which I gave him, and said that he would e-mail me lectures on the Koran and proofs of its truth. I told him I would pray for him, that God would give him the revelation of the truth of who Jesus is. So far I haven't heard from him. Pray for Ali and 1.4 billion Muslims like him.

- "Radical Islam blamed for French rioting." Seventy-five hundred cars were burned in three hundred cities as youth rioted throughout the country. The media downplayed the actual cause, saying the youth were "poor, unemployed and disenfranchised." The truth is that they were poor, unemployed, disenfranchised Muslims protesting the death of two youth who were being pursued by police.[17]
- "National Publisher Kills Spokane Journalist's Book." Random House, the world's largest English-language publisher, terminated publication of a book on Muhammad's child bride Aisha for fear that "it could incite acts of violence by a small, radical segment."[18]

MODERATE AND RADICAL ISLAM

Islam divides all of mankind into two categories: the House of Islam and the House of War.[19] This means that all non-Muslims are in opposition to the Koran's goal (Q 2:190–193) of seeing the entire world under Allah's rule and therefore must be brought into submission by any means necessary.

Moderate Muslims may seek peaceful means of accomplishing this objective, such as influencing the political process, outreach to the prisons and inner cities as is common in the US, education and community awareness programs, and distribution of Korans. Moderates, however, do not make the headlines as fundamentalists regularly do.

Radical Muslims will use violent means to terrorize and demoralize those who do not submit to Allah. The Ayatollah Khomeini, a deceased former ruler of Iran, said, "The purest joy in Islam is to kill and be killed for Allah."[20]

It is important to emphasize that the 80 to 85 percent of Muslims who do not hold to radical or violent views can be sincere in following the Koran and the Five Pillars of Islam. Unlike radical Muslims, they view Koranic passages advocating violence as historical rather than currently binding, or as metaphors rather than literal orders. Moderates have often been targets of violence for fundamentalists who view them as apostates and enemies of true Islam. Many moderate Muslims in the West have synthesized the comforts of a modern lifestyle and cultural values with the faith of their ancestors. They believe a correct interpretation of the Koran directs them to avoid compulsion in religion such as *sharia*, and for that reason they do not condone violence.

However, we must ask moderate Muslims some hard questions. Why do we not hear more moderates speaking out against terrorism, Koranic approval of violence against women, or honor killings? Why don't we see them using the weight of numbers to shut down terrorist organizations, voting out or overthrowing Islamist regimes, refusing to give to and denouncing any Islamic charity that supports terrorism, or identifying with and protecting minority religions who face severe persecution in nearly all Muslim dominated nations?

These issues raise the concerns that one of the following motives exists: that moderates live in fear of repercussions from radicals if they speak out; that they have an underlying agreement with the tactics and goals of radicals, even if they would not use the same tactics themselves; or that some moderate Muslims are actually silent fundamentalist Muslims.

The dividing line between moderate and fundamentalist Muslims is not fixed. Individuals or mosques may shift perspectives in either direction over time. Factors that can lead to increased radicalization include Imams (spiritual leaders in mosques) who declare that the true interpretation of the Koran is the literal one and stir up anti-Western or anti-Christian and Jewish sentiments, unemployed and angry young men who are ripe for a message of violence, and increasing numbers of Muslim immigrants whose cultures clash with host nations.

Recall the spirit that inspired Muhammad and the pattern of Mohammad's life and conduct. It is reasonable to consider that the demonic spirit behind Islam will always attempt to point its followers in the most destructive direction possible, as the history of the rise of Islam demonstrates. Current studies

THEOLOGY 101: The Trinity

Misunderstanding or denying the Trinity is common in cults and world religions. Some claim that the doctrine is unbiblical because the word *Trinity* is not found in Scripture. Although the word itself is not found in Scripture, the teaching of the Trinity is found throughout the Bible, and the term became the traditional Christian way of labeling the Godhead.

The triunity, or threeness, of God is a difficult concept, and our human brains, no matter how smart we are, are not able to grasp many aspects of the truth. We would have to be God to understand Him 100 percent, and contrary to false teachings, we are not and will never become divine. All our efforts to neatly package the doctrine of the Trinity fall short, and the analogies you may have heard are very imperfect attempts at making this easy. For example, people compare the Three-in-One to water, which can exist as a solid, liquid, or gas, or to an apple, with its peel, fruit, and seeds. These are helpful in realizing that one can be made up of three, but they fall short in that no single part (of the apple, for example) is the whole thing at the same time.

The Bible teaches that there is one God made up of three persons: the Father, the Son, and the Holy Spirit. The three persons are each fully and eternally God, differing in roles, able to interact with each other, separate yet One. There isn't just one God who acts in three different ways. This is the heresy of modalism. We often find all three persons of the Trinity in the same passage of Scripture, and we also find plural pronouns for God. The Old Testament word *Elohim,* meaning God, appears over two thousand times and is used with plural adjectives, pronouns, and verbs. Here are a few examples of the Trinity in Scripture:

Genesis 1:26: Then God said, "Let Us make man in Our image, according to Our likeness; let them have dominion over the fish of the sea, over the birds of the air, and over the cattle, over all the earth and over every creeping thing that creeps on the earth." *(See also Genesis 3:22 and 11:7.)*

Isaiah 6:8: Also I heard the voice of the Lord, saying: "Whom shall I send, and who will go for Us?" Then I said, "Here am I! Send me."

Isaiah 48:16: "The Lord GOD and His Spirit have sent Me."

Luke 1:35: And the angel answered and said to her, "The Holy Spirit will come upon you, and the power of the Highest will overshadow you; therefore, also, that Holy One who is to be born will be called the Son of God.

Matthew 3:16–17: When He had been baptized, Jesus came up immediately from the water; and behold, the heavens were opened to Him, and He saw the Spirit of God descending like a dove and alighting upon Him. And suddenly a voice came from heaven, saying, "This is My beloved Son, in whom I am well pleased."

Matthew 28:19: "Go therefore and make disciples of all the nations, baptizing them in the name of the Father and of the Son and of the Holy Spirit."

John 14:16–17: "And I [Jesus] will pray the Father, and He will give you another Helper, that He may abide with you forever—the Spirit of truth, whom the world cannot receive, because it neither sees Him nor knows Him."

2 Corinthians 13:14: The grace of the Lord Jesus Christ, and the love of God, and the communion of the Holy Spirit be with you all. Amen.

Galatians 4:6: And because you are sons, God has sent forth the Spirit of His Son into your hearts, crying out, "Abba, Father!"

Ephesians 2:18: For through Him [Christ Jesus] we both have access by one Spirit to the Father.

show that increased percentages of Muslims in a population result in increased conflict with the host nation, violent demonstrations, and movements toward Islamic law.[21]

In the end, Christians must take the perspective that moderate Muslims are just as lost without Christ as their fundamentalist cousins. Let's not let friendliness or the adoption of Western culture blind us to the fact that they still need the Savior.

Islam and Women

Strict Islamic societies require a separation of the sexes to "protect" the chastity of each gender. Because of this, most men and women have little opportunity before marriage to relate to one another outside of their immediate family. They develop all friendships and communication with their own gender. In conservative Muslim nations, women are not allowed to leave their houses without being escorted by a male relative. They must worship apart from men in these countries, usually at home, although some mosques have a separate, veiled section for women. As a result of isolation, abuse, and loneliness, many Muslim women commit suicide.[22] The only eternal hope of a Muslim woman is to be a servant to men in paradise. According to twelfth-century Muslim scholar Ghazali, women will not enter paradise without their husband's approval.[23] The birth of a daughter is traditionally considered a sorrowful event in a Muslim home. The Muslim system represses women, but women perpetuate the repression by teaching Islam to their children. Fatalism trains women to accept their sufferings and such things as sickness among their children as the will of Allah.

While abuse of women takes place in every nation and religion, it is a significant problem in Muslim nations. Note the following headlines and news stories about abuse of women from respected news sources from 2005 to 2008:

- "Yemen's 8-Year-old Divorcee." The girl said her father forced her to marry a 30-year-old man who constantly beat her and forced her to have sex.[24]
- "Father Kills Daughter; Doubted Virginity" tells the tragedy of a 17-year-old in Jordan.[25]
- "Slain Over Hijab? Father Allegedly Strangles Daughter Over Head Scarf: Clashing Over Western Culture May Have Sparked Canadian Teen's Death" tells of a 16-year-old's murder.[26]
- "Saudi Rape Victim Gets 200 Lashes and Jail" is the story of a nineteen-year-old gang rape victim who was subsequently imprisoned even though seven men were convicted of the rape. After an international outcry regarding this injustice, Saudi Arabia's King Abdullah pardoned the woman.[27]
- "Married at 9, slain by parents at 17" tells of a Pakistani child given as a wife to a 45-year-old man and also gives the story of three girls ages 16–18 being buried alive "because they wanted to marry men of their choice."[28]
- "Muslim Father Burns Christian Daughter Alive—Man slices out girl's tongue, ignites her after 'heated debate on religion.'" This Saudi Arabian father killed his own daughter when "the child became curious about Jesus Christ after she read Christian material online."[29]
- "Somali rape victim stoned to death" tells the story of a thirteen-year-old convicted of adultery after three men raped her, then executed by dozens of men in a stadium before one thousand spectators.[30]
- "Acid Attacks Keep Afghan Girls Away From Classes" states, "Men on motorcycles attacked 15 girls and teachers with acid."[31]

Islamic teaching, history, and current practice endorse marriage of men to children. "The Ayatollah Khomeini, himself, at age twenty-eight, married a ten-year-old girl. She became pregnant at eleven, but miscarried. Khomeini called marriage to a girl before her first menstrual period 'a divine blessing,' and he advised the faithful: 'Do your best to ensure that your daughters do not see their first blood in your house.'"[32] Sura 65:4 refers to marriage and divorce of girls before puberty. Muhammad married Aisha when she was six and consummated their marriage when she was nine and he was over fifty years old! This would be a felony in any modern society. In Iran, the legal age of adulthood for girls is nine.[33] There is no minimum legal age for marriage for girls in Saudi Arabia.[34]

On the basis of comparing the New Testament and the Koran, it is safe to conclude that Christianity raises the value and role of women while Islam decreases it. Muslims would protest this point by claiming that the laws, veils, and other traditional garb required of women in conservative Muslim nations are for their own safety, but the outworking of this concept leads to oppression.

ISLAM AND RELIGIOUS VIOLENCE

Many Christians are unaware that over 40 million young men are being trained around the world in Koranic schools called *madrassas* that frequently emphasize fundamentalist perspectives on America and Israel.[35] Some of these schools do not teach academic subjects such as math and science but teach only the Koran and *jihad*.[36] Thus, the young men who graduate from them have no

TRUE STORY

The Iranian businessman was getting frustrated with me. Although we were in the United States, in his car parts business it was customary to negotiate. With skills honed from bargaining for souvenirs in tourist markets all over the world, I asked for the best price on the parts I needed. He repeated the amount and said it was a good price. "Yes," I said, "but what is your *best* price?"

At this point the man's brother Behrouz, who was behind the counter, burst out laughing and agreed to a lower price, much to the other man's displeasure. I walked out with the amused brother and talked with him for a long time while we filled my order. I had heard Behrouz and his brother speaking in an unfamiliar language and asked what it was. It turned out to be Farsi, and Behrouz told me about emigrating to the United States from Iran as a young man. He confirmed that he was a Muslim, but his attitude was entirely different from the man in the previous True Story. We had a pleasant, low-stress conversation in which Behrouz asked me to tell him about myself and listened with an open mind. He was interested in my travels and experiences in other countries. I told him that despite the political tensions between our nations, I was sure that people in Iran were hospitable and friendly. This comment clearly pleased him as I showed respect for his people. He remarked that he believed that was what God required of people: to do good to others and try to live properly. This was the opening I was aiming for.

I replied that being better or worse than another person is not the standard we are called to live by. I spoke of Jesus' sacrifice for our sins. Behrouz was most likely a Shiite and would understand this more readily than a Sunni Muslim. He listened as I briefly told him what we believe about needing the Savior. As we walked to the front of the store, his scowling brother reminded me that I would need to come back to return my old parts, since he was not charging me a deposit for them.

The next week, Behrouz wasn't around, and his brother was surprised to see that I actually took the trouble to drive a long way and return the parts. "I am a Christian," I told him, "and I keep my word." With a thoughtful expression on his face, he reached out to shake my hand. I'm planning to do business with his company in the future so that I can continue the witness that began there, and I recently found out about a Christian man who is reaching out to another brother from their family.

marketable skills, have been inflamed with the passion of furthering Islam and the sexual rewards await-
ing them in paradise, and are perfect candidates for becoming terrorists. The name al-Qaeda means
"The Base," but its full name is "World Islamic Front for Jihad Against the Jews and the Crusaders."[37]

We must reach the conclusion that the politically correct view of Islam is wrong. It is not a religion
of peace. The vast majority of terrorist attacks worldwide, including those in Russia, England, and
Spain, are carried out by Muslims. The Koran commands and condones Islamic violence.

Let's deal honestly with violence in the Bible and in Christian history. Skeptics often point toward
the conquest of the Promised Land in the Old Testament as evidence that the Judeo-Christian God is
bloodthirsty and savage. Although it is true that God commanded the Jews to take over Canaan, keep in
mind that these kingdoms were in the land that He had allotted to the Jews. God never gave a command
to go beyond those boundaries to conquer other lands, and His wisdom is evident in that it proved
to be a source of temptation and downfall when the Jews allowed the idol-worshiping Canaanites to
remain among them. On a few specific occasions, God commanded the death of all in a particular village or locale, but this was not the norm. The Jews were generally commanded to drive out those who
didn't belong in Israel.

The New Testament does not encourage violent assault on people of other religions and, in fact,
commands Christians to love their enemies and turn the other cheek. There have been seasons in history in which professing Christians have committed atrocities. The most obvious are the Crusades, in
which European rulers sent armies to liberate the Holy Land and brutalized both Muslims and Jews.
Later, European nobles ordered the conquest of the Americas at the expense of native peoples who were
slaughtered in the process. In my own country, the mistreatment of African slaves at the hands of allegedly Christian masters is a stain on our history. We must call into question whether the people guilty
of these crimes were actually Christians, since they clearly went against Christ's commands. Doubtless
some genuine believers sinned against both God and their victims as they were caught up in these dark
seasons in history, but this is no excuse for present-day violence. Rather than endorse them, biblical
Christianity renounces these actions.

Genuine Christianity converts by free will surrendering to God, while Islam historically converts
by force and coercion. Radical Islam is like the bully on the playground, and often when Islam steps
forward, the church backs up. God's people must rise up with the truth, speak boldly, and not allow
their freedoms to be hindered by Islamic intimidation. This does not mean that Christians should have
a violent response to terrorism and return threats with conflict. We must act in the opposite spirit.
Governments should meet radical Islam with strength; Christians should meet Muslims with love. It is
the place of police and military to keep order in society, and Christians in these realms can righteously
use force to protect the innocent (Romans 13:4). It's our place as believers to represent Christ and reach
out to Muslims with the gospel.

KEY POINTS FOR EVANGELISM
1. Never insult Muhammad or Allah, which will unnecessarily alienate those you are trying to reach.
2. Realize that a past history of offense has created a barrier to the gospel. Many Muslims are still angry with Christianity over the Crusades, which ended in 1290, and the assistance the Western world
   has given to their greatest enemy, Israel. European nations colonized nearly all of the Muslim world
   and in many cases dealt brutally with Muslim people. All these offenses are viewed as coming from
   Christian nations.

3. Find out a person's level of devotion to the faith. Some Muslims are nominal in their faith, skeptical of the Koran, or lukewarm in following the essential points of Islam. Find out whether the Muslim you are sharing the gospel with is devout or nominal.

4. Find out which sect, or branch of Islam, the Muslims you are witnessing to belong to. Shiite Muslims accept the concept of atonement for sin, so it is easy to use the story of the death of Jesus with a Shiite.

5. Find out the level of openness Muslims have to non-Muslims. Islam teaches respect for "people of the book," which are Jews and Christians, although some Muslims will ignore those passages in favor of contradictory ones that emphasize conquering people of other religions.

6. Show Muslims that the attributes of the God we serve are different from those of Allah. The biblical view that God is love is replaced by emphasis on justice as Allah's major attribute. Allah shows forgiveness and mercy based on whims, not on eternal standards.

7. Explain the concept of intimacy with God. Because Allah is distant and unknowable, Muslims have exalted Muhammad to almost the level of deity. This is an attempt to satisfy the yearning of the human heart to relate to God and gives Christians an open door to talk about how intimacy with God is available through Jesus.

8. Portray the Jesus of the Bible. To Muslims, Jesus didn't die on the cross and rise from the dead, and He isn't God. The Koran implies that the angel Gabriel is His father (Q 19:17–19, a contradiction to Q 21:91 which says Mary remained chaste). Since Muslims believe in a different Jesus (as Galatians 1:6–9 warns against), don't carry too far the idea of leading a Muslim to the Lord using only the Koran. Keep in mind that the Jesus of the Koran is different from the Jesus of the Bible, so don't use the Koran as the source of authority when you share the gospel with Muslims, but use it only as a common-ground starting point.

9. Show Jesus' superiority over Muhammad. Some Muslims have been converted after recognizing the superiority of Jesus over Muhammad in the Koran. According to Muslim beliefs, Muhammad's only miracle was producing the Koran. Contrast this with the Koran's statements that Jesus did many miracles. Muhammad is seen as a prophet and messenger, but Jesus' Name in the Koran is Isa, which means Savior. Jesus is the second highest prophet in Islam out of 124,000 prophets. According to the Koran, Jesus was born of a virgin, lived a sinless life, worked miracles, was called the Messiah, was righteous, was a prophet, is alive in heaven with God right now, and will judge the world, yet Muhammad was a sinner, he died, and his tomb is in Medina today. Show Muslims the preeminence of Jesus from their own book, then correct their misunderstandings by giving them a complete and biblical picture of who Jesus really is.

10. See how the Lord is revealing Himself. Many Muslim converts testify to having dreams or visions of Jesus that caused them to become interested in Christianity or sometimes to instantly convert to following Him. Your friend may have already had experiences resulting in an interest in investigating Christianity.

11. Explain the inspiration and importance of the Bible. Muslims accept as divine revelation the Law of Moses, the Psalms, and the Gospels (Injil) but consider the Koran the last and greatest revelation of Allah. They claim the other books have been corrupted. Using the parts of the Bible that Muslims recognize as Scripture is an effective method of sharing the gospel. Use Old Testament prophecies and show how they point to Jesus being the Messiah. Point out that the Koran recommends using the Bible, and guide your discussion to the Bible's truths. Ask Muslims who reject

the validity of Scripture the following: If the Bible is corrupt, why does the Koran recommend using it?

12. Show man's need for forgiveness from sin. Muslims believe that man is a being who sins when he disobeys Allah, not a being having a sinful nature. Thus, to Muslims man is inherently good. Sin is an action against Allah's will and law, not an offense against a God whose heart is broken when sin is committed by a person He loves.

13. Be hospitable. Over 180,000 Muslim students are studying at US colleges and universities, and many more live and work near Christians.[38] Since hospitality is a key virtue among Muslims, show them friendliness and welcome them into your home and life. We have learned through ministry overseas that it is necessary for us to invite people to join us for a meal several times before they believe we really mean it. Because the same principle is true for Muslims, persist in invitations and hospitality.

14. Handle the Bible with respect. Don't put the Bible in your pocket or on the floor or put anything on top of it. Hold it above your waist so it is not near the unclean parts of the body. Don't use a Bible with writing in the margins or any underlining. These things will be interpreted as tampering with or showing disrespect for God's Word. Handle your Bible carefully.

15. Be careful quoting the Koran. It can be difficult to quote the Koran to Muslims because they can often find contradictory passages in the same book. This is because Muslims believe in the law of abrogation, which means that later revelations can contradict earlier ones (Q 13:39), and the Koran is not in chronological order. This gives them an easy way to overlook passages that are difficult to excuse, especially those dealing with violence. In addition, Muslims often disagree with Christians' quotations from the Koran. This is because they claim that translations are incorrect and that the Koran must be studied only in Arabic, even though only a small minority of Muslims worldwide can read Arabic. (Note with all references to the Koran that the numbering system in various translations varies slightly, and a verse may be one before or after the number shown in other versions.)

CONCLUSION

Only 6 percent of all missionaries are trying to reach the entire Muslim world.[39] It is illegal for Muslims to convert to Christianity in some countries, including Pakistan, Yemen, Saudi Arabia, and Bangladesh. Let's ask the Lord for opportunities to touch the lives of Muslims around us and pray to find out if He is calling us to bring the gospel to Muslim nations.

Always approach Muslims with a humble spirit, but be confident and firm in your witness. Your goal is not to destroy their religious beliefs but to show them the truth that will set them free. Set before them the difference between your faith and theirs, and show them the difference that knowing Jesus makes in your life. When you are trying to reach a Muslim friend, enlist others to help you pray for him or her to see the truth.

SCRIPTURE STUDY

Carefully read the beliefs in the left-hand column and ask yourself what is true, what is almost true, and what is completely wrong about them. In the right-hand column, write out Bible passages that correct or oppose each belief. Don't feel bad if you have a hard time finding biblical support to answer every belief. When you meet with your mentor or class, you'll find out what verses others have found and you can fill in what you lack.

MUSLIM BELIEFS	GOD'S WORD
The Nature of God "And the Word of thy Lord hath been fulfilled: Verily I shall fill hell with the jinn and mankind together" (Q 11:119; see also Q 4:168–169).[1]	
"Allah loveth not one who is treacherous and sinful" (Q 4:107).	
"Whom Allah will sendeth astray, and whom He will He placeth on a straight path" (Q 6:39; see also Q 13:33).	
Jesus, Mary, and the Trinity "And (remember) her [Mary] who guarded her chastity: We breathed into her of Our spirit, and We made her and her son a sign for all peoples" (Q 21:91).	
"That they said (in boast), 'We killed Christ Jesus the son of Mary, the Apostle of God'; but they killed him not, nor crucified him, but so it was made to appear to them. . . . For of a surety they killed him not: Nay, God raised him up unto Himself; and God is Exalted in Power, Wise" (Q 4.157–158). *[Note: Muslims are taught that Judas died on the cross in Jesus' place and that Jesus went to heaven without dying.]*	
"The Messiah, Jesus son of Mary, was only a messenger of Allah, and His word which He conveyed unto Mary, and a spirit from Him. So believe in Allah and His messengers, and say not	

"Three"—Cease! (it is) better for you!—Allah is only One God. Far is it removed from His Transcendent Majesty that He should have a son" (Q 4:171; see also Q 19:35).

Salvation
"Then those whose balance (of good deeds) is heavy, they will attain salvation: But those whose balance is light, will be those who have lost their souls, in Hell will they abide" (Q 23:102–3; see also Q 21:47).

"So know (O Muhammad) that there is no God save Allah, and ask forgiveness for thy sin and for believing men and believing women" (Q 47:19; see also Q 40:55, Q 4:110).

"God accepts the repentance of those who do evil in ignorance and repent soon afterwards; to them will God turn in mercy" (Q 4:17).

"No laden soul [other translations, "no sinner"] can bear another's load" (Q 17:15; see also Q 35:18).

The Law and the Gospel
"Before thee, also, the apostles We sent were but men, to whom We granted inspiration: If ye realise this not, ask of those who possess the Message" (Q 21:7; see also Q 10.94).

"O ye who believe! Believe in God and His Apostle, and the scripture which He hath sent to His Apostle and the scripture which He sent to those before (him). Any who denieth God, His angels, His Books, His Apostles, and the Day of Judgment, hath gone far, far astray" (Q 4:136; see also Q 4.163).

"And in their footsteps We sent Jesus the son of Mary, confirming the Law that had come before him: We sent him the Gospel: therein was guidance and light, and confirmation of the Law that had come before him: a guidance and an admonition to those who fear God" (Q 5:46; see also Q 2.136).

"Say: 'O People of the Book! ye have no ground to stand upon unless ye stand fast by the Law, the Gospel, and all the revelation that has come to you from your Lord'" (Q 5:68).

Treatment of Non-Muslims
"O ye who believe! Take not the Jews and the Christians for friends. They are friends one to another. He among you who taketh them for friends is (one) of them" [other translations say, "becomes one of them"] (Q 5:51).

"Then, when the sacred months have passed, slay the idolaters wherever ye find them, and take them (captive), and besiege them, and prepare for them each ambush. But if they repent and establish worship and pay the poor-due, then leave their way free. Lo! Allah is Forgiving, Merciful" (Q 9:5).

"Fight those who believe not in God nor the Last Day, nor hold that forbidden which hath been forbidden by God and His Apostle, nor acknowledge the religion of Truth, (even if they are) of the People of the Book, until they pay the Jizya with willing submission, and feel themselves subdued" (Q 9:29).

"Therefore, when ye meet the Unbelievers (in fight), smite at their necks. . . . But those who are slain in the Way of God, He will never let their deeds be lost. Soon will He guide them and improve their condition, And admit them to the Garden which He has announced for them" (Q 47:4–6).

"The only reward of those who make war upon Allah and His messenger and strive after corruption in the land will be that they will be killed or crucified, or have their hands and feet on alternate sides cut off, or will be expelled out of the land" (Q 5:33).

"Fight in the way of Allah against those who fight against you, but begin not hostilities. Lo! Allah loveth not aggressors. And slay them wherever ye find them. . . . And fight them until persecution is no more, and religion is for Allah" (Q 2:190–193).

_____
_____
_____
_____
_____
_____
_____
_____
_____

PRAYER TIME

List the major prayer needs of Muslims and pray for them.

-

-

-

SCRIPTURE MEMORY

Hebrews 9:27
And as it is appointed for men to die once, but after this the judgment.

1 Peter 5:7
[Cast] all your care upon Him, for He cares for you.

DAILY BIBLE READING

✓ Check when completed		
Sunday	Ezra 4–6	_____
Monday	Ezra 7–8	_____
Tuesday	Nehemiah 1–3	_____
Wednesday	Nehemiah 4–5	_____
Thursday	Nehemiah 6–7	_____
Friday	Nehemiah 8–10	_____
Saturday	Nehemiah 11–13	_____

BIBLE READING QUESTIONS/THOUGHTS

_____
_____
_____
_____
_____
_____
_____
_____
_____
_____
_____

PRAYER NEEDS THIS WEEK

_____
_____
_____
_____
_____
_____
_____
_____

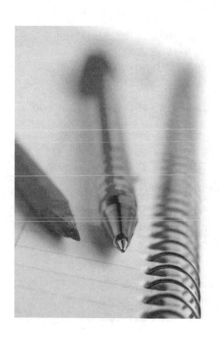

6

Lesson six

Hinduism

No single individual is responsible for founding Hinduism, as is the case with Buddhism and Islam. Hinduism is a fluid and all-encompassing religion of many different beliefs and deities. It is held together by a core of centralized beliefs, including caste, karma, polytheism, sacrifice, and reincarnation, which we will define and study. These beliefs manifest in a variety of expressions.

Hinduism began about 3,500 years ago with a series of rituals designed to honor many deities. These rules became formalized over time, and written instructions for the ceremonies developed into the Hindu scriptures called Vedas and Upanishads. The Bhagavad Gita is the best known of the Hindu scriptures in the Western world. The majority of Hindu scripture is poetry, which makes it easier to memorize. The primary gods of Hinduism are Brahma the Creator, Vishnu the Preserver, and Shiva the Destroyer. Behind these principal gods lies an impersonal force known as Brahman. From the principal gods come many incarnations of lesser gods, totaling 330 million deities, which include the same gods appearing multiple times in different forms.[1] However, there is no list of the 330 million, and that number is symbolic of the endless number of gods in Hindu belief. Hindus in one area may never even have heard of the gods worshiped by Hindus in another area. Because Hinduism is rooted in India, we'll refer to that nation throughout this chapter.

Hinduism Today

There are approximately 900 million Hindus worldwide. Over one million Hindus live in the United States. Other Western nations with a large Hindu population are Suriname and Trinidad. In Asia, Hindus make up the majority of the population in India and Nepal and a minority in other nations. The largest gathering of people in the history of the world for a single purpose was the Kumbh Mela festival in

Terms and Concepts

atman: the individual soul.

avatar: an incarnation of a god as a human being.

Brahman: the universal soul that absorbs the individual souls when they reach *moksha*. Hindus compare this to a raindrop falling into the ocean and becoming one with it.

caste system: the division of society in India based on the belief that people were created from different parts of the original man's body, giving them varying levels of status and privilege in Indian culture.

karma: a person's good or bad deeds that earn reward or punishment; Hindus believe that karma carries over into the next reincarnated life.

mantra: a religious word or name of a Hindu god, repeated to produce a trancelike state in meditation.

maya: the illusion or appearance of everything in the world. According to the Hindu belief that the material world is an illusion, there is no such thing as suffering (it is maya), and thus there is no need to help the poor, the sick, or others in need.

moksha: the end of (escape from) the cycle of reincarnation and the realization that we are part of the divine nature of Brahman and that nothing else is real.

pantheism: belief that God's nature is found not in a separate personal being but in all aspects of nature and in every person. This is a feature of monism, the belief that all is one.

polytheism: the belief in multiple gods.

puja: a worship ceremony or ritual.

reincarnation: life after death in the form of returning to earth in another body to live out the karma one has earned in past lives. This can include a human coming back as an animal.

satguru, guru, swami, and sadhu: levels of rank from highest to lowest among Hindu holy men.

TRUE STORY

Can you find me in this picture? These are mostly pastors who came as far as 112 miles one way by bus, motorcycle, and bicycle for a two-day pastors conference. When I arrived, the host pastor introduced me to a group of men and explained in his heavily accented English a story that I didn't quite understand.

The men were leaders from the Mali tribe. They had come to the conclusion that Hinduism and idolatry are wrong, and they came—uninvited and unexpected—to the city to investigate Christianity as the new religion for their people. The idea of tribal leaders may bring to your mind pictures of people wearing feathers and loincloths. Instead, the group consisted of well-dressed businessmen, a doctor, and elegant women in colorful saris, all carrying cell phones.

Without fully understanding what was taking place, I taught what the Lord was directing me to teach. Some of it seemed painfully basic, but I felt God's leading and wisdom flowing. Slowly I put the pieces of the puzzle together and grasped the fact that this was a moment of destiny. There are 8.4 million Mali people in India, and the local Mali leaders—the leaders of 8.4 million people with no known Christians among them and zero churches—were listening to me teach the Bible for two days! The host pastor said, "On the day that you came, they came!" He is the head of four hundred churches in central India and told me he had been trying unsuccessfully for six years to get a foot in the door of the Mali people.

> **Micah 4:1–2:** Now it shall come to pass in the latter days that the mountain of the Lord's house shall be established on the top of the mountains, and shall be exalted above the hills; and peoples shall flow to it. Many nations shall come and say, "Come, and let us go up to the mountain of the Lord, to the house of the God of Jacob; He will teach us His ways, and we shall walk in His paths.

While sitting, talking, and praying with the Mali leaders, communicating through an interpreter, I faced many hard questions. The leaders wanted to choose a new faith for their people carefully.

> **Habakkuk 1:5:** "Look among the nations and watch—be utterly astounded! For I will work a work in your days which you would not believe, though it were told you."

In mission terminology, there is a concept known as a people movement. This means that rather than individuals making separate personal decisions, an entire culture or tribe will collectively decide to follow the Lord. This seems impossible to us because in the Western world we are so individual-oriented, but it's the way people think in Eastern cultures. Could a people movement take place among the Malis?

> **Revelation 5:9:** And they sang a new song, saying: "You are worthy to take the scroll, and to open its seals; for You were slain, and have redeemed us to God by Your blood out of every tribe and tongue and people and nation."

Toward the end of the conference, about sixteen of the leaders and some others surrounded the host pastor and me. On behalf of the group, one Mali leader said in his language, "When you are speaking, we understand you before the translator translates." He turned to the others and said, "This God does not require sacrifices of incense and coconuts like the others." I could see that the light was going on. He was getting it.

Will you take a few minutes and join me in praying that the 8.4 million Malis who don't know the Lord will find Him? Pray that the searching leaders who are still undecided will have revelation of the truth in their hearts and lead their people to Jesus. Pray for my church-planter friends who will be beginning new home churches in the Mali villages as soon as the doors are open. Some Malis are now committed Christians and attend the church where the conference was held.

As the conference ended, a man came to the microphone and said, "All my life I searched for the true guru (teacher). Now I have discovered that Jesus is the true guru!"

2001, in which 25 million Hindus gathered at the Ganges River, whose polluted waters are believed to wash away sins.[2]

Although much of the emphasis in missionary circles and Christian media is on Islam because of its geopolitical significance, wars, and terrorism, Christians need to remember that there are two-thirds as many Hindus as there are Muslims in the world. The fact that Hinduism, unlike Islam, is not an aggressively missionary-focused religion does not negate the reality that Hindus need to be reached for Christ and should have as much intercessory prayer and effort to reach them. We must also recognize that the persecution from Hindu radicals against Christians is every bit as lethal as Islamic persecution of believers. We have a great obligation to stand together with the persecuted church (Hebrews 13:3).

Beliefs and Practices

Let's first look at the foundations of Hindu doctrine and learn some vocabulary that's necessary to understand their worldview, and then see the outworking of these doctrines in the lives of the Hindu people.

Karma. Karma is the belief that the consequences of a person's good or bad deeds carry over into the next life. Fatalism, acceptance of suffering without trying to change it, is based on the concept that one is living out the karma one deserves from previous lives. Poor people are taught that they deserve their place in life and thus should be content with the kind of lives they have. Avoiding suffering would be postponing the inevitable law of karma. (In some aspects, Karma is similar to the biblical principle of sowing and reaping. But, in contrast, Christians believe that not everything that happens to us is a consequence of our doing right or wrong, that God is sovereign and controls our situation in life, and that He allows some things to happen to us that are not punishments.)

Reincarnation. Reincarnation is life after death through being born into another body. Belief in reincarnation will cause a rich person to think that he or she shouldn't help the needy, because that would interfere with poor people's karma and doom them to another life of suffering. In addition, because the higher castes believe they have earned everything they have in this life through good karma in previous lives, they are not inclined to give their own resources to help others who they believe don't deserve anything but their sufferings. This aloof attitude often prevents them from showing mercy and being involved in social action on behalf of others. Most programs for the handicapped, widows, or orphans are run by ministries with a Christian worldview. Throughout the world, most nations owe the roots of their modern medical systems to Christian missionary doctors who saw the exercise of compassion as a fulfillment of God's commands.

The caste system. The caste system rigidly defines social class levels in Hindu culture. It is based on reincarnation. Originally there were four castes, but now there are thousands. The castes correspond to various parts of the body of the original man. The highest caste, the Brahmin (those who know Brahma), was made from Brahma's head, and the status of the other castes goes downward from there, with the "untouchables" believing they were made from the dust under Brahma's feet. Lower castes are taught that they exist to serve the higher ones. Although it is now illegal, the caste system remains in the hearts and minds of many Hindus and often determines the level of education children can receive, their professions, and the people they will marry. Family members have been known to kill young couples in love because they came from different castes.[3]

The Sanskrit language of ancient India relates caste to color. Hindu society is founded on the division of peoples by their ethnic ancestry, which results in the light-skinned Brahmins at the top and the

TRUE STORY

This is an excerpt from one of our newsletters while we were ministering in India:

The experience here is like living in a *National Geographic* magazine. There's no more exotic place in the world. Here are some word pictures so you can get a sense of what the kids feel: the browns of mud, rust, and decrepit buildings contrast with the bright saris worn by women lined up to pump water at the village wells. Laughing children greet us, want to be picked up and carried, like to play catch, and have taught our kids cricket. Some of the constantly staring young men are smiling, but others give the girls the creeps and we stand in front of them. Many have never seen blonde hair or white skin before—ever. Everything we do attracts attention, so we limit their exposure in the city, going out to get cold drinks or snacks in groups of four. We are being careful of government officials and Hindu radicals.

Streets are packed with goats, holy cows with painted horns, massive black water buffalo with three-foot horns and eerie blue eyes, bicycle and motorcycle drawn taxis, bikes and motorcycles, but few privately owned cars. Trucks and buses blast on their horns constantly, as do our drivers, warning the mobs of pedestrians. Roadside stands sell produce and flowers, clothes and tools. There is no store bigger than your garage in the entire city of 140,000. Beggars, Hindu holy men, many Muslims in head-to-toe black gowns or small round caps on the men, Buddhist monks, demonized street people with cow dung smeared in their hair, ordinary people, kids in school uniforms—all turn to look at the foreigners as we pass in three SUVs. Once we're out of the city we watch for the monkeys and cobras, driving through the fields of bananas, papayas, and magnificent scenery. There are 1,400 villages in this county alone, and the people in every one we've passed through gawk at us as you would if aliens landed in your yard.

To give you an idea how far off the beaten path we are, in a Kolowar tribal village, people were told we were from the United States. They asked where in India the United States was located and were told it is a separate country, so they asked how many hours it takes to drive there! Going into primitive villages of stick huts is a step back in time a few thousand years, but in any village with electricity we see a satellite dish! Some have no electricity. At the end of a winding one-lane road through fields plowed by ox-drawn wooden plows, the people asked if we were from north India; they had no concept of light-skinned foreigners, and we were the first people to bring the gospel.

A Paradha village of the fortune-teller caste was quite a sight: the men with flowing beards and their hair in topknots, wearing long skirts. The crowd was very large, and the first one to respond to the salvation invitation was the headman or village chief. There was a loud collective gasp from the people at his decision, and about one-third of the village followed him forward. Our pastor friends were very happy about this and have planted a church there already!

darkest castes at the bottom of the socioeconomic structure. Castes pass along trades or professions to their children: there are castes of thieves and castes of human-waste handlers, with each generation limited by the type of work done by their ancestors.[4] The treatment that higher-caste members give to lower castes is similar to the segregation and mistreatment of African-Americans in the United States until the 1960s: lower castes can't drink from the same cups in restaurants, and if their shadow falls on a Brahmin, it makes him unclean. The ancient Code of Manu commands cutting out the tongue of a low-caste man who insults one from a high caste, and branding or cutting a low-caste man who tries to sit with a high-caste man. The Code also excuses high-caste criminals from capital punishment, replacing it with cutting their hair or banishment. It even states that a high-caste man's name should mean something favorable, while a low-caste man's name should mean something disgraceful.[5]

Leaving the caste system in India is possible through changing religions, but forms of class discrimination carry over into the Christian and Muslim communities. Thousands of Hindus have converted to Buddhism in recent years.[6] Tired of caste segregation yet either ignorant of or unwilling to turn to Christianity, they trade one lie for another. However, the lowest caste Dalits, with 360 million people, are the most responsive group to the gospel.[7]

Other Beliefs and Practices

Astrology is a favorite Hindu practice. Most marriages are arranged, and weddings are held at times determined by astrologers. Government leaders often consult astrologers on official policies, and some families deliver their babies by Caesarian section so that the babies will be born at a time with favorable astrological significance.

A popular exercise in the Western world, yoga has unwisely been practiced in a Christianized form in some churches. In the Hindu religion, yoga is seen as a means of recognizing one's unity with Brahman through disciplined control of the body, mind, and soul. Each yoga position corresponds to the worship of a Hindu deity, and the underlying philosophy of yoga makes the practice incompatible with Christianity.[8]

Ahimsa is the doctrine of nonviolence that results in most Hindus following a vegetarian diet so that they are not responsible for the death of any animal. This belief reaches its most radical form in the religion of Jainism, some of whose followers carry a small broom with them to sweep bugs off the road to safety and wear a small screen over their nose and mouth so they don't accidentally inhale an insect.[9]

Social and Spiritual Conditions in India Resulting from Hinduism

Most of India's sufferings trace back to Hinduism, the caste system, and the law of karma. India is rich in natural resources, but injustice and prejudice keep the wealth in the hands of the higher castes. Much of India's crop harvest is destroyed by rats and other vermin, which the doctrines of transmigration (reincarnation between human and animal forms) and Brahman protect, since these creatures are of one essence with man (monism) and could be incarnations of people. In addition, there are temples dedicated to rat gods and other animals, and nearly 200 million holy cows roam the streets and are not used for food in a nation where millions go hungry.[10] The Hindu priests tell fearful worshipers that the gods demand sacrificial offerings every time their crops come in, keeping the poor in the cycle of poverty while transferring their limited financial resources to the higher castes. Thus, worship of the gods is rooted in fear of them rather than love for them and in a desire to appease gods who might otherwise be angry and bring punishment upon the people.[11] Hinduism has kept India as one of the poorest and most backward nations in the world, yet the New Age Movement looks to India for answers. "Their sorrows shall be multiplied who hasten after another god; their drink offerings of blood I will not offer, nor take up their names on my lips" (Psalm 16:4).

My extensive travels throughout India have caused me to have a great love for its people, including many personal friends, appreciation for its history and natural beauty, and enjoyment of its cuisine. And yet I have a deep awareness and concern that India's millions do not know their Creator. It is my hope that you will join me in this burden for India and the Hindu people, and that we will take all necessary steps to reach out to them both in our nations and in their homeland.

The following are some interesting facts about India:

- About 1.2 billion people—more than the entire population of North America, Central America, South America, and the Caribbean combined—live in an area one-third the size of the US.
- Indians speak 1,612 languages and dialects, but the Bible or New Testament is available in only 81 of them.[12]
- The apostle Thomas brought the gospel to India around AD 50, but only about 3 percent of Indians are born-again Christians.[13]
- India is mentioned in the Bible in Esther 1:1.
- There is one missionary in India for every 1.2 million people.
- India has over 600,000 villages without a Christian church.[14]
- India has 10 million blind people and 1.5 million lepers.[15]

The following paragraphs discuss examples of the destructive results of Hinduism from our experiences ministering in India.

One day a pastor came to us and told us that it would be too dangerous for us to even leave the house that day. When we asked why, he explained that it was a feast of the cobra god. The way people celebrated this feast was to drink wine all day, then go into the jungle and catch cobras to bring home in baskets. How many of the people are killed by the gods they bring home in their baskets?

We observed that the lowest-caste people in poor and primitive villages had no idea about even the most basic rules of sanitation. Many lives could be saved each year if the people were taught to wash their hands before preparing food, keep their wells from being polluted, build outhouses, and care for their children's health. However, higher-caste, educated Hindus who believe in karma generally are not motivated to help the lower castes with foundational healthcare instruction that would prevent many

TRUE STORY

It would be easy to look at Hindu (or another religion's or a cult's) doctrines and assume that only poor and ignorant people could believe them. An example from our experience ministering in India will illustrate that this is not the case. Once we went to a poor village where most houses were made of sticks. We waited in the village square as a crowd gathered, and our Indian Christian friends asked the village chief's permission to share the gospel there. One of the pastors warned us not to sit on the village idols. We were shocked as he pointed not to carved idols but to three plain rocks painted orange and set in a cement slab. As we carefully avoided them, a well-dressed young man ran up. Speaking perfect English, he introduced himself as a graduate student at the university and said he would be our guide while we were there. He was so excited that foreign visitors would come to his remote village. We went to his home to meet his family. They were much better off than the rest of the villagers, with a nicer home and a tractor instead of a cow to plow their fields. As we returned to the village square to end our tour, the young man pointed to the orange rocks and said, "These are our village gods!" I looked at him quickly to see whether he, a highly educated man, was mocking the mostly illiterate villagers. I saw no trace of sarcasm. I'll never forget his expression, showing reverence, awe, and the deepest respect for those rocks. Deception can't be cured by education or Western sophistication. It can be cured only by Jesus.

Hosea 8:6: A workman made it, and it is not God.

unnecessary deaths, and the mindset of accepting suffering as a result of the inevitable law of karma keeps many from taking steps to make their lives easier or more comfortable.

Because of reincarnation, suicide is common, since there is no fear of judgment after death and Hindus believe they will go directly into another life. In just seven Indian states, over eight thousand farmers have committed suicide in recent years because droughts have ruined their crops and the thought of starvation and failure caused them to take their own lives, believing they will get another chance in the next incarnation.[16] We have seen their funerals, with processions of mourners who have lost their friend, father, husband, or son to a lie.

Women suffer because of Hindu practices. Rape of lower-caste women by upper-caste men is rampant and seldom prosecuted.[17] Although it is illegal, temple prostitution continues to this day, with young girls being used by men in sexual rituals.[18] Many contract AIDS, which is widespread in India. Suttee, or sati, the illegal practice of burning a widow alive when her husband's body is cremated, still continues in remote areas.[19]

ANSWERING IDOLATRY

In 1998 the pastor of a church in the small Indian town where we lived for seven weeks asked me to preach on idolatry. The church had nearly doubled in size because of the curiosity of the people in the town about why light-skinned foreigners were living there, and people pressed in around the doors and windows to see what was going on inside. Many of the new men likely came from the bar across the street, where crowds gathered just to stare at us. Realizing that many of the people weren't yet converted and that this was such a touchy subject that we could be in great danger after preaching it, I prayed hard for God's wisdom in explaining it. The response was interesting: many of the Christians nodded favorably while others, likely Hindus who came out of curiosity, made brief, angry sounds at points they didn't like.

Here's how the Lord showed me to present this message:

God	
Angels	Demons
Saved Men	Lost Men
The Rest of Creation	

This is a chart of everything in the universe. God is separate from creation. He is the Creator, and He is all good. There is no bad god to compete with Him (Isaiah 45:5–6, 18). If no other gods exist, what else is there? There are spirits, both good and bad. The good ones are angels, and they are servants of God. Angels protect us. They would never accept worship, which belongs to God alone. Only God is worthy of worship. The bad spirits are demons. They are the enemies of God who rebelled against Him. They desire worship and want to harm us.

All men know that something greater than themselves exists. We are made to worship (Romans 1:20–23). Saved men know to worship the true God. Lost men don't know what to worship—good spirits, bad spirits whom they fear, bad spirits who pretend to be good, or even creation itself.

It makes no sense to worship creation, which consists of the things God made. God is greater than His creation, just as man is greater than the things man makes. We wouldn't worship a chapatti (flat Indian bread) or an auto rickshaw (three-wheeled motorcycle taxi).

THEOLOGY 101: Salvation by Grace through Faith

A common theme in many belief systems is the self-reliant perspective that humans can do all that is necessary to make themselves right with God or that they can improve their spiritual condition through good works. Christians believe that our own efforts are completely insufficient to make us righteous or to cancel even the smallest of our sins. Even our attempts to obey the Ten Commandments are not enough to overcome our past failures, and none of us has obeyed the commandments perfectly. Our efforts only serve to remind us of our sinful condition and point us toward the cross. If they could do anything to save us, Jesus' brutal death would have been unnecessary.

The Bible teaches that we are saved by God's grace. *Grace* means undeserved favor and shows that the work in salvation is what Christ did, not what we do. Because of His mercy, God reaches into our darkened minds, dead spirits, and sin-ravaged hearts to give us the ability to believe in Him. Apart from His grace, we would have no hope.

God has given each person a measure of faith (Romans 12:3). We don't have to work up a feeling of faith but need only to use what faith God has given us. A small amount of faith is sufficient for God to respond by doing great things in and through us (Matthew 17:20). The greatest challenge of faith is not that it is absent or too weak but that we place faith in the wrong object. Most often people put their faith—the God-given ability to believe—in themselves, trusting their human goodness as being sufficient to earn rewards, including eternal life. Faith can also be aimed at false gods, human leaders, and unreliable scriptures, but no matter how sincere or heartfelt that faith may be, its object cannot deliver what the person hopes to receive.

The work of the Holy Spirit, God's promises in Scripture, and the Bible's revelation of who He is are the means by which the Father develops saving faith in a lost person. Only faith placed in the person of Jesus will result in receiving God's grace and salvation.

Here are some key verses to use with people who put their faith in their own efforts through religion or good deeds to make them right with God.

Ephesians 2:8–9: For by grace you have been saved through faith, and that not of yourselves; it is the gift of God, not of works, lest anyone should boast.

Titus 3:4–5: But when the kindness and the love of God our Savior toward man appeared, not by works of righteousness which we have done, but according to His mercy He saved us, through the washing of regeneration and renewing of the Holy Spirit.

Galatians 2:16: Knowing that a man is not justified by the works of the law but by faith in Jesus Christ, even we have believed in Christ Jesus, that we might be justified by faith in Christ and not by the works of the law; for by the works of the law no flesh shall be justified.

Galatians 2:21: I do not set aside the grace of God; for if righteousness comes through the law, then Christ died in vain.

Only God deserves worship. His first two commandments tell us this (Exodus 20:1–6). People offend God and disobey Him when they love, serve, or fear anything else and call it their god (Jeremiah 44:4–6; 25:6; Hosea 8:6).

Who actually receives the honor that people give to an idol? Demons—God's enemies (Deuteronomy 32:16–17; 1 Corinthians 10:14, 20–22). We can't both have a relationship with the true God and have idols or other gods. Let's use the example of marriage. What if your wife spends some time with you and some time with another man? What man would allow this? It would cause the deepest anger. What if your wife said she was married to you but she kept a picture of the other man to honor him each day? God feels the same way you would feel. Christians must separate themselves completely from idols. In the old days the penalty for idolatry was death, and now the penalty is that it will keep a person

THEOLOGY 101: Biblical Answers to Reincarnation

More than half the world's population believes in some form of reincarnation. Because this belief is so widespread in Hinduism, Buddhism, the New Age movement, and American culture, you can use the following scriptures as tools to answer those who believe in it.

Hebrews 9:27: And as it is appointed for men to die once, but after this the judgment.

Hebrews 10:12–14: But this Man, after He had offered one sacrifice for sins forever, sat down at the right hand of God, from that time waiting till His enemies are made His footstool. For by one offering He has perfected forever those who are being sanctified.

Luke 16:19–31: [The story of Lazarus and the rich man shows judgment, not reincarnation, after death.]

2 Corinthians 5:8–10: We are confident, yes, well pleased rather to be absent from the body and to be present with the Lord. Therefore we make it our aim, whether present or absent, to be well pleasing to Him. For we must all appear before the judgment seat of Christ, that each one may receive the things done in the body, according to what he has done, whether good or bad.

John 9:1–3: Now as Jesus passed by, He saw a man who was blind from birth. And His disciples asked Him, saying, "Rabbi, who sinned, this man or his parents, that he was born blind?" Jesus answered, "Neither this man nor his parents sinned, but that the works of God should be revealed in him.

Luke 23:39–43: [In the story of the thieves on the cross, Jesus tells one of them, "Assuredly, I say to you, today you will be with Me in Paradise."]

Matthew 25:31–46: [The parable of the sheep and the goats shows the judgment of both righteous and wicked people after death.]

Romans 9:11: For the children not yet being born, nor having done any good or evil, that the purpose of God according to election might stand, not of works but of Him who calls. [This shows that the unborn are not carrying with them any guilt from a previous life.]

out of heaven (Deuteronomy 17:2–5; 1 Corinthians 6:9–10). God tells us to choose between Him and His enemies (Judges 10:12–14; Jeremiah 2:27–28)

If we choose to worship the true God alone, He offers us blessing (Isaiah 30:22–23; Psalm 144:15). If we choose to dishonor God by having idols in our homes, we will be under His curse (Deuteronomy 7:25–26). Now God calls us to choose between Him and idols (Joshua 24:14–15).

KEY POINTS FOR EVANGELISM

1. Emphasize grace. In Hinduism, everything is the result of human effort and achievement. The concept of reincarnation is rooted in the belief that one lifetime is not enough for a person to reach perfection. Hindus are ignorant of the truth that God gives us the status of an unfallen, perfect man through redemption in Christ. Talk with a Hindu about the exhausting task of always trying to achieve a higher level of human perfection, without ever having the assurance of progress, and about the daily reminders that we fail to be what we have hoped to become. Show your gratefulness that Jesus has taken you out of the futility of self-perfection by His grace.

2. Focus on forgiveness. The law of karma means judgment in the next life for every imperfect person, with no way of escape. With proper explanation, a Hindu can realize that Jesus took our bad

karma. Although we definitely don't believe in karma as Hindus do, it is a great starting point for the gospel message. Christians don't carry the sense of dread that Hinduism gives its followers, who see their sins stacking up daily and know that they will have a terrible price to pay in their future incarnations. We can look toward our death with peace and assurance, something an honest Hindu cannot do.

3. Teach an "only Jesus" mentality. The Hindu scriptures emphasize that each person should be devoted to a god.[20] As a result, Hindus pick favorites among the multitude of gods and devote themselves to them. Various regions of India have different favorite gods. Since gods have diverse specialties, Hindus believe it is useful to pray to the correct one at appropriate times: Laxmi for money, Shiva for healing, Durga as the goddess of motherhood, Ganesh the god of luck, and many others. In their way of thinking, all gods trace back to the primary three gods, who trace back to Brahman. As a result, all worship is legitimate regardless of which god receives it. The danger of this belief is that Hindus can add Jesus to the list of gods they worship instead of believing in Him to the exclusion of all other gods. Hindus who seemingly convert to Christianity are not genuinely converted until they believe in Jesus, forsaking idols to follow Him alone.

4. Explain that Christianity is about God becoming man. Hinduism is about man becoming god. Show people the admirable qualities of Jesus' life and quote Mohandas Gandhi, who said, "I shall say to the Hindus that your lives will be incomplete unless you reverently study the teachings of Jesus."[21]

5. Explain the concept of sin. Hindus see the root of sin as ignorance of knowing that at the core we are one essence with Brahman. Hinduism has no concept of sin being an offense against a Person, as we know it to be, but sees sin as a failure to follow the laws of a system. Show by your testimony the understanding that you offended the God who loves you, understood that only Jesus could carry the penalty of sin for you, humbled yourself, repented toward God, and found peace through Christ. This is an entirely different paradigm than Hinduism teaches.

6. Carefully distinguish between reincarnation and being born again. Realize that the Christian term *born again* has a very different meaning to someone who believes in reincarnation. Ask those who believe in reincarnation, "If reincarnation is true, how could the population increase? There would be a fixed number of people in the world. Then, as some reach *moksha,* the population would decrease, but this is not happening."

7. Also ask, "Why isn't mankind improving if we are slowly evolving toward Brahman as we work out our bad karma? Is there any evidence that there is less selfishness, suffering, war, or poverty now than in the past? Since India has taught the concepts of karma and reincarnation for centuries, it should be the most highly evolved nation in the world. Instead, it is a place of immense need, with hundreds of millions who suffer daily. Why is this so?"

8. Teach true salvation. The term *salvation* carries a different meaning to Hindus, who believe that being saved from the cycle of reincarnation matters most, not being saved from sin. Hindus believe salvation can be achieved in one of three ways: by knowledge (understanding that all is *maya,* through Hindu scripture and holy men), by works (pilgrimages, good deeds to gain good karma), or by devotion (to a god or guru).

9. Explain that the worship of other gods and all idolatry is the worship of demons. Hinduism is not merely a colorful religion of uneducated farmers and villagers but is a spiritual bondage of the enemy.

TRUE STORY

The big Christian conference in central India was going to begin the next day, when my friend came to me with a worried look on his face. He told me that the RSS—the 750,000-member radical Hindu paramilitary organization that persecutes Christians and has its headquarters fifty miles away from where I was—had found out I was in town and had made threats. The photograph here shows the conference poster with my name, which was also on flyers and the big banner. When I asked what the threats were, my friend wouldn't tell me, but his expression said plenty.

The RSS is the group that severely beat our pastor friends and all the men in a village church the first time we were in India. A related Hindu radical group, the VHP, had attacked Australian missionary Graham Staines and his two sons, ages nine and seven, in 1999. After stabbing them with traditional Hindu tridents, the group threw gasoline into the car they were in and set it on fire. Villagers nearby ran to rescue them, but the radicals beat them back until Graham and his two little boys were dead.

I went to bed that night before the conference very concerned. My mind ran through all the possibilities. Leaving just wasn't an option; I had come to encourage the churches and pastors. How would it encourage them if the guest speaker decided to run away? I had to stay and face it. All night long I prayed, fell asleep, woke up, and prayed some more, asking the Lord to make me ready for whatever I would face. The next morning I decided not to e-mail my family and tell them about the threat so that they wouldn't be 8,700 miles away worrying. It was time to practice what I preach and trust the Lord. My major emotion was not fear but uncertainty of whether I was ready to face things I had never faced before.

When I woke up the next day, a clear thought came immediately to mind: *What if I have counted you worthy to suffer for the Name?*

Acts 5:41: So they departed from the presence of the council, rejoicing that they were counted worthy to suffer shame for His name.

Peace flooded through me. The brooding heaviness of the night before lifted. All the anxiety from the night of tossing and turning was gone. If God was in this, then it must be okay, regardless of the outcome. This was more than a rush of courage—it was God overcoming my uncertainties. He was in control, regardless of what the RSS had planned.

My pastor friend wouldn't let me go to the first morning's sessions. He wanted me to stay away until they could see what the RSS might do. I stayed at his house and read the book of Acts to prepare my heart. After a few hours, I had absolute peace and went to the conference. When they honored the Indian pastor (who is shown in the photo) and me as the main speakers, they gave us badges to wear. I thought, how crazy is this! Not only am I utterly conspicuous as the only white person in a fifty-mile radius (literally true—tourists don't come to this part of India, and a Canadian missionary told me she's the only white person in her city fifty miles away), and I've been threatened by Hindu terrorists who have a history of violence, but now I'm wearing a target! I put on the badge and wore it all three days.

Those days were full of preaching, teaching, worship, and prayer. The people were very open and responsive. The hardest part was the breaks—during every break I was mobbed by people wanting me to pray for the sick, mostly children with overwhelming needs and parents in desperation—lame, blind, deaf, mute, infections, tumors, mental handicaps, wasting disease, demonization. I prayed the best prayers I know but didn't see much. It was very frustrating. I hate to see the people disappointed, believing for a breakthrough, but we have to just pray the prayer of faith and leave the results to the Lord. We had many testimonies come back to us later of people being healed after prayer. When the conference was over and no persecution had taken place, I told my pastor friends that we had made it through. It was then that they told me that the RSS men had been in every meeting. Without knowing it, I had preached the Word to Hindu terrorists for three days.

1 Corinthians 10:20: Rather, that the things which the Gentiles sacrifice they sacrifice to demons and not to God, and I do not want you to have fellowship with demons.

Revelation 9:20: But the rest of mankind, who were not killed by these plagues, did not repent of the works of their hands, that they should not worship demons, and idols of gold, silver, brass, stone, and wood, which can neither see nor hear nor walk.

Deuteronomy 32:16–17: They provoked Him to jealousy with foreign gods; with abominations they provoked Him to anger. They sacrificed to demons, not to God, to gods they did not know, to new gods, new arrivals that your fathers did not fear.

10. Use drama ministry. Hindu doctrines are often taught by traveling teachers and actors who portray stories from the lives of the gods.[22] This gives Christians a culturally relevant opportunity through drama and preaching, as we found in Central India with puppet shows portraying the story of the Prodigal Son (Luke 15:11–32) as an example of God's grace and forgiveness.
11. Recognize doors open to Westerners. Because of the wealth and power in America, Indians often consider America the highest caste. This, coupled with racist beliefs instilled by the Brahmins, gives light-skinned Westerners a place of respect among lower-caste Hindus. While we understand that there is no validity whatsoever to this belief, those who are pale like I am can make use of the openness the belief brings among the lower castes, as long as we walk in humility and with Christlike character.

    (See the chapter on Buddhism for additional evangelism pointers in areas where Buddhist beliefs are similar to Hinduism.)

CONCLUSION

Your Hindu friends are on an impossible quest, looking for peace and assurance from a system built on human effort, karma, and reincarnation. Point them toward new concepts: grace, forgiveness, and a personal fellowship with a God who loves them. Tell your own testimony of the ways He has proven Himself to be real, to care about your needs, and to answer your prayers.

Scripture Study

Carefully read the beliefs in the left-hand column and ask yourself what is true, what is almost true, and what is completely wrong about them. In the right-hand column, write out Bible passages that correct or oppose each belief. Don't feel bad if you have a hard time finding biblical support to answer every belief. When you meet with your mentor or class, you'll find out what verses others have found and you can fill in what you lack.

Hindu Beliefs

God's Word

The Nature of God
Krishna said, "I am all-devouring death."[1]

"O Lord of lords, O refuge of the worlds, please be gracious to me. I cannot keep my balance seeing thus Your blazing deathlike faces and awful teeth. In all directions I am bewildered."[2]

A multitude of gods exist.

Some gods are good, and some are evil.

Hindu gods exhibit character traits that are patterned after the sins of the people.

The fire god, Agni, is the most truthful god. (What does this tell you about the others?)

Some gods are part human and part animal.

Vishnu incarnated "for destruction of evil-doers."[3]

Vishnu said, "Time I am, the great destroyer of the worlds, and I have come here to destroy all people."[4]

The gods are indifferent; they do not love people or care about their problems.

The gods may do something harmful to humans if they are not appeased.

Jesus
Jesus was one of the many incarnations (avatars) of God.

Salvation
"By following his qualities of work, every man can become perfect."[5]

Salvation comes through good works, bathing in the Ganges River, many reincarnations, and sacrifices.

Krishna said, "Being freed from attachment, fear and anger, being fully absorbed in Me and taking refuge in Me, many, many persons in the past became purified by knowledge of Me—and thus they all attained transcendental love for Me."[6]

Life, Death, and Enlightenment
"From the highest planet in the material world down to the lowest, all are places of misery wherein repeated birth and death take place. But one who attains to My abode, O son of Kunti, never takes birth again."[7]

Humans who escape the cycle of life, death, and rebirth and reach enlightenment become merged with divine oneness. The individual self ceases to exist.

Roles in Society
"Day and night a woman must be kept in subordination to the men in the family."[8]

_____

_____

_____

_____

The caste system: "According to the three modes of material nature and the work associated with them, the four divisions of human society are created by Me. And although I am the creator of this system, you should know that I am yet the nondoer, being unchangeable."[9]

_____

_____

_____

_____

_____

Astrology
Astrologers should be consulted about important decisions, such as planning the date and time of a wedding.

_____

_____

_____

_____

Prayer Time

List the major prayer needs of Hindus and pray for them.

•

•

•

SCRIPTURE MEMORY

Ephesians 2:8–9
For by grace you have been saved through faith, and that not of yourselves; it is the gift of God, not of works, lest anyone should boast.

Titus 3:4–5
But when the kindness and the love of God our Savior toward man appeared, not by works of righteousness which we have done, but according to His mercy He saved us, through the washing of regeneration and renewing of the Holy Spirit.

DAILY BIBLE READING

✓ Check when completed		
Sunday	Esther 1–2	_____
Monday	Esther 3–4	_____
Tuesday	Esther 5–7	_____
Wednesday	Esther 8–10	_____
Thursday	Job 1–3	_____
Friday	Job 4–7	_____
Saturday	Job 8–10	_____

BIBLE READING QUESTIONS/THOUGHTS

_____
_____
_____
_____
_____
_____
_____
_____
_____
_____

PRAYER NEEDS THIS WEEK

_____
_____
_____
_____
_____
_____
_____
_____

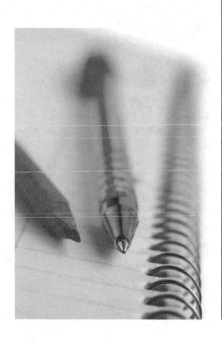

7

Lesson seven

BUDDHISM

T he first Buddha was born as Siddhartha Gautama in India around 563 BC. "Buddha" is a title and not the name of an individual. The son of a regional king, Siddhartha lived in luxury and was carefully kept from observing any of life's sufferings. As a young adult he left home and tried to find spiritual enlightenment as directed by local monks. He was frustrated by the lack of progress as he practiced asceticism, which is self-imposed denial and suffering. After a confrontation with an evil spirit who tempted him away from pursuing spirituality, he developed what is called the Middle Way between luxury and pleasure on one hand and asceticism on the other.[1] This revelation earned him the title of Buddha, which means the Enlightened One. With a growing following of monks to spread his teachings, Buddha's influence grew among the poor who made up the lower castes of Hinduism because Buddha emphasized equality instead of the caste system. After Buddha's death his teachings were written and formed into the primary Buddhist scripture, the Tripitaka, which contains rules for ethical living and teachings on how to attain spiritual enlightenment. The Tripitaka is eleven times longer than the Bible![2]

Buddha did not claim he was a god, and his teachings focus not on the worship of a personal deity but on a proper approach to living. Without a god, there is no place for prayer or worship in classical Buddhism. After his death many followers exalted him to the level of a god, and Buddhists often add traditional or regional gods such as Kuan Yin, Matsu, and Kuan Kung to their religion. This is a result of the innate desire in human beings for something greater than themselves to worship and follow.

BUDDHISM TODAY

Wandering monks have traveled throughout Asia spreading the teachings of Buddhism for over 2,400 years. Fiercely persecuted by Hindu leaders in India during its early years, Buddhism is strongest in Southeast Asia. Many boys and young men in Asia devote a few years of their lives to being Buddhist monks and learning about their religion. A smaller number of women become Buddhist nuns. Both shave their heads and renounce worldly comforts, dressing in robes, living a celibate life, begging for their meals, and giving blessings and spiritual advice in exchange for food.[3]

This Asian religion now has 400 million followers and is growing rapidly in the United States.[4] It has more appeal than Hinduism to the Western mindset because it is a religion of personal effort, which furthers pride in one's self-reliance, rather than worship of strange deities found in Hinduism. The author Henry David Thoreau practiced Buddhism in America in the mid

Terms and Concepts

nirvana: the extinguishing of the separate identity of a person when he or she has reached enlightenment through multiple reincarnations. At this point, all suffering has ended, but personal consciousness also ends. Buddhists compare this state to a candle whose flame has been extinguished. This is not a place like heaven but a condition of existence.

monism: the belief that all is one. This means that no distinction exists between the Creator and the creation, between humans and animals or even rocks and plants. Thus, everything is alive and has a spiritual life as part of the whole.

dharma: the duties of man taught by Buddha.

samsara: the cycle of reincarnation through death and rebirth.

satori: the goal of understanding that is reached by contemplating some of the seventeen hundred nonsense riddles, called *koans*. The most well-known koan is "What is the sound of one hand clapping?"

1800s.[5] Companies use Buddhist themes in advertising, and music groups, such as Nirvana, have promoted Buddhist doctrines. Movies like *Bulletproof Monk* and *Seven Years in Tibet* and well-known Americans who are Buddhist (including Adam Yauch of the Beastie Boys, Richard Gere, Tina Turner, Coach Phil Jackson, and Steven Seagal, who was proclaimed a reincarnation of a seventeenth-century Tibetan teacher) have generated increased interest in Buddhism.[6] Buddhist leaders in the West are often strongly critical of Christianity and mock the Bible.[7] Followers in the US include thousands of refugees and immigrants from Southeast Asian nations. Because Buddhism is currently trendy in the Western world, many people will claim to be Buddhists, although they have only a basic understanding of what Buddhism teaches. Some even go by the oxymoron "Buddhist Christians," but the two faiths are mutually exclusive and cannot be synthesized into one belief system. People who use this label generally are taking elements of each belief and trying to merge them while not having a real understanding of either one.

BELIEFS AND PRACTICES

The lines between Buddhism, Taoism, Confucianism, and Shinto are sometimes blurred, because Buddhism adapts to each of these beliefs and philosophies in the countries that historically believe in them. Buddhism grew from Hinduism and shares its beliefs in reincarnation

TRUE STORY

The architecture of the Taiwanese temples was ornate and impressive, but it disguised the evil within. Throughout our five weeks of ministry with the aboriginal tribes in the mountains and at youth camps in major cities, we saw people go into complete demonic seizures requiring deliverance, a new experience for some of the youth on our team. Most of the individuals had been forced by older family members to perform worship rituals to Buddha and the various gods: being dedicated to the rat as a totem of fertility; having Buddhist priests write "blessings" on paper scrolls that turned out to be curses, then burning the scrolls and mixing the ashes in water for them to drink; and dancing before the idols. One young girl had four intense deliverance sessions lasting several hours and found much more freedom but still had some strongholds of the enemy in her life when we had to leave. Her spiritual bondage was as severe as any of the Satanist kids I used to deal with in my days as a youth pastor in the US. An update from our missionary friends there told us that the girl has now come to complete freedom in Christ and is actively involved in her church.

and karma. It teaches that the way to knowing spiritual enlightenment or understanding is through meditation and thinking right thoughts. Buddhists don't believe there is a God or a heaven and are convinced that when a person becomes perfected through reincarnation he will stop being a separate person and become part of nothingness. There is no soul or life after death in Buddhist theology.

Buddhism teaches that eventually all of its followers could become Buddhas by following the principles of their religion through a series of reincarnations. This results in several different Buddhas being worshiped in various parts of Asia. The most recent incarnation of Buddha in 2008 is alleged to be Ram Bahadur Bamjan, an eighteen-year-old man in Nepal who is revered by thousands of followers.[8] Buddhism, like Islam and Hinduism, teaches that Jesus was a great teacher and a prophet. Buddhists see Jesus as one of many who have attained enlightenment or Buddha status.

Buddhist beliefs can be summarized into four points called The Four Noble Truths:[9]

1. Everyone suffers.
2. Suffering originates from selfish desires.
3. Suffering can be overcome by ending these desires, which means ceasing to care about anything and even losing the desire to live to the point that one can be dying without continuing to grasp for life.
4. The Noble Eightfold Path will lead people from suffering to spiritual enlightenment. The eight aspects of the path are right views or understanding, right resolve, right speech, right behavior, right livelihood, right effort, right mind control or concentration, and right meditation.

In addition, there are ten commandments for monks, with four of them matching those in the Bible, plus 251 precepts,[10] and 227 regulations.[11] There are also "3 praiseworthy acts, the 4 places of pilgrimage, the 5 obstacles, the 6-fold duty of a monk, 7 kinds of wealth, 8 causes of the earthquake, 9 types of person, 10 objects of contemplation, and 11 kinds of happiness."[12] A Buddhist will encounter these as he or she progresses through the thirty-one planes of existence.[13] Does Buddhist doctrine confuse you? It should! Part of Buddhism's appeal is that it doesn't make rational sense, which gives it a mystical quality that draws in spiritually hungry people. The contradictions and confusion in this and all false religions are a natural result of their not being inspired by the one true God.

DIFFERENT FORMS OF BUDDHISM

Theravada Buddhism holds to the original and purest form of Buddha's teachings, viewing Buddha only as a great teacher and not as a deity.[14] In practice, many Theravada Buddhists mix the traditional teachings of their religion with animism, the belief that everything in nature has a spirit and that people must keep the spirits happy or suffer the consequences.[15] Theravadans believe there is only one Buddha and don't emphasize the existence of God, but focus on seeking individual spiritual perfection. This branch of Buddhism is most often found in Cambodia, Vietnam, Laos, Myanmar, Thailand, and Sri Lanka.[16]

Mahayana Buddhism often considers Buddha to be a god and includes many occultic practices.[17] This branch is more outwardly focused than Theravada and desires to help others achieve enlightenment. Mahayana Buddhism continues to add books to its scripture and now has over five thousand books in several languages.[18] Nations with a large Mahayana following are Japan, Korea, India, Mongolia, Nepal, Bhutan, and China.

Several branches of Mahayana Buddhism have developed through the ages: Zen, Tibetan, and Nichiren Shoshu Buddhism.

Zen Buddhism is gaining popularity in the US, as the culture moves away from rationalism and toward existentialism. *Zen* means meditation and uses meditation and chanting to seek spiritual enlightenment through the experience of "nonthinking."[19] The danger in emptying one's mind, as in hypnotism and non-Christian meditation, is that when one willingly relinquishes control, he or she can be controlled by outside forces, whether human forces, as with a hypnotist, or demonic powers. Christian meditation is entirely different: it's an active event rather than a passive one. When Scripture tells us to meditate, the focus is on seeking greater understanding of God's Word (Psalms 1:1–2; 119:15), God's nature (Psalm 63:6), or His works (Psalm 77:12). Zen focuses on realizing the Buddha nature already within each person.[20] The appeal to people is that by learning how to avoid thinking while meditating, they can escape from their sufferings for a while. In this way meditation is similar to the use of alcohol or other drugs as escapism. The Beat poets of the 1950s and '60s, such as Jack Kerouac, practiced and endorsed Zen Buddhism.[21]

Tibetan Buddhism (also called Tantric) is led by the Dalai Lama. (The current Dalai Lama left Tibet when the Chinese invaded and annexed it.) The title of Dalai Lama (which means "Ocean of Wisdom") is passed down through generations and given to a boy believed to be a reincarnation of the previous Dalai Lama. The current Dalai Lama won the Nobel Peace Prize in 1989 and in the West is considered a leading spiritual example on the level of Mother Teresa. The roots of Tibetan Buddhism are found in a mixture of Mahayana Buddhism and an ancient religion called Bon, which centered on shamans (witch doctors) and animism.[22] Tibetan Buddhists believe chanting can break the cycle of reincarnation and

TRUE STORY

We still underestimated the spiritual power behind the ever-present idols and altars until several experiences in Danshui, Taiwan, opened our eyes. During free time one afternoon, I stood in front of a temple to a Buddhist goddess to watch the people worship and to learn more about their practices. We teach the kids who go on our mission outreaches that they must not enter the temples, because they would be required first to take off their shoes, a universal sign of reverence to a deity (Exodus 3:5). As I watched the people bowing and burning incense, an overwhelming impression came to my mind: bow…just bow…*bow…BOW!* I felt pressure pushing downward on my head to force me to bow down. This feeling was shocking and scary—so much so that I made the mistake of not calling on the Lord but just tried to withstand it by my own will-power. It was so incredibly strong that I had to leave. I realized that if I, after twenty-five years as a believer and experienced in dealing with spiritual things, could hardly resist it, these poor, lost people must be completely under its control.

Looking back on this unforgettable experience, I understood several things much more clearly:

1. Going to a place of strong demonic power alone was foolish and prideful. Jesus sent His disciples two by two, and we aren't being wise when we ignore this example.

Mark 6:7: And He called the twelve to Himself, and began to send them out two by two, and gave them power over unclean spirits.

2. Satan has kept the same goal for thousands of years: to receive worship that only the Lord deserves.

Isaiah 14:12–15: "How you are fallen from heaven, O Lucifer, son of the morning! How you are cut down to the ground, you who weakened the nations! For you have said in your heart: 'I will ascend into heaven, I will exalt my throne above the stars of God; I will also sit on the mount of the congregation on the farthest sides of the north; I will ascend above the heights of the clouds, I will be like the Most High.' Yet you shall be brought down to Sheol, to the lowest depths of the Pit."

Matthew 4:9: And he said to Him, "All these things I will give You if You will fall down and worship me."

3. We must never try to face the devil with our own strength. Even if we have made a mistake and find ourselves in over our heads, the Lord is our refuge and strength, and we must call on Him.

Jude 9: Yet Michael the archangel, in contending with the devil, when he disputed about the body of Moses, dared not bring against him a reviling accusation, but said, "The Lord rebuke you!"

allow people to go to nirvana when they die. The leaders of the religion are called *lamas,* and they seek occult powers through contact with spirits and sexual practices.

Nichiren Shoshu Buddhism is the foundation of an offshoot called Soka Gakkai. It is the only branch of Buddhism to encourage materialism, health, and power.[23] This is why it is popular in Japan and the Western world. Chanting is the means to both worldly and spiritual benefits but can be used to call down evil on others as well as good on the one chanting. Both good and evil spirits are part of the daily ritual performed at an altar at home that also includes rosaries[24] and prayers to the dead.[25]

KEY POINTS FOR EVANGELISM

1. Recognize that many people mix Buddhism with other beliefs. Frequently those who call themselves Buddhists actually practice more animism (the belief that natural objects and animals have spirits) than Buddhism. They may not be familiar with much Buddhist doctrine and often live in fear of evil spirits. Present to them the peace and confidence we have as Christians, knowing that the God we serve is all-powerful and has complete dominion over demonic powers. God extends this power to us as His servants when we take that authority over evil spirits in the Name of Jesus. Also look for the emptiness of idolatry when they mix Buddhism with belief in traditional or regional gods and ask them if the gods of wood or stone have brought them peace of mind, a cleansed conscience, or answers to any of their prayers.

2. Be careful with the term *born again.* Buddhists may confuse the Christian teaching of being born again, or spiritual rebirth, with reincarnation and being born naturally into another body countless times. Use this term with a thorough explanation that it means a new start in *this* lifetime, with freedom from the guilt of the past rather than an incarnation into another lifetime.

3. Explain the biblical concept of eternity. In a similar way, Buddhists may reject our offer of eternal life through Christ because of their misunderstanding of what it would be like. Since life results in suffering, they wouldn't want to continue suffering forever in new incarnations or live forever on earth. Explain to them the biblical perspective of a perfect place called heaven, which is a radically different destination for the soul than nirvana.

4. Contrast self-perfection with the transforming power and grace of God. Ask questions like these: Have you achieved your goal yet? (An honest Buddhist will have to say no.) How many more lifetimes will it take until you reach nirvana? (They can't answer this.) How do you know you're making progress, since you can't remember any of your past lives? Will you ever get there? These questions will bring up valid doubts about the insufficiency of Buddhism to perfect the soul, which in turn will open the door for your testimony about the sufficiency of Jesus.

5. Show the evidence of God's grace in your life. Grace is unearned, undeserved favor. It is merit credited to our account on the basis of what Christ has done, not on what we do. This is a humbling factor for Christians as we realize we are incapable of doing anything that will impress God but that the work of salvation has been done for us. Explaining our testimony of understanding grace provides Buddhists with an opportunity to compare the constant striving of their works-based religion with the peace and freedom we have in knowing the Lord.

6. Give them a new perspective on "doing good." The entire goal of doing any good work in Buddhism is earning merit toward the goal of enlightenment and eventually reaching nirvana. Buddhists believe that even thinking about good works, without doing them, earns merit. Although Buddhists may do good things, the root of all their actions is selfishness. Any giving of alms to a beggar or

helping a neighbor is done not from a motivation of love, compassion, or care for another person but out of self-interest.[26] Contrast this with the Christian perspective that we even do good to our enemies, not for what we can get out of it or to earn points with God but because of the love of God in our hearts. Since we don't have to earn any merit because of grace, we are free to do good without the taint of selfish motivation.

7. Explain the concept of sin. A significant difference between the Buddhist and Christian views of obedience is that Buddhists do not consider sin as an offense against a Person (God), as we know

---

THEOLOGY 101: Eternity and the Afterlife

Buddhists await being extinguished, Hindus view time and eternity as a cycle with endless rotations, Muslims and Mormons look forward to a sensual paradise, and Jehovah's Witnesses expect to be servants of other human beings. Let's look at the Bible's teachings on this subject.

Since elsewhere we have shown from Scripture that there is no reincarnation, the Bible leaves only two choices for human beings once they die: heaven and hell. (There is no biblical basis for the concept of purgatory, a place where people pay for their sins in order to be righteous enough to enter heaven. This is entirely contrary to salvation by grace and to believing that Jesus' death was sufficient atonement or payment for our sins.)

Heaven is a place of conscious fellowship with God, with its focus on Him rather than on carrying over earthly pleasures into eternity (Revelation 22:3–5). None of the troubles of our former life on earth, such as fear and sorrow, will be there (Revelation 21:4). God seemingly removes our capacity to feel eternal sadness over those who don't make it into heaven. Worship and adoration of the Lord is a primary activity, but God will have some responsibilities for us to accomplish in heaven (Revelation 5:6–14; 1 Corinthians 6:2–3). People will know each other from the past, although marriage will not carry over into eternity (Matthew 22:30). At the point of death, the spirit of a redeemed person immediately goes into the presence of the Lord (2 Corinthians 5:6–8). All believers will face a separate judgment from that of unbelievers, at which judgment God will reward faithfulness, obedience, and martyrdom (2 Corinthians 5:10; 1 Corinthians 9:25; Revelation 2:10). Although all Christians enter heaven by grace, some will receive varying amounts of eternal rewards, and some will get into heaven without reward (1 Corinthians 3:15).

Hell is eternal torment for the unforgiven, which includes all who have not come to God through Jesus (Matthew 18:8; 25:41). It is a place of unimaginable suffering (Matthew 13:40–42; Luke 16:22–28; Revelation 14:11). Although a common perspective is that God loves people so much that He would never send anyone to hell, He will keep His promise to punish the wicked (Revelation 20:15; 2 Thessalonians 1:8–9). Punishment in hell will vary according to the awareness the lost person had of God's laws and his or her choices to break them (Luke 12:47–48).

Many people prefer to believe in annihilationism, the belief that people who are sent to hell cease to exist and are burned up in an instant with no conscious suffering. This doctrine was invented to deny judgment and make the wrath of God against sin and sinners more palatable. Scripture is clear that it is not only the fire that is eternal but also the suffering of those in it (Matthew 25:46).

Despite the fact that we may recoil from the hard truth of hell, we must accept what the Bible says about it as the fate of the lost. If we can't believe what the Bible says about hell, how can we believe what it says about heaven? If Jesus exaggerated the terrors of hell, did He exaggerate the blessings of heaven? How can we know whether any of God's promises are true if parts of the Bible are wrong? Can you see that it's all or nothing—either we take this Book as the infallible revelation of truth, or we have nothing for our faith to stand on? Having a biblical perspective on eternity will cause Christians to appreciate our salvation more and to seek the lost with fervent effort. It also reminds us of the truly good news of salvation, which we are to spread throughout the earth.

TRUE STORY

One blistering hot day in Taiwan, we had to make our usual fifteen-minute walk from our lodging to the subway station to go to minister in a church. We put several sick kids in two taxis and began walking. Just around the corner from us, a procession for one of the Buddhist deities was beginning. Men in twelve-foot-high puppet costumes representing hideous demons walked among others with grotesque face paint, ceremonial clothing, and masks that portrayed all kinds of fanged evil spirits. Flat trailers filled with huge drums pounded out a rhythm for worship, and throngs of people dressed in red filled the street. Men carried the fifty-foot-long dragon puppets you've probably seen on TV, but this wasn't a show for tourists—it was being done out of reverence, fear, and devotion.

The kids walked as fast as they could through the crowd, but the procession took the same route we had to take to the subway. We all took note of an altar with idols and flapping banners carried on poles—a counterfeit of the Ark of the Covenant—and sensed an intense demonic force. It was obviously the power center of the whole event. Everyone was praying, some were in tears, and we thought at least the kids in the taxis were somewhat shielded. However, the kids were stuck in the traffic of the festival, surrounded on all sides by the costumed worshipers for much longer. Then their taxi driver, responding to the demonic presence in the festival, started shuddering and convulsing, making unnatural sounds. Our nine-year-old daughter Julie was terrified but was stuck in the taxi—there was no place to go. Getting out and walking through the crowd of worshipers wasn't an option. Some of the kids were quite traumatized by the time we met at the subway, so we had a time of worship there, right in front of everyone, and prayed to put off the spiritual defilement we all felt.

---

sin to be, but consider it as a violation of a principle for proper living.

8. Talk about the difference between escaping suffering and resolving it. A major value in Western culture is avoiding suffering, which explains the appeal of a religion that promises escape from stress, worry, and trouble. Ask Zen Buddhists why they want to only temporarily escape sufferings rather than find the help of a loving God to resolve them. Point out examples from your own life showing that your sufferings have accomplished important changes, such as developing character, causing you to draw close to God, and finding that He is compassionate and understanding.

9. Reference our natural will and desire to live. Ask Buddhists whether they really want to lose themselves in nothingness after death or, instead, wish deep inside that life would go on after death. The will to live is a part of every creature and results in humans' instinctual understanding that there must be something after this life is over. Although atheists try to deny a yearning for life after death, such yearning is foundational to mankind. People's wondering or worrying about what they will face after their last breath is a door into their hearts.

CONCLUSION

Show your Buddhist friend the reasonableness of God being a Person and the benefit to mankind of God's love, mercy, and patience. We do not deal with an impersonal force or the laws of the universe but with a Creator who has a personality, thoughts, and emotions. He is the One to whom we can take our deepest concerns, because He cares for us. And once we are reconciled to Him through Jesus—who understands suffering more than any other person—we can partake of the blessings He promises.

SCRIPTURE STUDY

Carefully read the beliefs in the left-hand column and ask yourself what is true, what is almost true, and what is completely wrong about them. In the right-hand column, write out Bible passages that correct or oppose each belief. Don't feel bad if you have a hard time finding biblical support to answer every belief. When you meet with your mentor or class, you'll find out what verses others have found and you can fill in what you lack.

BUDDHIST BELIEFS	GOD'S WORD
Scriptures Buddhists believe that their holy books accurately depict Buddha's life and teachings, although their scriptures were written beginning four hundred years after Buddha's death.	
The Nature of God "God," or ultimate reality, is an impersonal and abstract void.	
The Way to Truth and Wisdom "Strive hard and become wise! Rid of impurities and cleansed of stain, you shall enter the celestial abode of the Noble Ones."[1]	
"By yourself must the effort be made: the Tathagatas [Buddhas] only make known the way."[2]	
"Draw yourself out of this bog of evil, even as an elephant draws himself out of the mud."[3]	
"Lo, no man can purify another."[4]	
"Be a lamp unto yourself."[7]	

"Right meditation leads to spiritual enlightenment, or the development of that Buddha-like faculty which is latent [hidden] in every man."[5]

Jesus
"Because of his love, Jesus of Nazareth is comparable to a Bodhisattva (an enlightened person reaching the status of Buddha)."[6]

The Natural World
The natural world is impermanent and fragmentary. (Buddhism gives no explanation for its existence.)

Life, Death, and Enlightenment
The purpose of life is to escape suffering and reach nirvana.

After death, the soul will be reborn in a new body (human or animal).

All our actions determine our fate in future existences.

Prayer Time

List the major prayer needs of Buddhists and pray for them.

-

-

-

SCRIPTURE MEMORY

2 Corinthians 5:18–19
Now all things are of God, who has reconciled us to Himself through Jesus Christ, and has given us the ministry of reconciliation, that is, that God was in Christ reconciling the world to Himself, not imputing their trespasses to them, and has committed to us the word of reconciliation.

2 Corinthians 5:20–21
Now then, we are ambassadors for Christ, as though God were pleading through us: we implore you on Christ's behalf, be reconciled to God. For He made Him who knew no sin to be sin for us, that we might become the righteousness of God in Him.

DAILY BIBLE READING

✓ Check when completed		
Sunday	Job 11–14	_____
Monday	Job 15–17	_____
Tuesday	Job 18–19	_____
Wednesday	Job 20–21	_____
Thursday	Job 22–24	_____
Friday	Job 25–28	_____
Saturday	Job 29–31	_____

BIBLE READING QUESTIONS/THOUGHTS

_____
_____
_____
_____
_____
_____
_____
_____
_____
_____
_____

PRAYER NEEDS THIS WEEK

_____
_____
_____
_____
_____
_____
_____
_____
_____

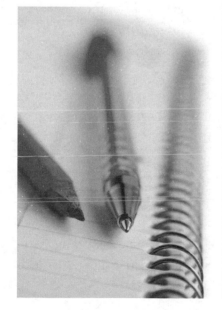

Lesson eight
WITNESSING SCENARIOS FOR ROLE-PLAYING

Use this class session to see how much you have learned. If you are taking the course alone, use the following scenarios to role-play with your mentor. If you are part of a class, divide into groups to act out the scenarios, with one person representing the other religion in the scenario and one person speaking as a Christian. Then have the rest of the group evaluate how effective you were in sharing the gospel, whether your attitude reflected the Lord, and what you could do to improve your witness. Be sure that when you are playing the part of those in false religions, you do not blaspheme or misuse the name of the Lord. For example, you can say something like "Buddhists believe that Jesus was only a great teacher" rather than saying that Jesus isn't God.

Scenario 1: It's your first day of college. As you walk into your dorm room, you see that your roommate, Habib, has already moved in. He's kneeling facedown on a small square of carpet. His shoes are off, and he's praying out loud. As he hears the door open, Habib's smiling, bearded face turns toward you, and he welcomes you in thickly accented English. During the semester, you build a friendship and find that he's very open to discussing religious beliefs. What will you say?

Scenario 2: You just graduated from nursing school and have been hired on the staff of a successful pediatrician. After work one day, Dr. Banerjee invites you into his office, where you notice a photo of his wife and daughters in saris, with the traditional Hindu bindi dot on their foreheads. Behind his desk is a painting of blue-skinned Krishna, and a small bronze statue of a six-armed Durga sits on his bookshelf. Dr. Banerjee had noticed the cross you wear around your neck and remarks that he never hears you gossip or criticize others like the rest of his staff do. He compliments you and asks whether your conduct has anything to do with your religious beliefs.

Scenario 3: She speaks in awe of the Dalai Lama's latest travels and speeches. She recommends meditation to another student who is having a hard time, and she talks in class about the Noble Eightfold Path. Her conversations are sprinkled with words like *karma* and *dharma*. She's your English teacher. One day you ask if you can visit with her after school, and she says yes.

These scenarios provide the setting for your witnessing opportunity. Take these practices seriously and prepare for them as though they were real-life situations. Plan ahead for the conversation so that you can keep it aimed at the most significant points. While it is good to answer honest questions, don't let the other person direct the conversation, or he or she may keep it focused on points of lesser importance, attempt to convert you to his or her beliefs, or bring up points for which you are not prepared to give an answer. You can overcome these obstacles by firmly and repeatedly going back to the main focus: to exalt the Lord Jesus Christ and point the person to Him. Promise to answer difficult questions at a later time, and if you ever see that you are outnumbered and need backup in an actual evangelistic setting, reschedule the meeting and invite your mentor or a knowledgeable Christian leader to join you.

Answer the following questions to help you plan your approach to each scenario.

1. What points do you expect the other person to bring up?

Scenario 1:

_____

_____

_____

_____

Scenario 2:

_____

_____

_____

_____

Scenario 3:

_____

_____

_____

_____

2. What are the main points you will bring up?

Scenario 1:

_____

_____

_____

_____

Scenario 2:

_____

_____

_____

_____

Scenario 3:

_____

_____

_____

_____

3. What parts of your own testimony and personal walk with the Lord would relate to the person's life and beliefs?

Scenario 1:

_____

_____

_____

_____

Scenario 2:

_____

_____

_____

_____

Scenario 3:

_____

_____

_____

_____

SCRIPTURE MEMORY

2 Corinthians 4:3–4
But even if our gospel is veiled, it is veiled to those who are perishing, whose minds the god of this age has blinded, who do not believe, lest the light of the gospel of the glory of Christ, who is the image of God, should shine on them.

Galatians 1:6–8
I marvel that you are turning away so soon from Him who called you in the grace of Christ, to a different gospel, which is not another; but there are some who trouble you and want to pervert the gospel of Christ. But even if we, or an angel from heaven, preach any other gospel to you than what we have preached to you, let him be accursed.

FINISH READING YOUR BOOK AND COMPLETE BOOK REPORT 2 ON THE NEXT PAGE.

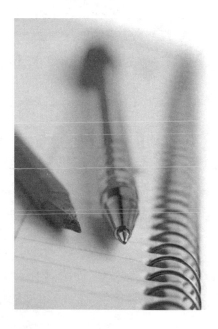

DAILY BIBLE READING

✓ Check when completed		
Sunday	Job 32–34	_____
Monday	Job 35–37	_____
Tuesday	Job 38–39	_____
Wednesday	Job 40–42	_____
Thursday	Psalms 1–6	_____
Friday	Psalms 7–12	_____
Saturday	Psalms 13–18	_____

BIBLE READING QUESTIONS/THOUGHTS

_____
_____
_____
_____
_____
_____
_____
_____
_____
_____

PRAYER NEEDS THIS WEEK

_____
_____
_____
_____
_____
_____
_____
_____
_____

BOOK REPORT 2

Book title: _____

Author: _____

What did you like about it?

_____
_____
_____
_____

Would you recommend it to others?

_____
_____

What impressed you most about this book?

_____
_____
_____
_____
_____

How did God use the book to speak to you?

_____
_____
_____
_____
_____

Other comments or thoughts about the book:

_____
_____
_____
_____
_____

Lesson nine

Mormonism

The world's largest cult began in New York in 1820 with a vision that came to fifteen-year-old Joseph Smith. Smith later told several contradictory versions of who appeared to him and what they said, but the basic story is that God told him not to join any of the churches around him, since they were all corrupt. Smith had a reputation in his town of being an untrustworthy character, although Smith's mother said that Joseph had a great imagination and entertained the family with tales of past civilizations and great battles.[1] Mormon history refers to Smith's father as a lazy man, interested in divination and treasure hunting.[2]

Smith was involved in occultism throughout his life and died wearing an occult medallion.[3] He was a member of the Masons, an occult group still popular today, and drew heavily from Masonry in developing Mormon practices such as secret handshakes, blood oaths of secrecy, Masonic symbols, and many aspects of Mormon temple ceremonies.[4] Some Mormon temples use the upside-down pentagram, a symbol of Satanism, in their architecture.[5] Mormonism endorses the biblically forbidden (Deuteronomy 18:11) practice of necromancy, or communicating with the dead, beginning with Joseph Smith's vision. "Ye Latter-day Saints! Ye thousands of the hosts of Israel! Ye are assembled here today, and have laid these Corner Stones, for the express purpose that the living might hear from the dead, and that we may prepare a holy sanctuary, where the people may seek unto their God, for the living to hear from the dead."[6]

Three years after the initial vision, Smith claimed that the angel Moroni appeared in his room and told him the location of a book written on gold plates, which could be translated using special glasses called Urim and Thummim. This book was said to hold the fullness

Similarities between Islam and Mormonism

A comparison of the remarkable similarities between the world's second largest religion and the world's largest cult shows that there must be common spiritual roots between them.

> "[I] will be to this generation a second Mohammed…whose motto in treating for peace was 'the Alcoran [Koran] or the Sword.' So shall it eventually be with us 'Joseph Smith or the Sword!'"[1]

- Both began through visions of an angel.
- Both visitations resulted in new scriptures.
- Both have varying and conflicting stories of what happened in their original vision.
- Both leaders had a delay of years before telling others of their visions.
- Both referred to flaws in Christian belief and practice to support beginning a new religion.
- Both have a history of violence.
- Both taught polygamy.
- Both believe in later revelations replacing earlier ones (Muslims call this the law of abrogation).
- Both have a missionary orientation.
- Both plan for world domination.
- Both have a subservient role of women.
- Both promise a sensual afterlife for men.
- Both prohibit the use of alcohol.
- Both teach a lower status of women than men in the afterlife.
- Both give men responsibility for the way women enter the afterlife.
- Both believe in the fallibility of the Bible.
- Both give death sentence for apostates.
- Both have equated books of their founders' sayings with scriptures.
- They comprise the fastest growing religion and fastest growing cult.
- When the founder died, followers of both split into factions over controversies regarding a successor.

of the gospel. Stating that the Book of Mormon was written in reformed Egyptian hieroglyphics, a language that no non-Mormon scholars believe exists, Smith attracted a group of followers and moved to Ohio. He then wrote the Book of Commandments, now called the Doctrine and Covenants, and revised the King James Bible to suit his beliefs. History shows that Joseph Smith married forty-eight wives,[7] as young as age fourteen,[8] but counts of the multiple wives and children of early Mormon leaders vary according to different sources. Smith battled with critics, developed a small army, and was imprisoned in Missouri first and later in Illinois, where a mob stormed the jail. Smith shot and killed two men and wounded another before being shot himself. Although he died with a gun in his hand, Mormons to this day call him a martyr.[9] After Joseph Smith's death, his persecuted followers settled in Utah under the leadership of Brigham Young, who had twenty wives and forty-seven children and continued to develop the distinctive teachings of the church.[10]

Mormonism Today

Now called the Church of Jesus Christ of Latter-Day Saints (LDS) and numbering over ten million, Mormons spread a false gospel worldwide through fifty-four thousand missionaries.[11] The headquarters of the church is in Salt Lake City, Utah. Mormon churches are called wards. More than one hundred temples found in major cities throughout the world are reserved for secret ceremonies not only closed to outsiders but also not open to all Mormons. Offshoots of the LDS church number over one hundred different factions, with the largest being the Reorganized Church of Jesus Christ of Latter-Day Saints (RLDS), which has moved closer to some biblical teachings in recent years.

Gaining converts is one of the primary goals of the Mormon church today. Mormon missionaries (called elders) are young men and women who devote two years and raise their own expenses to dedicate themselves to spreading their religion. They live under strict accountability and are seldom converted to Christianity during their mission because of their immersion in Mormon influences through living with other missionaries and working hard to make converts. However, Christian witnesses can plant seeds of the genuine gospel message in an elder's life that may bear fruit later. The elders' goal is baptism, which shows a genuine commitment to the LDS church. Baptism is more than a symbolic event in Mormonism and likely has a great spiritual significance in finalizing the grip of deceiving spirits on the life of the convert. Mormons believe that baptism into their church is being born again and that only the Mormon church has authority to give valid baptism.

Elders are trained to tell prospective converts what they want to hear, presenting themselves as a Christian church and trying to show similarities between Mormonism and Christianity. However, they consistently give new definitions to biblical terms.[12] They wait until after they have gained a convert to begin to talk about the unorthodox teachings of the church.

When Mormons don't have an answer to outsiders' questions, they resort to "bearing their testimony." This is a completely subjective basis for faith, which is based on a "burning in the bosom" experience of knowing in their hearts that Mormonism is true.

The status of women is low in LDS teachings. Multiple wives are to gratify lustful desires.[13] Early Mormon leader Heber Kimball once referred to his forty-three wives in a sermon as "my cows."[14] The church teaches that a woman's salvation depends on her husband. A woman can't make it to paradise unless her Mormon husbands chooses to call her forth from the grave at the resurrection. So a Mormon wife hopes that her husband, as a faithful missionary, will make it to the highest level of heaven and will want her to join him there. (From my many conversations with Mormon missionaries, I have observed how this idea affects the motives of Mormon missionaries. One young elder I was witnessing to on a weekly basis became very honest one night. He said the reason he became a missionary was that at the end of his mission he could have his pick of any girl in the church. A Mormon girl would presumably go along with this since her salvation is dependent on her husband.)

The Mormon church has done an excellent job in presenting itself to the public. The image from their television commercials and spokesmen in the realms of entertainment and public service is one of close-knit families, all-American values of patriotism and hard work, high moral standards, and conservative politics. Individual Mormons are often people of integrity and sincerity. This image attracts potential converts who want to separate themselves from the moral decline in the Western world and gives misguided credibility to Mormon doctrines. Mormons freely help one another, find jobs for fellow believers in Mormon-run corporations, and provide a sense of community often lacking in our society. When one of my Mormon relatives died and we went to the funeral, I was impressed by the care and concern the church showed to the family, both before and after his death.

Although in some ways the structures of Mormon relationships and social networks are more organized and effective than those found in many Christian churches, we must note several things that balance this observation. First, Mormonism is intensely concerned about image, while God is concerned with the heart. The Pharisees were also notable for their image-consciousness, but the Lord wasn't pleased when He looked within. Second, good works do not save anyone and can become a basis for self-righteous pride and the error of presenting one-self to God on the basis of human goodness, which falls far short of the righteousness Christ provides and is insufficient to cancel even the least of our sins. Third, public image is seldom reality. Considering Utah is a predominantly Mormon state, its divorce rate is average as compared with the rest of the country; its

TRUE STORY

The phone rang about 10:00 PM while we were still in the church office after a youth service. On the other end a woman's voice asked, "Can you tell me how to become a Christian?" Thinking this was too easy and must be a joke, I waited to hear the punch line, but the woman was serious. She told me that her former professional athlete husband was a heavy cocaine user, and she had left him, taking their child. While in a hotel room, she watched the *700 Club* and prayed to give her heart to the Lord. She called her husband, and he agreed to see a pastor with her. They looked in the phone book for a church with Jesus in its name. Our church was called Jesus Chapel.

They came to the church, and the husband, desperate for help, prayed with me to meet the Lord. The family began coming every Sunday and were growing in their walk with the Lord. They were celebrities because his athletic career caused many people to recognize his name. All was well until about four months later, when they called to tell me they weren't going to come to the church again. I was shocked as they explained that Mormon missionaries had come to their door shortly after they came to Christ. Hearing the young men were from the Church of Jesus Christ of Latter Day Saints, they had eagerly invited them in. The Mormons encouraged them not to tell anyone at our church about their visit, and the new believers fell for their lies. Weekly "Bible studies" lured them into deception, and once they were firmly gripped by the new doctrines and the spirit behind them, they were baptized into the Mormon church. No amount of talking could dissuade them. The family moved away shortly after that, and we've never seen them again.

TRUE STORY

Rita was the leader of a small group of Christians who met at their high school to pray before school every morning. When a Mormon girl started to come, no one objected, thinking it would be a good witness to her. The situation changed when the girl invited the Christian kids to a Mormon meeting, called a fireside, at her home, and most agreed to go. Rita was horrified. She told me the kids were not mature believers and that they would end up being deceived. I agreed to go with Rita, and we prayed and fasted, knowing a spiritual battle was looming. I had studied Mormonism as a new Christian and felt prepared for this encounter, but I was only nineteen at the time.

None of the other prayer group members showed up, and the Mormon youth made room for Rita and me to sit on the couch. Two enthusiastic young elders suggested we open with prayer, and one of the most unusual and intense experiences of my life took place. From the first word of the elder's prayer, I can only describe the sensation as though a powerful bird of prey had reached its talons into my mind and had slowly begun pulling it outward. I had the impression of evil and hatred masked by a sweet and smiling exterior. It was a direct contact with the demonic spirit behind the Mormon church. Reeling from the impact of this experience, which ended with the amen, I looked at Rita and saw by her expression that she had felt it too.

The elders used a flip book with pictures of ancient civilizations, Moroni, and the golden plates as they worked to convince us of the truths of Mormonism. We noticed the continual emphasis on being baptized if we would receive the truth of their doctrine, which told us that either their baptism had a powerful spiritual significance or that the elders were eager for the credit of our conversions that baptism would bring. At the end of their message, Elder Gonzalez asked whether I had any questions.

"Yes," I began, with a look toward the Lord for help in quoting the Book of Mormon. "Why do you believe there is more than one god, when in Alma 11:26–31 Amulek told Zeezrom that there was only one?"

With a collective gasp, all the Mormon kids turned toward the elders. God was with me as the elders fumbled for an answer and counterattacked. This continued as every deceitful doctrine faced the light of the Bible. It seemed as though every point the elders made was exactly what I had studied to answer, and the Lord gave me wisdom and boldness for the moment (Matthew 10:19). With arguments coming from various people and God coming through powerfully, the climax came when Elder Gonzalez said, "You are right and I am wrong. You are right and I am wrong!"

Chaos broke loose. Soon the door swung open, and two more missionaries came in. Not pausing for introductions, they immediately began with a doctrinal blitz. Anytime they were cornered and didn't have an answer, their reply was that they had a burning in their bosom that Mormonism was true. Finally one said, "Let's close in prayer." Oh, no! Rita and I braced ourselves, but I still felt the same spiritual attack as in the first prayer. The Mormon kids served refreshments, and the night ended.

I never saw Elder Gonzalez again. But the next week at a Mormon exhibit at the university I attended, I ran into one girl who had really seemed to understand the truth of the Christian gospel that night. When I asked her how she saw Mormonism and Christianity now, her answer shocked me.

"I'm so much more confident of my faith now," she replied. "I know that the Mormon church is the true church."

How could this have happened? Did the elders and her family do some spiritual damage control to convince their youth that they shouldn't believe the genuine Christian message? Maybe. But I prayed a lot and believe that the biggest influence was the spiritual power I felt during their prayers. Although the gospel of Jesus Christ can liberate captives (John 8:32, 36; Romans 1:16), this young woman didn't turn to Christ when she heard the truth, and the talons of the spirit behind Mormonism had returned to grip her even more tightly than before.

rape statistics exceed the national average, with 86 percent of victims being under age eighteen;[15] domestic violence is one of its fastest growing violent crimes;[16] suicide rates are consistently above the national average;[17] and antidepressant prescription rates are nearly twice the national average.[18] It is likely that the expectation to keep up the public image of perfection is the cause for the last two unfortunate statistics.

BELIEFS AND PRACTICES

Although Mormonism uses much of the same terminology as Christianity, the foundational beliefs of the church are entirely opposed to the revelation of God found in the Bible. Let's take a look at their scriptures and doctrines.

The Book of Mormon. Joseph Smith allegedly translated the Book of Mormon from the gold plates he received from Moroni. He hid behind a curtain and dictated the translation to Oliver Cowdery, David Whitmer, and Martin Harris. These witnesses claimed to have seen the Book of Mormon's golden plates, but later Martin Harris said he saw them only through the eyes of faith.[19] The famed three witnesses all eventually left the Mormon church, and the only ones who continued to claim they had seen the golden plates were two of Smith's brothers and his father. Smith later wrote fierce articles denouncing Cowdery, Whitmer, and Harris.

The Book of Mormon tells the story of a small group of Jewish settlers who came to the Promised Land of America in 600 BC and continued to AD 421. The settlers built great civilizations, fought huge battles, and received a visit from Jesus after His resurrection, which was supposedly a fulfillment of John 10:16. These Jewish settlers split into two groups, the Lamanites and the Nephites. The Lamanites are said to be the ancestors of the Native Americans, although no non-Mormon anthropologists believe there are any racial similarities between Native Americans and Jews.[20] Before the Lamanites killed off the Nephites, the angel Mormon wrote their history on gold plates and buried them. Interestingly enough, Mormon wrote the history in "reformed Egyptian hieroglyphics" (not in the Jewish language of Hebrew or Aramaic), which has no archaeological or historical connection to the Jews.

Considerable evidence exists against Joseph Smith's story of the origin of the Book of Mormon. In an era before TV, movies, and the Internet, people often amused each other by storytelling. Several men in Joseph Smith's town were known for telling similar stories about ancient civilizations, and the Book of Mormon stories have great similarities to book manuscripts written by ministers Solomon Spaulding and Ethan Smith.[21] The presence of twenty-five thousand words taken directly from the King James Bible, which was translated twelve hundred years after the Book of Mormon was supposedly written, makes sense if the theory that Smith plagiarized their works is true.[22]

Other Mormon scriptures. Other Mormon scriptures include the *Pearl of Great Price,* which contains a variety of "translated" documents, some of Joseph Smith's autobiography, and the LDS Articles of Faith. The *Book of Abraham* came from Egyptian papyri that Joseph Smith purchased and claimed to translate, but reputable Egyptian scholars say not a single word of the document is translated correctly. It is actually a standard funeral document full of Egyptian mythology.[23] The *Doctrine and Covenants* holds most of the distinctive LDS teachings not found in the Book of Mormon.

Significant Mormon doctrines. Many Mormon doctrines are not found in the Book of Mormon. The *Doctrine and Covenants* 20:9 says the Book of Mormon contains the fullness of the gospel, and Joseph Smith said it was "the most correct of any book on earth."[24] A serious contradiction in the Mormon faith comes from the lack of most of its significant doctrines in the original scripture of the church. The following key Mormon doctrines are *not* found in what is claimed to be the most true book:

God has a body. He is an imperfect, exalted man, and men can become gods. This is called "eternal progression" and leads to questions that Mormons cannot answer. If all gods were once men, where did the original god come from? Who began creation? Mormons teach polytheism, including both father and mother gods who are married and are eternally conceiving spirit children.

Jesus attained godhood. "Lucifer [is the] spirit-brother of Jesus [who] desperately tried to become the Savior of mankind."[25] Both Jesus and Lucifer wanted to be Savior of the world, but God chose Jesus, and Lucifer rebelled and took one-third of the spirit children with him. Jesus was not born to a virgin; God had an incestuous relationship with His own daughter, Mary. Jesus participated in polygamy; he married Mary, Martha, and Mary Magdalene and had children (Jesus was the groom at the wedding in Cana). Jesus' blood can't atone for all sin, so for some serious sins the sinner's own blood must be shed. This is why Utah uses the firing squad to execute criminals.

The Holy Spirit is different from the Holy Ghost. There is no Trinity.[26]

Salvation is for all of creation, including animals. This is a form of universalism; however, Mormonism excludes apostates from heaven because of their rejection of the Mormon gospel and says they will go to outer darkness.[27] Salvation is available after death to those who believe the Mormon gospel in the afterlife. It is a combination of works and faith. "All who hear and believe, repenting and receiving the gospel in its fullness, whether living or dead, are heirs of salvation in the celestial kingdom of God."[28] Mormons practice baptism for the dead by proxy (substitutes who undergo baptism in place of dead relatives and friends) with an emphasis on genealogy to keep accurate records for this purpose.

Pre-earth life, heaven, and the afterlife. Mormons teach the doctrine of preexistence of souls in a heavenly realm before coming to live in human bodies on earth.[29] Three degrees of heavenly glory are levels of heaven designed to include most of mankind and reward the most faithful Mormons. They believe in celestial marriage for time and eternity which does not cease at death.[30] Mormonism teaches a sensual view of heaven, similar to Islam, with multiple partners and eternal sex. Each Mormon man will receive ten virgins, "to multiply and replenish the earth."[31] Brigham Young said, "I shall have wives and children by the million, and glory and riches, and power and dominion, and kingdom after kingdom and reign triumphantly."[32]

Earthly conduct. Mormons follow the "Word of Wisdom" (a section in the *Doctrine and Covenants*), which warns them to avoid wine, strong drinks, tobacco, and hot drinks. Mormons who are qualified to participate in temple ceremonies are given special garments, called a temple garment, which they are told never to remove except to bathe.[33] This is supposed to protect them from harm. Families have set evenings at home together and keep food stored to prepare for future famines.

MORMON USE OF THE BIBLE

"We believe the Bible to be the Word of God insofar as it is translated correctly" (Articles of Faith, article 8). With this statement the LDS church is able to ignore anything in the Bible that contradicts its teachings, claiming that it must be translated incorrectly. In addition, 1 Nephi 13:26–27 claims that many important parts of the gospel have been removed. This allows Mormon doctrines to fill in the alleged gaps. Since Joseph Smith retranslated the Bible, why don't Mormons accept this as a restored edition of God's Word? Smith changed parts of fifty books of the Bible and removed the Song of Solomon completely. Isn't that interesting—the great biblical analogy of an intimate relationship with God, which Mormons discourage, was the one book Smith chose to remove. Although Mormons claim to

THEOLOGY 101: Can We Trust the Bible?

Every few years, alleged evidence that the Bible is false comes out. The secular media are no friend of biblical Christianity and often hype the latest exposé that claims "absolute proof" that a core doctrine of Christianity has been disproven. Christians tend to worry that these attacks on the truth will shatter the faith of many and discredit the gospel. But the attacks usually die down quickly, and often even unbelieving but fair-minded experts show the errors in reasoning, flaws in scientific methodology, and specious arguments. However, the attacks can destroy the faith of some Christians who are not strong enough in the knowledge of the truth and especially of those who are already looking for an excuse to turn away from the Lord.

Often we hear the claim that the Bible has been changed through the centuries. However, overwhelming evidence shows the consistency and accuracy of the Bible.

- Consider that the 24,000 ancient manuscripts and portions of the New Testament do not disagree on any major doctrines,[1] and the total amount of disputed passages, which are mostly spelling differences, equal about a half page. For anyone to have successfully changed the Bible, including passages quoted in sermons of early church leaders, all the copies would have had to be discovered, confiscated, changed in the same way, and redistributed. Surely an organization or individual responsible for the greatest fraud in history would have been discovered after two thousand years of scholarly research.
- The Bible quotes in sermons of early church leaders, called patristic citations, cover nearly the entire New Testament and agree with the thousands of scrolls and parchments.
- "The New Testament documents, for example, have more manuscript authority than any 10 works of antiquity put together.... We have over 24,000 manuscript copies of portions of the New Testament dating from before AD 350. In comparison, the number two book in all of ancient history for manuscript authority is the *Iliad* with 643 manuscripts."[2]

- The books of ancient authors such as Plato and Aristotle are considered to be the authors' words and thoughts despite the fact that there is only a tiny fraction of manuscripts for those books compared to the Bible. For example, only ten copies of *Julius Caesar* exist.[3] Isn't it logical to apply the same standard, yet with far greater confidence, to the thousands of copies of the New Testament?
- "The Dead Sea Scrolls were discovered beginning in 1947 in desert caves about 15 miles from Jerusalem. There are more than 100,000 scroll fragments from 930 documents, including text from every book of the Hebrew Bible except Esther."[4] The scrolls show that the books we have today were considered to be authentic Old Testament books in Bible times.
- Changes to the scrolls and parchments would have introduced scientific or archaeological errors, yet archaeological discoveries consistently support statements in Scripture, even proving the Bible's statements that historians have strongly doubted. Examples of this are discoveries relating to the Hittites, Sargon, and Belshazzar that were questioned by critics and then proven to be genuine.

Skeptics often deny that the Bible is divinely inspired, but more than adequate support exists for the truth and inspiration of the Bible and the belief that it is a supernatural book.

- Fulfilled prophecy points to divine inspiration. For example, the events surrounding Jesus' crucifixion were described in detail in Psalm 22 and Isaiah 53 about one thousand years before crucifixion became a means of capital punishment. Jesus fulfilled about three hundred specific and detailed prophecies from the Old Testament, in contrast to the vague generalizations given by others, such as Nostradamus, who falsely claimed to be prophets. No other book considered divinely inspired by any of the world's religions can show the proof of fulfilled prophecy.

- Scientific discoveries confirm biblical statements given centuries earlier, as in the fact that the earth is round (Isaiah 40:22), the hydrologic cycle (Job 36:27), and the life-giving nature of blood (Leviticus 17:11).

God claims He has inspired and preserved the Bible.

2 Timothy 3:16: All Scripture is given by inspiration of God, and is profitable for doctrine, for reproof, for correction, for instruction in righteousness.

2 Peter 1:21: For prophecy never came by the will of man, but holy men of God spoke as they were moved by the Holy Spirit.

Isaiah 40:8: The grass withers, the flower fades, but the word of our God stands forever.

Eyewitnesses claim that the Bible's stories are accurate, and ten of the original twelve apostles died as martyrs for their faith (not including Judas, who killed himself, and John, who died in exile). Why would anyone die for that which he knew was false? The apostles were convinced of the truth of Jesus Christ and the events surrounding His life. Their writings were distributed during their lifetimes, when other eyewitnesses could have come forward and denied the events, yet no exposure of falsehood by contemporary critics took place.

2 Peter 1:16: For we did not follow cunningly devised fables when we made known to you the power and coming of our Lord Jesus Christ, but were eyewitnesses of His majesty.

Luke 1:1–4: Inasmuch as many have taken in hand to set in order a narrative of those things which have been fulfilled among us, just as those who from the beginning were eyewitnesses and ministers of the word delivered them to us, it seemed good to me also, having had perfect understanding of all things from the very first, to write to you an orderly account, most excellent Theophilus, that you may know the certainty of those things in which you were instructed.

honor the Bible, in practice it is the least used of their four holy books, and key Mormon leaders have claimed that every verse in the Bible may have been corrupted.

Though Mormons do not believe in the core doctrines of Christianity, the Book of Mormon does contain some biblical doctrines, which contradict the teachings of Mormonism as found in their other scriptures.

- God has always been God—no eternal progression (Book of Mormon 9:9–11, 19; Moroni 7:22; 8:18)
- God is spirit (Alma 18:24–28; 22:9–11)
- There is only one God (Alma 11:26–31, 38–39; 14:5; 1 Nephi 13:41; 2 Nephi 31:21; 3 Nephi 11:14, 27, 36; Mosiah 15:1–5; Book of Mormon 7:7)
- Polygamy is wrong (Jacob 1:15; 2:23–31; Mosiah 11:2; Ether 10:5–7; DC 42:22)
- You must be born again (Mosiah 27:24–28)
- The cleansing of Jesus' blood (Alma 5:26–27)
- As many as received Him became sons of God (3 Nephi 9:17)
- Virgin birth of Jesus (Alma: 7:10; 1 Nephi 11:13–21)
- There is no salvation available after death for those who rejected it during their lifetime (Alma 34:31–35; 2 Nephi 9:23–24, 27; Mosiah 2:38–39)
- Eternal hell (1 Nephi 14:3; 2 Nephi 9:16; 28:21–23; Mosiah 3:25; Alma 34:35; Helaman 6:28; and at least thirty other references)

- The Holy Spirit dwells in man (Alma 18:35; Moroni 7:32)
- Jesus is God (2 Nephi 10:3; 11:7, 3; Nephi 11:27; 9:15; Alma 11:38–39)

CHANGING REVELATIONS AND FALSE PROPHECIES IN MORMONISM

In addition to the discrepancies between the Bible and the Mormon scriptures, there are practical and logical reasons to believe that the Latter Day Saints are following a system that does not have genuine authority and cannot lead them to the truth. The following paragraphs discuss several points for consideration.

Changing revelations. Throughout Mormon history, Joseph Smith and other notable leaders received "revelations" from God to change a significant doctrine when it became important or convenient to do so.

Polygamy is one of the most telling examples of these changing revelations. Polygamy was the official Mormon doctrine until the Utah Territory found it was a major obstacle in obtaining statehood in the United States, at which point a new revelation changed the practice.[34] Although polygamy is officially banned, Mormons still practice it secretly in several states, and some offshoot Mormon groups require it. Current estimates say that 60,000–100,000 Americans and Canadians are part of a polygamous "family."[35] The way they can get around charges of breaking the law is to legally marry only one wife and have other women and their children living in the same house as sister wives. *Doctrine and Covenants* 132:1–4 says those who don't practice polygamy will be damned.

Priesthood is another example of changing revelations. Women still can't hold the Aaronic and Melchizedekian priesthoods, which are reserved for boys and men ages twelve and nineteen. Both were originally only for white-skinned Mormons until a new revelation in 1978 opened the priesthoods to dark-skinned males. Mormon doctrine has supported racism, teaching that people are born with dark skin because of their failures in the preexistent world. "It is alleged that they were neutral, standing neither for Christ nor the devil. But, I am convinced it is because of some things they did before they came into this life that they have been denied the privilege. The races of today are very largely reaping the consequence of a previous life."[36] Second Nephi 5:21 says that sin causes people's skin to become black but righteousness causes black skin to turn white. Why aren't we seeing this happen in the world today?

These are two of many instances in which Mormon doctrine has changed as a result of the discovery of contradictions and outside political or social pressure. About four thousand changes in grammar, spelling, and contradictions have been documented in the Book of Mormon since 1830.[37]

False prophecies. Mormonism claims prophet status to Joseph Smith as well as an office of the prophet that continues to the present day. Each president of the LDS is said to be a prophet, providing the church with ongoing revelation. Mormons believe that current revelations are much more in tune with modern life than reading a two-thousand-year-old Bible. However, Mormonism's prophetic track record falls far short of the biblical standard, which shows that even one false prophecy makes the speaker a false prophet (Deuteronomy 18:20–22). The following are a few false Mormon prophecies and revelations:

- The Civil War will spread worldwide, with England fighting on the side of the South (*Doctrine and Covenants* 87:1–6).
- Brigham Young will become president of the United States (*Journal of Discourses,* vol. 5, 219).
- Jesus will return by 1891 (*History of the Church*, vol. 2, 182).

- "So it is with regard to the inhabitants of the sun. Do you think it is inhabited? I rather think it is. Do you think there is any life there? No question of it; it was not made in vain" (*Journal of Discourses*, vol. 13, 271).

Past leaders have made statements that most Mormons don't know about (for example, Brigham Young said that Adam is our god, and Joseph Smith said that tall men dressed like Quakers live on the moon).[38]

Archaeological Evidence against the Book of Mormon

A Mormon organization called the Foundation for Ancient Research and Mormon Studies (FARMS) has been trying for years to find evidence for the Book of Mormon. Its far-fetched claims are unconvincing. The Smithsonian Institution, one of the United States' foremost museums and research centers, sees "no direct connection between the archaeology of the New World and the subject matter of the book."[39] Much of the technology mentioned in the Book of Mormon (swords, steel, glass windows, compasses, chariots, cement, candles, highways) was unknown when the Lamanites and Nephites were supposed to have existed, and none of the cities or rivers mentioned in the Book of Mormon have ever been discovered.[40] The Book of Mormon contains no maps to give clues about the alleged cities and rivers, nor does it mention any of North America's prominent geographical features. A recent explanation from FARMS claims that the events in the book actually took place in Central America, although Joseph Smith stated that he found the golden plates in New York.

Many of the Book of Mormon's archeological findings have simply never been verified in the Americas. Middle Eastern crops are an example of this. According to 1 Nephi 18:24, the Jews planted crops when they came here, but none of these crops have been found growing wild in the Americas.[41] Book of Mormon animals such as cumoms and cureloms have never been identified, and there are complications with the other animals the book references. According to 1 Nephi 18:25 and Ether 9:18–19, domesticated cows, chickens, dogs, sheep, pigs, horses, donkeys, and elephants were discovered here in ancient times by the Lamanites and the Nephites. However, none of these animals were found in the US when European explorers and settlers came.[42] In addition, no traces of Egyptian or Hebrew script have been discovered in any archaeological site in the Americas.[43]

The golden plates themselves raise some questions. Joseph Smith claimed to have discovered and carried them for three miles through the woods, although the golden books would have weighed 230 pounds.[44] How could Smith alone have carried these plates for such a distance? Also, since there is no record of written language in the Americas at the time the golden books were supposed to have been written, the plates could not possibly have been transcribed as Smith claimed.

In contrast to the Book of Mormon, the Bible has significant and compelling archaeological roots. Nearly all of the locations named in the Bible have been found, twenty-four thousand New Testament manuscripts exist, and most are in agreement with each other on all but the smallest details.[45] Despite so much evidence for the validity of the Bible, Mormons believe the Bible is untrustworthy. And yet zero manuscripts, scrolls, or plates of the Book of Mormon exist.

Key Points for Evangelism

1. Love Mormons and show them that your goal is not to tear apart their beliefs but to point them to the true Savior. Realize the price a Mormon would pay to leave the church—loss of friends, family,

and possibly a job and education. The all-encompassing Mormon system and emphasis on family are what draw many people to Mormonism in the first place. Be patient and compassionate.

2. Talk about divine authority. With the motivation just explained, patiently show Mormons that their church does not have divine authority. Highlight Mormon contradictions and false prophecies, but not as weapons against them. Mormons are familiar with anti-Mormon literature, videos, and websites. Your goal is not to win the argument but to win their souls.

3. Spend time in prayer. Because of the inconsistencies, false prophecies, reputation of Joseph Smith, bad fruit as shown by the social problems in Utah, evidence against the Book of Mormon, contradictions between their scriptures, and other flaws, it is easy to think we can convince Mormons that their religion is false. However, spiritual deception can be broken only through prayer. Bind the deceiving spirits in Jesus' name, and fast for a breakthrough. Logic alone isn't enough.

4. Emphasize salvation by grace, not by works. Perfectionism and public image are very important to Mormons. Help them see their lost condition according to God's Word, and point out that even Mormon scriptures would tell them they are lost. Show them that they aren't fulfilling all of God's laws and that their own righteousness is insufficient.

5. Don't ridicule their more outrageous beliefs, including core doctrines such as the plurality of gods and men becoming gods.

6. Encourage their invitation to investigation. Mormon leaders and scriptures invite investigation of the truth of their beliefs. Show these invitations to Mormons and hold them to the test:

> Mormonism, as it is called, must stand or fall on the story of Joseph Smith. He was either a prophet of God, divinely called, properly appointed and commissioned, or he was one of the biggest frauds this world has ever seen. There is no middle ground. If Joseph Smith was a deceiver, who willfully attempted to mislead the people, then he should be exposed; his claims should be refuted, and his doctrines shown to be false. . . . There would appear many errors and contradictions which would be easy to detect. (*Doctrines of Salvation*, vol. 1, 188)

> Take up the Bible, compare the religion of the Latter Day Saints with it, and see if it will stand the test. (*Journal of Discourses*, vol. 16, 46)

Conclusion

Mormons, some of whom may be your friends, are part of an all-encompassing religious system that mimics the high moral standards, devotion, and biblical terminology of Christianity without pointing its members to a genuine relationship with Jesus Christ. It will take much love, patience, and prayer on your part to enable your friends to understand that they are caught in a false belief—that Joseph Smith, Brigham Young, and others in their organization are false prophets whose teachings are inconsistent with the Bible and the facts of archaeology and science.

Scripture Study

Carefully read the beliefs in the left-hand column and ask yourself what is true, what is almost true, and what is completely wrong about them. In the right-hand column, write out Bible passages that correct or oppose each belief. Don't feel bad if you have a hard time finding biblical support to answer every belief. When you meet with your mentor or class, you'll find out what verses others have found and you can fill in what you lack.

Mormon Beliefs

God's Word

Salvation and the Church
There is no salvation without accepting Joseph Smith as a prophet of God.[1]

"No man or woman in this dispensation will ever enter into the celestial kingdom of God without the consent of Joseph Smith. From the day that the Priesthood was taken from the earth to the winding-up scene of all things, every man and woman must have the certificate of Joseph Smith, junior, as a passport to their entrance into the mansion where God and Christ are."[2]

All non-Mormon churches are corrupt.

Mormons are "the only true and living church upon the face of the whole earth."[3]

"Salvation is not a gift of God which comes to man through the decree of Deity or through the sacramental action of the Church. It is a gift of God which man must work diligently to achieve."[4]

The idea of "gaining a special, personal relationship with Christ . . . is both improper and perilous. . . . Some misguided members of the Church may 'begin to pray directly to Christ because of some special friendship they feel has been developed' with him. This is wrong, said Elder McConkie."[12]

The dead may be baptized vicariously into the Mormon church.

Jesus
"The birth of the Savior was as natural as are the births of our children; it was the result of natural action. He partook of flesh and blood—was begotten of his Father, as we were of our fathers."[5]

Jesus and Satan are spirit brothers.

God and Man
"We will become gods and have jurisdiction over worlds, and these worlds will be peopled by our own offspring."[6]

The doctrine of eternal progression: "As man now is, God once was; as God now is, man may be."[7]

"God himself was once as we are now, and is an exalted man, and sits enthroned in yonder heavens! That is the great secret. If the veil were rent today, and the great God who holds this world in its orbit, and who upholds all worlds and all things by his power, was to make himself visible, . . . you would see him like a man in form—like yourselves in all the person, image, and very form as a man. . . . I am going to tell you how God came to be God. We have imagined and supposed that God was God from all eternity. I will refute that idea, and take away the veil, so that you may see. . . . You have got to learn how to be Gods yourselves, and to be kings and priests to God, the same as all Gods have done before you. . . . He was once a man like us; yea, that God himself, the Father of us all, dwelt on an earth, the same as Jesus Christ himself did; and I will show it from the Bible."[8]

"The Father has a body of flesh and bones as tangible as man's; the Son also."[9]

Knowing Truth
To know the truth, Mormons trust in a subjective "burning in the bosom."

Revelation and Doctrine
Revelation is ongoing through prophets who teach and change doctrine.

The Bible is not the sole source of revelation. The Book of Mormon is subtitled "Another Testament of Jesus Christ."

Marriage
"The only men who become Gods, even the Sons of God, are those who enter into polygamy."[10]

Equality
"You see some classes of the human family that are black, uncouth, uncomely, disagreeable and low in their habits, wild, and seemingly deprived of nearly all the blessings of the intelligence that is generally bestowed upon mankind ... they should be the 'servant of servants.'"[11]

PRAYER TIME

List the major prayer needs of people caught in the deceptions of Mormonism and pray for them.

-

-

-

SCRIPTURE MEMORY

Colossians 2:8–9
Beware lest anyone cheat you through philosophy and empty deceit, according to the tradition of men, according to the basic principles of the world, and not according to Christ. For in Him dwells all the fullness of the Godhead bodily.

1 Timothy 2:5
For there is one God and one Mediator between God and men, the Man Christ Jesus.

DAILY BIBLE READING

✓ Check when completed

Sunday	Psalms 19–24	_____
Monday	Psalms 25–30	_____
Tuesday	Psalms 31–36	_____
Wednesday	Psalms 37–39	_____
Thursday	Psalms 40–42	_____
Friday	Psalms 43–49	_____
Saturday	Psalms 50–54	_____

BIBLE READING QUESTIONS/THOUGHTS

_____
_____
_____
_____
_____
_____
_____
_____
_____
_____
_____

PRAYER NEEDS THIS WEEK

_____
_____
_____
_____
_____
_____
_____
_____

10

JEHOVAH'S WITNESS

The Jehovah's Witness cult began after a season of intense interest in the return of Christ in America in the 1840s. Charles Taze Russell, a former Presbyterian and successful businessman, started the group in 1870 in Brooklyn, New York, that is officially known as the Watchtower Bible and Tract Society. The budding movement was later led by Joseph Rutherford, the author of numerous books and new doctrinal positions, and grew worldwide under Nathan Knorr, whose leadership skills brought rapid numerical growth. Using Isaiah 43:10 as a theme verse, members are commonly called Jehovah's Witnesses and are known within the group as "publishers." *Jehovah* is a twelfth-century mistranslation of the Hebrew name Yahweh ("I Am"), which was originally written YHWH.[1]

JEHOVAH'S WITNESS TODAY

Jehovah's Witnesses are known to outsiders by their distinctive practices more than their doctrines and are often marginalized because the rules of the Watchtower keep them from participating in many facets of modern culture. The Watchtower is less visible than Mormonism in the mainstream of American life, since it is smaller and its followers avoid politics. It does, however, have a few well-known followers, including the late Michael Jackson (who was raised in the cult but converted to Islam in 2008)[2] and Prince (who joined in 2001 after being converted by his bassist).[3] The low profile of Jehovah's Witnesses in public life is matched by consistent visibility in residential neighborhoods as they systematically and persistently ring doorbells in search of potential converts.

In 2008 Jehovah's Witnesses spent 1.5 billion hours preaching and witnessing, usually in pairs of Witnesses going from door to door.[4] These Witnesses are characterized by an aggressive and argumentative spirit, often intimidating those who would hear them by quoting Greek and appearing to have a tremendous command of Scripture. This apparent knowledge of Scripture comes from thorough indoctrination, including ways to answer biblical objections from Christians. Official Watchtower publications even call their witnessing "argumentation."[5] Members are required to attend meetings five times each week, and one meeting is devoted to teaching members to share their faith and to learn the counterarguments against it.[6] The average Witness spent 209 hours "preaching" in 2007.[7]

Jehovah's Witnesses use the New World Translation of the Bible. This translation changes key Bible verses to fit Watchtower doctrines. No Greek or Hebrew scholars outside the Watchtower support this translation, and no other Bible translation agrees with the changes found in it.[8] The five-member translation committee included four men with no higher education after high school and one with two years of college, which hardly qualified any of them to translate the Bible accurately.[9] For example, they added the word *Jehovah* 237 times in the New Testament, although in the Greek texts it isn't used even once.[10] Additional words are added to change the meaning of Scripture to support Watchtower beliefs, ignoring the warning of Proverbs 30:5–6. Jehovah's Witnesses also generate literature, particularly *The Watchtower* and *Awake!* magazines, for use in teaching their beliefs. Their printing presses had produced over one billion publications by the year 2000.[11] *The Watchtower* is published in 168 languages and *Awake!* in 81 languages.[12] These magazines are often the first step toward conversion for many outside the group because they use contemporary topics to capitalize on common fears and concerns, offering the Watchtower organization as an authority with answers. The Watchtower considers its magazines the sole source of God's revelation to mankind today. One of the primary goals of Witnesses is to convince people to take and read the magazines, then come to a meeting at a Kingdom Hall.

Through the efforts of Jehovah's Witnesses, the cult following has seven million baptized members and fifteen million people involved in Bible studies.[13] It baptized nearly 300,000 converts in 2008 and has 103,000 churches called Kingdom Halls worldwide.[14]

BELIEFS AND PRACTICES

Jehovah's Witness beliefs about the nature of God show that the group is not part of orthodox Christianity. The Watchtower repeats the Arian heresy, dealt with by the early church at the Council of Nicaea in AD 325. Arius taught that Jesus was a created being and not eternally coexistent with God.[15] Jehovah's Witnesses deny that the Holy Spirit is a Person but say He is merely a force. Witnesses usually refer to holy spirit (without "the" preceding it and without capital letters). They also deny the Trinity, although references to the Trinity are found throughout their Bible and all Witnesses are baptized in the Name of the Father, Son, and Holy Spirit.

The Watchtower teaches that Witnesses must have faith in their organization, which provides salvation, rather than in a Person. Watchtower members are taught that they are unable to understand the Bible without their leadership teaching them proper interpretation and that God speaks to the world only through this leadership, never directly to individual Witnesses.[16]

Jehovah's Witnesses' believe that only 144,000 people, called the Little Flock, will become bodiless spirits and make it to heaven, and the rest of the faithful Witnesses, called the Great Multitude, will serve them on earth forever in physical bodies.[17] Witnesses ignore the fact that in Revelation

TRUE STORY

Maria was really nervous about the upcoming visit from her two aunts. She was a converted Jehovah's Witness who had begun coming to my youth group. Maria's parents didn't care much about religion, but her aunts were aggressive Witnesses who had brought her to the Watchtower as a young girl. Now Maria was a sincere Christian facing an impending conflict: her aunts hadn't yet heard about her leaving the Watchtower.

Just as Maria feared, the aunts cornered her to check on her faithfulness to the cult. Maria lost her nerve and gave answers that didn't fit her aunts' questions.

"Have you been baptized yet?" they demanded.

"Oh, yes, just a few months ago," Maria replied, although I, not a Jehovah's Witness minister, had baptized her!

"How many hours are you doing weekly?" they asked, referring to her commitment to door-to-door proselytizing.

"Twelve! And I talk to people at school all the time about my beliefs!" she blurted, referring to the number of class hours she was taking in college and her witness there for Jesus, not for the Watchtower.

Impressed at their niece's devotion, the aunts backed off, and Maria breathed a sigh of relief.

When Maria told me this story, I didn't chew her out for chickening out or for deceiving them. If points were awarded for creativity, she would have won that discussion. She was a new believer and needed to grow in confidence and the understanding of how the Holy Spirit gives us power to be Jesus' witnesses (Acts 1:8). It's been about twenty years since this incident, and today Maria is still walking with the Lord, is living a victorious Christian life, and has never gone back to the Watchtower.

THEOLOGY 101: The Resurrection of Jesus

If Jesus had merely lived a good and upright life, taught insightful thoughts about God, and died as any normal person, history would remember Him as a wise man and philosopher but not as the divine Son of God, time would not be split into before and after His birth (BC and AD), and one-third of the human race would not profess faith in Him. It is Jesus' resurrection from the dead that causes a stumbling block for unbelievers (just as Jesus had prophesied and promised) and brings into sharp focus the uniqueness of the Christian faith. No other major religious leader claimed that he would come back to life after death, and no followers except Jesus' past and present-day disciples believe their leader has done so. Without the resurrection our faith would be in vain, because if Jesus had died and remained dead, the power of sin would be in effect and salvation would not be available to mankind. We could not expect to rise from the dead to eternal life with the Father unless Jesus Himself rose.

1 Corinthians 15:12–19: Now if Christ is preached that He has been raised from the dead, how do some among you say that there is no resurrection of the dead? But if there is no resurrection of the dead, then Christ is not risen. And if Christ is not risen, then our preaching is empty and your faith is also empty. Yes, and we are found false witnesses of God, because we have testified of God that He raised up Christ, whom He did not raise up—if in fact the dead do not rise. For if the dead do not rise, then Christ is not risen. And if Christ is not risen, your faith is futile; you are still in your sins! Then also those who have fallen asleep in Christ have perished. If in this life only we have hope in Christ, we are of all men the most pitiable.

Believing the Bible's account of the resurrection is not an option but is one of the core doctrines of our faith. Let's look at the primary excuse given in Scripture for Jesus' enemies denying the resurrection and the answers for this belief, which we still hear unbelievers profess today.

Matthew 28:11–15: Now while they were going, behold, some of the guard came into the city and reported to the chief priests all the things that had happened. When they had assembled with the elders and consulted together, they gave a large sum of money to the soldiers, saying, "Tell them, 'His disciples came at night and stole Him away while we slept.' And if this comes to the governor's ears, we will appease him and make you secure." So they took the money and did as they were instructed; and this saying is commonly reported among the Jews until this day.

If Jesus' body had been stolen and the disciples had claimed that Jesus had risen, the Jews would have needed only to produce His body to destroy Christianity's credibility forever, yet they could not do so. Note that this excuse arose from the desperation of the Jewish leaders after hearing from the soldiers of Jesus' miraculous resurrection. If their report was true, why would the disciples willingly have died as martyrs for a faith they knew was a lie?

The alibi offered to protect the soldiers also fails to support this denial of the resurrection. The strict discipline of Roman soldiers would have brought punishment as in Acts 12:19. How could the Jewish leaders have rescued the Roman soldiers from punishment or execution after they failed to carry out a direct order, slept while on duty, and allowed a condemned criminal's followers to perpetrate a massive fraud in Jerusalem?

Another common though far-fetched scenario denying the resurrection has been called the swoon theory, which states that Jesus was merely unconscious when taken down from the cross and that He recovered in the tomb and lied to the disciples. Sound reasoning shows the flaws of this theory: The Roman soldiers were men familiar with death and were charged by their superiors to see that Jesus' sentence was carried out. They plunged a spear into Jesus' side and saw blood and water flow out, showing the separation of the blood into its parts that takes place after death. The disciples wrapped Jesus' body in a shroud with one hundred pounds of spices (John 19:39–40) and placed it in the tomb (John 19:41–42), in front of which they rolled a large rock.

Considering the lashing Jesus endured before carrying His cross; the weakness evidenced by His falling three times; and the dehydration, shock, and trauma of the crucifixion, is it reasonable to assume that He could have regained consciousness, unwrapped Himself, and rolled away the stone—all without food, water, or medical care to help Him recover His strength? Would the disciples have been inspired to forsake all to follow a man who had lied to them, required medical care and recuperation after a falsified death and resurrection, and made false promises and outlandish claims that He could not keep? After the resurrection the disciples had already gone back to their old professions (John 21:3), so how did these men gain the inspiration to wait in prayer until they were filled with the Holy Spirit, then proclaim Jesus' resurrection from the very first sermon on the day of Pentecost?

Acts 2:29–32: "Men and brethren, let me speak freely to you of the patriarch David, that he is both dead and buried, and his tomb is with us to this day. Therefore, being a prophet, and knowing that God had sworn with an oath to

him that of the fruit of his body, according to the flesh, He would raise up the Christ to sit on his throne, he, foreseeing this, spoke concerning the resurrection of the Christ, that His soul was not left in Hades, nor did His flesh see corruption. This Jesus God has raised up, of which we are all witnesses.

Add to this the more than five hundred witnesses who claimed to see Jesus alive after the cross (1 Corinthians 15:3–8) and the numerous appearances to disciples individually and in groups. We truly have "many infallible proofs" to believe in the resurrection of Jesus from the dead.

Acts 1:3: To whom He also presented Himself alive after His suffering by many infallible proofs, being seen by them during forty days and speaking of the things pertaining to the kingdom of God.

14 the 144,000 are all virgin Jewish males. This doctrine worked well when the Watchtower was small, but as its numbers grew past 144,000 in 1935, it realized the need for some way to offer salvation to new converts. Thus, the Great Multitude, or "Jonadab class" of "faithful slaves," was added.[18] Because of the teaching that the majority of Witnesses have a lower standing with God, only a small number of elderly Witnesses who believe they are part of the 144,000 are officially qualified to take communion when it is offered to them annually. In 2008 this was 9,986 out of the 17,790,631 who participated in the Memorial celebration, or only one of every eighteen hundred Witnesses![19]

It's sad to realize that despite their zeal, only a tiny percentage of Jehovah's Witnesses believe they will make it to heaven. On a side note, the number of Witnesses taking communion has been increasing slightly in recent years. The leadership of the cult is concerned about this, noting that the reason must be misunderstanding of Watchtower doctrine, since more people cannot be added to the already completed 144,000 members of the Little Flock.

Jehovah's Witnesses believe that hell is only the grave and that the lost experience no conscious, eternal punishment. Their concept of annihilation means that the unrighteous dead simply cease to exist.[20]

Restricted practices (some of which are currently permitted, since the Watchtower often updates and changes doctrines) include all of the following: blood transfusions, organ transplants, vaccinations, college education, saluting the flag, military service, and celebrating birthdays and Christmas or other holidays.[21] These practices separate them from mainstream American life. Many Jehovah's Witnesses avoid outsiders and form friendships only with other Witnesses.

Realize that the life of a Witness is difficult. Figuring the math from their own statistics shows that it takes 5,100 hours of preaching on average to gain one baptized convert. Their determination is admirable, but their message has enslaved them and will bring spiritual bondage instead of freedom to all

TRUE STORY

They just left five minutes ago. We have to give Jehovah's Witnesses credit for persistence and hard work, but I always feel so sad for the stream of the ones who come to my door. In our border city many people speak Spanish, and we almost always get Witnesses who don't speak English. It's a dual challenge as I try to communicate truth through the means of my not really fluent Spanish, but I see the Lord come through, giving me wisdom and helping me recall Spanish words.

They come two at a time, but when I go onto the front porch to speak to them, I see pairs at doors up and down my block. They are nicely dressed, carrying shoulder bags full of magazines and umbrellas to ward off the hot southwest sun, but they are lost and deceived by a false gospel. As with Mormon missionaries, Witnesses are paired up, usually with one more experienced than the other. I aim my comments at the one who seems less confident in the message, more open, or more vulnerable. Once a college-age Witness who spoke English was very open and translated my message for her partner. They were joined by two others, and it seemed so ironic that *she* was helping *me* tell them the truth about God.

My tactic is to exalt Jesus and speak of my relationship with Him, something no Witness can testify to having. I explain that we can put our trust in Jesus to save us and that no church, religion, or system can save our souls. Witnesses are often surprised to hear that we Christians have a faith as serious and foundational as theirs, with Bible study, devotions, real scriptural knowledge, and evangelism. This may be because they run into so many token Christians whose faith is merely an addition to their lives rather than life itself. Although I've never seen any of the Witnesses converted, those encounters on Saturday mornings have planted many seeds, and I trust that the Lord will speak through other genuine believers who cross paths with these evangelists of a lie.

who receive it. We must see them through God's compassion as His lost sheep. Mental illness in Witnesses is ten to seventeen times higher than in the general population.[22] One explanation for this sad fact is that people who struggle with mental illness may be attracted to and find comfort in the highly controlled, structured life of a Witness in which they can simply follow the rules and avoid having to make many decisions for themselves. In addition, confusing and contradictory revelations, guilt, and other factors contribute to paranoid schizophrenia and depression.[23]

Many Witnesses see evidence that the Watchtower isn't the true church but consider the cost of leaving it to be too high, since they would face shunning and persecution from family and friends. This puts them in a difficult situation and adds to their psychological burden. Children who are raised in strict Witness homes are often ridiculed and isolated from others because of the unusual beliefs they hold. This sets them up for mental problems in adult life. The Watchtower forbids them from involvement in organized sports and making friends who aren't Witnesses. This contributes to a sense of separation and loneliness. Both suicide and murder are more common among Witnesses than the general population.[24]

FAILED PROPHECIES

Because Jehovah's Witness began with an intense focus on the end times, it continues to emphasize eschatology (the study of the end times), with an expectation of Armageddon taking place in the near future. The date for Armageddon has been set and passed on many occasions, with the church making excuses and repeatedly setting a new date. For example, Jesus is said to have returned to earth invisibly in 1914, and the next prophetic event will be Armageddon.[25] Witnesses were told in 1938 to avoid marrying and having children because the end of the world was so near.[26] Imagine the disappointment of those who believed this false prophecy and remained single or refused to have children until it was too late in life for them to do so. Many who were affected by the false prophecies left the Watchtower, but other Witnesses made excuses or denied the failed prophecies that would show their leaders to be false prophets. Witnesses' fear of contradicting or leaving the organization keeps doubt in check.

The Watchtower organization has gone as far as to change past publications to cover up false prophecies. The standard response of a Witness when confronted with evidence of a false prophecy is that they now have more light than in prior years. This doesn't stand, however, because clearer revelations from God should not contradict older ones but should enhance them. Also, it is a contradiction to claim to be the only true prophetic organization that speaks for God to mankind and yet claim that men are fallible and make mistakes. According to the biblical test of true and false prophets, the Watchtower has no authority to speak on behalf of God.

> **Deuteronomy 18:21–22:** "And if you say in your heart, 'How shall we know the word which the LORD has not spoken?'—when a prophet speaks in the name of the LORD, if the thing does not happen or come to pass, that is the thing which the LORD has not spoken; the prophet has spoken it presumptuously; you shall not be afraid of him."

Leaders of the Watchtower falsely predicted the end of the world in 1889, 1914, 1915, 1918, 1925, 1941, 1972, 1975, and 2000. The teaching that the generation alive in 1914 would see the end has been modified many times as that generation has aged and is now nearly gone.[27] Many of these false prophecies came from Charles Russell, but later leaders have updated them as the original dates passed without the prophecies coming true. Beth Sarim is a huge home the Watchtower built in San Diego, California, for resurrected Old Testament prophets to live in. These prophets were supposed to return to earth in 1925, then in 1942.[28] Rutherford also prophesied that in 1925 churches would be destroyed and millions of apostate professing Christians would be killed.[29]

Exactly 100 percent of all prophecies from the Watchtower have failed to come to pass. Hundreds of thousands of Witnesses, many of whom had quit their jobs and sold their homes to devote themselves to preaching their gospel and preparing for the end, left the cult after the 1975 end-of-the-world prophecy didn't come true.[30] The Watchtower now admits that date setting has not worked, that those who prophesied were missing God's truth and the evidence He was using and guiding them. What does this say about the trustworthiness of the Watchtower?

KEY POINTS FOR EVANGELISM

1. Understand the motivation of Witnesses who come to your door. Fear of the Watchtower organization and a quota system of house-to-house visitation drive the Witnesses who walk through your neighborhood in pairs. Under their system of earned righteousness, Witnesses are unable to experience the peace of God. Each rejection when witnessing their false gospel only convinces them that they are suffering as martyrs for the true faith.

2. Use the Watchtower record of failed prophecies to help Witnesses see that their organization doesn't have authority or credibility. Then follow through with truth from Scripture.

3. Lead the conversation. Don't let them use the programmed approach to witnessing that they have studied. Take charge in the conversation by questioning their beliefs, using your Bible, and asking questions that will cause them to think for themselves rather than quote a memorized script.

4. Explain the true concept of heaven. Since few Witnesses expect to go to heaven, the standard evangelistic question of asking whether they know where they will go when they die doesn't work. They expect to remain as slaves on a perfected earth after Armageddon. Point out to them that Revelation 7 plainly says that both the 144,000 and the Great Multitude are found in heaven. Why has the Watchtower stolen their hope of going to heaven? Has anyone ever explained to them the gift of salvation that Jesus has provided to all people?

5. Emphasize Jesus' promise for salvation. Fear of the prospect of eternal annihilation or ceasing to exist after death is a strong motivation. Since Witnesses believe that truth is found only in the Watchtower, leaving the organization equals an end to their eternal existence. While the hope of being slaves in earthly bodies to other humans may sound unappealing to those of us with a hope in Christ of going to heaven, to Witnesses it is the best available option, and they don't want to miss their reward for being faithful slaves.

6. Use your Bible to show error in their translation. When Witnesses claim that your Bible is corrupted, point out the same passages in their version. Many times their version will convey the genuine meaning, but keep your Bible open to check for changes. Show them verses that they have taken out of context. Ask them why they are not quoting the verses in a context that explains them properly. Since Witnesses emphasize that Jesus isn't God, point out passages that use the same terms and descriptions of both Jesus and God the Father. Here are some significant ones: Psalm 68:19 with Romans 10:9; Revelation 22:13 with Revelation 1:8; Psalm 50:6 with 2 Timothy 4:1; Malachi 3:6 with Hebrews 13:8; Isaiah 45:21 with Acts 4:12; Isaiah 9:6 with Isaiah 10:21; Deuteronomy 10:17 with Revelation 17:14; Psalm 23:1 with John 10:11; Isaiah 45:23 with Philippians 2:10–11.[31]

7. Show them the true nature of Jesus. Remember that according to the Bible, those who do not have the Son do not have the Father (1 John 2:23). Show them that Jesus is part of the Godhead. Witnesses often use John 1:1, which they mistranslate to say Jesus is *a* god. They also emphasize that He is a mighty god, while Jehovah is Almighty God. Ask them how many gods they believe in. Their doctrine says there is only one, while their argument to lower the status of Jesus shows two. Witnesses are unable to adequately explain this contradiction.

8. Explain that Jesus is superior to the angels. Ask them where the Bible teaches that Jesus is the archangel Michael. There are no references to this belief even in their translation, and Scripture is clear in showing that Jesus is above all the angels (Hebrews 1:5–8). Jesus accepted worship and angels always refused it in scriptural accounts, and the Bible shows prayers to Jesus, while it never shows prayers to angels.

9. Show them the truth of Jesus' crucifixion. Ask them where the Watchtower finds the belief that Jesus wasn't crucified on a cross but instead had His hands attached with one nail above His head on a torture stake. John 20:25 lists two nails, and the New Testament is full of references to the cross. The essential point, however, is not the shape of the cross but rather the Watchtower's factual errors and lack of emphasis on the redemption Christ purchased on the cross.

10. Explain the truth of Jesus' resurrection. Ask where the Bible gives any indication that Jesus resurrected as a spirit only and not in a body. No one else in Scripture resurrected without a body, and Jesus said that the temple of His body would rise after three days, not that He would merely appear in a vision to His disciples as they teach. The Watchtower claims that Jesus' body turned into

gases or was destroyed in some unknown way.

11. Emphasize love and relationship with Jesus. A Witness can have no sense of intimacy with God, peace, or the experience of God's love. A Witness's commitment and devotion are to an organization rather than to God Himself, and the demanding organization does not meet any of the inner needs that knowing Jesus meets. Use your testimony of a personal, genuine relationship with God through His Son and the fulfillment and joy that that relationship brings you.

12. Respond to Witnesses in the opposite spirit. In place of joining their argumentative and legalistic spirit, show peace, gentleness, and patience. It is far too easy to respond to them in a spirit similar to theirs, which will cause them to believe they are being persecuted for the truth and will take them into deeper bondage.

13. Never accept literature from a Witness. If you do, he or she will assume you believe the Watchtower has credibility and will use the literature as a basis for attempting to convert you. The Witnesses' standard approach is to leave literature with a prospective convert, then return to discuss it in the hopes of bringing the person to church for further indoctrination. When you tell Witnesses that you believe their publications

TRUE STORY

He was one of the rare English-speaking Witnesses to come to my neighborhood. As always, I tried to point him to faith in Jesus by contrasting it with his faith in an untrustworthy organization. He listened as I listed the failed prophecies of the return of Christ that have come forth for many years from the Watchtower. When I waited for his reply, he simply smiled and said, "Some of the brethren have been a little too enthusiastic in years gone by." That's it. No refuting the facts, justifying their failures, or claiming they have been misunderstood.

Now I understood more clearly what we are up against in trying to reach cultists for Christ. It's not a matter of logic, having all the details at our disposal, or changing their minds. Deeper and more sinister issues keep them from seeing what is so plain to us. Deceiving spirits cause them to turn off their ability to reason and think for themselves. Considering the cost of leaving a group that may include family, friends, and employers can cause a fear response that shuts their minds to the possibility of being wrong, and they soothe their minds with their identity in a system that insists it is the only truth.

are apostate (not faithful to religion or faith), which is exactly what they believe about Christian literature, they will understand why you refuse to accept it. Your certainty about this will cause some to question whether or not they should put their trust in their own literature. Don't expect Witnesses to accept literature from a Christian perspective unless they are already very open to the gospel and have begun to move out of the authoritarian Watchtower control. Witnesses are taught to reject non-Watchtower literature as they would pornography.[32]

Conclusion

The Watchtower emphasis on avoiding friendships outside the group makes relational evangelism difficult. If you work with, go to school with, or live near a Jehovah's Witness, it will take an investment of your time and effort to gain his or her trust and open the door for evangelism. Help the person to see that there is life outside of the rigidly defined boundaries he or she is used to living within, and pray that the person will let down his or her guard and open his or her heart to the truth.

SCRIPTURE STUDY

Carefully read the beliefs in the left-hand column and ask yourself what is true, what is almost true, and what is completely wrong about them. In the right-hand column, write out Bible passages that correct or oppose each belief. Don't feel bad if you have a hard time finding biblical support to answer every belief. When you meet with your mentor or class, you'll find out what verses others have found and you can fill in what you lack.

JEHOVAH'S WITNESS BELIEFS

GOD'S WORD

Jesus' Divinity
"Jesus was a created spirit being, just as angels were spirit beings created by God. . . . The fact is that Jesus is not God and never claimed to be."[1]

Jesus is not God but an incarnation of Michael the archangel.

Jesus' Resurrection
Jesus did not rise from the dead bodily.

Jesus as the Christ
Jesus became the Christ at His baptism.

"Jesus Christ, who is God's executioner today, cannot be tricked."[2]

Jesus' Return
Jesus returned to earth invisibly in 1914.

The Holy Spirit
The Holy Spirit "is not a person but is a powerful force that God causes to emanate from himself."[3]

The Trinity
"Satan is the originator of the Trinity doctrine."[4]

Salvation
"To get one's name written in the Book of Life will depend upon one's works."[5]

"Come to Jehovah's organization for salvation."[6]

Heaven and Hell
Only 144,000 will go to heaven.

The 144,000 will be mediators between God and man.

There are two categories of the saved—those who go to heaven and those who will live forever on earth.

There is no existence of the consciousness or soul after death.

There is no hell; the wicked dead cease to exist (the doctrine of annihilationism).

PRAYER TIME

List the major prayer needs of people caught in the deceptions of the Watchtower and pray for them.

-
-
-

SCRIPTURE MEMORY

2 Corinthians 11:14
And no wonder! For Satan himself transforms himself into an angel of light.

Matthew 24:4–5
And Jesus answered and said to them: "Take heed that no one deceives you. For many will come in My name, saying, 'I am the Christ,' and will deceive many.

DAILY BIBLE READING

✓ Check when completed		
Sunday	Psalms 55–59	_____
Monday	Psalms 60–66	_____
Tuesday	Psalms 67–72	_____
Wednesday	Psalms 73–75	_____
Thursday	Psalms 76–77	_____
Friday	Psalms 78–83	_____
Saturday	Psalms 84–89	_____

BIBLE READING QUESTIONS/THOUGHTS

_____
_____
_____
_____
_____
_____
_____
_____
_____
_____

PRAYER NEEDS THIS WEEK

_____
_____
_____
_____
_____
_____
_____

11

Lesson eleven

THE NEW AGE MOVEMENT

The New Age movement is different from other world religions and cults in several ways. It has no single founder, no scriptures or required beliefs, and no formal places of worship.[1] Instead, it is a loosely structured approach to faith in which participants can choose from a variety of doctrines and practices in a way similar to eating at a cafeteria or a buffet. One can take two helpings of this and none of that, making each person's meal unique while still eating at the same restaurant. Interest in the New Age comes from a spiritually bankrupt Western world forsaking its biblical foundation and looking for answers in ancient civilizations, mystical philosophies, and pagan religions. The New Age movement is primarily found in the West (Europe and the Americas), but some of its foundations come from the East (Asia).

Isaiah 2:6: For You have forsaken Your people, the house of Jacob, because they are filled with eastern ways; they are soothsayers like the Philistines.

Some of the founding voices and popular proponents of the New Age movement in the West over the past two centuries were Madame Helena Blavatsky, Alice Bailey, George Gurdjieff, H. G. Wells, Phineas Quimby, Mary Baker Eddy, Charles and Myrtle Fillmore, Henry David Thoreau, Ralph Waldo Emerson, Abner Doubleday, Thomas Edison, and Carl Jung.

THE NEW AGE TODAY: THE AGE OF AQUARIUS

Based on astrology, the New Age movement teaches that mankind left the Age of Pisces in the year 2000 and is coming into an age of universal peace, happiness, and perfection, brought about by realizing our divinity and by man's efforts apart from God.[2] The Age of Aquarius will end war, famine, and ignorance and restore the environment. Pisces is the fish

New Age in Western Culture

Western culture is becoming more oriented toward New Age thought than toward a biblical worldview, as shown by the following results of recent polls in the US:[1]

- 55% believe in psychic or spiritual healing or the power of the human mind to heal the body.
- 41% believe in ESP (extrasensory perception).
- 32% believe in ghosts, or that spirits of dead people can come back in certain places or situations.
- 31% believe in telepathy/communication between minds without using traditional senses.
- 26% believe in clairvoyance, or the power of the mind to know the past and predict the future.
- 24% believe that extraterrestrial beings have visited earth at some time in the past.
- 21% believe that people can communicate mentally with someone who has died.
- 9% believe in channeling, or allowing a "spirit-being" to temporarily assume control of the body.
- 25% believe in reincarnation.
- 29% believe astrology is scientific.
- 66% do not believe that moral truth is absolute.
- 73% are not convinced that Satan is a real force.
- 72% believe that it is possible for someone to earn their way into heaven through good behavior.

American teenagers show significant belief in and practice of occultism and New Age teachings:[2]

- 73% have engaged in at least one type of psychic or witchcraft-related activity.
- 10% have participated in a séance.
- 8% have tried to cast a spell or mix a magic potion.
- 30% have had their palm read.
- 80% have read their horoscope.
- Over 30% have encountered an angel, demon, or some other supernatural being.
- 10% say they have communicated with a dead person.
- Nearly 10% claim they have psychic powers.

in the Zodiac and symbolizes the Christian era, which New Agers believe is ending.[3] New Agers see a transition taking place from belief in a male deity above (God the Father) to a female deity beneath (Mother Earth or Gaia, the earth goddess). To the New Ager this means an end to belief in a God with authority and law, and a coming era of freedom and independence from religion. Radical environmentalism results in worship of Gaia. This concept is especially popular with radical feminists and lesbians. The planet itself is seen as a living being, and mankind's offenses against the environment are the reasons for natural disasters as the Earth Mother takes revenge on the human race. Planetary cleansing is a coming judgment from Gaia, when she will destroy much of mankind. "Even if we stopped immediately all further seizing of Gaia's land and water for food and fuel production, and stopped poisoning the air, it would take the Earth more than a thousand years to recover from the damage we have already done. . . . Like an old lady who has to share her house with a growing and destructive group of teenagers, Gaia grows angry, and if they do not mend their ways, she will evict them."[4] A common New Age belief is an ideal population for the earth that is significantly smaller than the current population, so that fewer people pollute and offend Gaia.

An avatar (incarnation of a god) comes to earth to help mankind make the transition into each new Zodiac era. The next avatar will fulfill

TRUE STORY

Have you ever boarded a plane and wondered who would be sitting next to you? Once I was seated on a plane headed for Chicago and looked up the aisle as passengers compared their boarding passes to the seat numbers. A middle-aged woman approached. As I saw her, I immediately felt a strange reaction in my spirit. I thought maybe she was a Christian, but as she came closer, I became certain that what I felt was not the presence of the Lord in her life but a counterfeit, and that she would come to sit next to me. Sure enough, the seat was hers. After a little small talk to let her know I was friendly, I pulled out my Bible and began reading it. When I finished and put it away, she wanted to talk. She told me about my color aura, her experiences while living in the desert with a "holy man," and other bizarre beliefs. A former schoolteacher, she was an intelligent person but so very lost. She reacted against my description of God as Father and told me she was exploring goddess worship. I recognized the symptoms of a person who was very wounded by the men in her life and tried to share the hope I have in Jesus, but the door of her heart was closed tightly.

all the roles expected in major world religions: the return of Christ to Christians, the Messiah to the Jews, the Imam Mahdi to Muslims, Krishna to Hindus, and the fifth Buddha to Buddhists. Benjamin Creme, a leading New Age spokesman, says that this man was born in 1962, lives in London, and will be known as Lord Maitreya. This figure has made public appearances in various parts of the world since 1988.[5]

Since the New Age is a category of beliefs rather than an organization, its followers often use catchphrases, such as "I'm a very spiritual person," to identify themselves rather than say they are in the New Age Movement. Other catchphrases and buzzwords include "global village," "reaching your potential," "unlocking the power within to achieve health, love, and harmony," and "balancing energies." The goals of a one-world government, one currency, one religion, and one judicial and banking system are common. Frequently used symbols include pyramids, the all-seeing eye, the peace sign, the yin and yang symbol, and Hindu and Buddhist imagery such as mandalas (geometric designs used in meditation) and deities.

CORE VALUES OF THE NEW AGE MOVEMENT

The New Age movement will look to any source of spiritual input for truth with one exception: biblical Christianity. Any past religion, mystical aspects of current world religions, obscure philosophy, pagan practice, or bizarre belief system, including ancient and aberrant Christian mysticism, is considered valid, but the simple message of repentance and faith in Jesus as the sacrificial Lamb is viewed with a condescending smile. In this way, it shows rebellion against the message of the gospel and the pride of self-sufficiency. All religious roads lead to the same goal in their highly valued mindset of religious tolerance, as opposed to the perceived exclusiveness and narrow-mindedness of Christianity. However, New Age tolerance does not extend to biblical Christianity. Current leading New Age writer Eckhart Tolle quotes the Bible frequently but applies New Age thought to reinterpret every passage to suit his ends.[6]

The New Age teaches a type of evolution, with mankind progressing toward realizing its own divinity and developing a perfected world, similar to the future Kingdom of God but without the King. Maharishi Mahesh Yogi, founder of Transcendental Meditation, said, "I will fill the world with love and create Heaven on earth."[7] By misapplying Jesus' statement that the kingdom of God is within you (Luke 17:21), New Agers look in the wrong direction.

As the human race evolves toward godhood, spirit guides allegedly accompany New Agers on the journey. These are beings who help mankind, giving wisdom and comfort, and can include dead relatives and warriors from Atlantis.[8] Some of these spirit guides are ascended masters: those who have reached a state of cosmic consciousness, including Jesus, Krishna, Buddha, and certain saints known as mystics. They speak through channeling and automatic writing, processes that allow a spirit to communicate through an individual who becomes a medium for wisdom from the spiritual dimension. Note the current popularity in the United States of TV programs dealing with ghosts, communication with the dead, and other occult themes.

The New Age movement teaches pantheism. Similar to the Force in *Star Wars,* this belief states that God does not exist as a Person but that divinity resides in creation through an impersonal cosmic energy. Learning to tap into this energy or consciousness is the primary goal of the New Age.[9] The New Age movement teaches the Hindu concept of monism—if all is one essence, then we are all gods. A consequence of this belief is the concept that Jesus and Satan are ultimately of the same fundamental nature. Man is basically good and must learn to look within for answers instead of to an external God. Believing that God is found in everyone and everything means that there is no Person who can make laws, have a claim on His creation, be offended, or bring judgment or reward. Thus there are no universal laws, no sin, no guilt, no need for a Savior.

Significant New Age teachers, authors, thinkers, and spokespeople include Andrew Weil, David Spangler, Marianne Williamson, Deepak Chopra, Shirley MacLaine, Carlos Castaneda, Benjamin Creme, Barbara Marx Hubbard, Fritjof Capra, Bernie Siegel, Anthony Robbins, M. Scott Peck, Matthew Fox, Joseph Campbell, Al Gore, J. Z. Knight, Jane Roberts, Arthur Clarke, José Silva, Werner Erhard, Helen Shucman, Napoleon Hill, Neal Donald Walsch, Doreen Virtue, Sylvia Browne, Rhonda Byrne, Oprah Winfrey, and Eckhart Tolle.

New Age books include those with a clear agenda of altering the perspective of the reader toward a non-biblical view of the spiritual dimension and those with a more subtle message that shows the author is personally influenced by New Age views. Current popular titles include *The Celestine Prophecy; Embraced by the Light; The Power of Myth; The Reappearance of the Christ and the Masters of Wisdom; Chicken Soup for the Soul; Jonathan Livingston Seagull; A Course in Miracles; The Road Less Traveled; The Aquarian Conspiracy; The Urantia Book; The Coming of the Cosmic Christ; Ageless Body, Timeless Mind; The Way of the Wizard; Out on a Limb; Tales of Power; Dancing in the Light; The Aquarian Gospel of Jesus the Christ; A New Earth; The Power of Now;* and *The Secret.*

BELIEFS AND PRACTICES

The New Age teaches that all spiritual expressions are correct, since there is no external standard by which to judge them. Because reality is different for each person, the emphasis is on subjective experience. There are no moral absolutes, standards, or universal truths. When asked how to make the right choice, Deepak Chopra said, "It is the one that brings joy and fulfillment to me. . . . I ask my heart, not my brain."[10]

Some New Age beliefs assign new meanings to biblical concepts. For example, angels play a prominent role in Scripture, but angels in the New Age are entirely different. God's Word teaches that angels are God's messengers and

TRUE STORY

It was a street festival for the Fourth of July, with mariachi bands, food, and fireworks, but the fortune teller's booth caught my attention. I watched the woman in gypsy attire reading palms until the chair before her was empty, then went in and sat down. "Give me your hand," she said in a voice modeled after the Count from Sesame Street.

"I'm not here to have my palm read," I replied.

"Then why are you here?"

"Because you may not know this, but you are not using a gift from God. Fortune telling is of the devil, and—"

Before I could get any further, she shrieked and leapt from her chair. With a contorted face and shaking with intense emotion, she pointed all ten fingers at me in a gesture I've never seen before or since. She screamed curses at me in the devil's name while I sat in amazement (but not in fear—1 John 4:4). I guess she did know who she was serving! A crowd began to gather, and I realized that the police from the festival would be there soon. Since they would likely think that I had caused the disturbance, it seemed like a good time to leave. Deeply shaken, she watched as I walked away unshaken.

that they worship God in heaven, protect us, and bring God's judgments. True angels refuse worship and encourage people to glorify God. Scripture warns us about angels of light, which masquerade as being good when they are, in fact, fallen angels. In the New Age movement, people are encouraged to get in touch with their angels, talk with them, pray to them, and receive direction for their lives.

The New Age buffet of sources for spiritual truth is huge. Here are some of the choices on the menu:

- *Astrology.* Nearly every American newspaper has a horoscope column, which tells eager readers that the placement of the stars determines their destiny and gives daily guidance.

- *Egyptian religion/pyramid power.* Note the scarab beetle, jackal-headed Anubis, winged Isis, the ankh (a cross with a loop at the top symbolizing reincarnation), and fascination with the tomb of King Tutankhamen. "From time immemorial, Egypt has been known as the home of sorcery. This is why the Talmud states in *Kiddushim 49b*, 'Ten measures of sorcery came into the world, Egypt took nine of them for herself and the rest of the world took one.'"[11]

- *Native American religion.* The Great Spirit is not another name for the true God. Note the popularity of the Kokopelli flute player, who is the traditional link between our world and the next; dreamcatcher weavings; kachina dolls; medicine wheels; and power animals in Southwestern art and décor. Mayan and Aztec religions are also seen as sources of truth.

THEOLOGY 101: The Deity of Jesus

A major point of disagreement between Christians and people of other religions is exactly who Jesus is. Most people of other religions do not deny that Jesus existed but assign to Him a role very different than the only begotten Son of God, Savior, and Lord. They call Him by lesser names or descriptions, such as a great moral teacher, prophet, good example, a god among many gods, ascended master, or one who got in touch with His own deity (as New Agers allege we all can do). They erase the distinct difference in nature that the Bible ascribes to Jesus: God Himself, eternally coexistent with the Father and the Holy Spirit; Creator and Sustainer of the world; Redeemer of mankind; Judge of the earth; returning King of kings; Messiah; and Lord.

If Jesus was not God as He claimed, the idea that He was a great moral teacher is worthless: great moral teachers don't lie about their nature and claim divinity. We can't waver on the foundational belief that Jesus is God, or all else He said and did would be worthless. His atoning death would be invalidated if He were a mere man with His own personal guilt, which would prevent Him from being the spotless, sacrificial Lamb of God. All His promises would be groundless, and we would have no reason to consider His words as distinct from any other philosopher or thinker. There is no middle ground on this point. Either He is or is not God.

Many Bible passages show Jesus as having characteristics that can apply only to God, and the biblical authors use titles for Him that refer to God. Following are some such passages that reveal the full deity of Jesus:

Isaiah 9:6: For unto us a Child is born, unto us a Son is given; and the government will be upon His shoulder. And His name will be called Wonderful, Counselor, Mighty God, Everlasting Father, Prince of Peace.

John 1:1: In the beginning was the Word, and the Word was with God, and the Word was God.

1 Timothy 3:16: And without controversy great is the mystery of godliness: God was manifested in the flesh, justified in the Spirit, seen by angels, preached among the Gentiles, believed on in the world, received up in glory.

Titus 2:12–13: We should live soberly, righteously, and godly in the present age, looking for the blessed hope and glorious appearing of our great God and Savior Jesus Christ.

Hebrews 1:8: But to the Son He says: "Your throne, O God, is forever and ever; a scepter of righteousness is the scepter of Your Kingdom.

1 John 5:20: And we know that the Son of God has come and has given us an understanding, that we may know Him who is true; and we are in Him who is true, in His Son Jesus Christ. This is the true God and eternal life.

Some people claim that Jesus did not think he was God, but numerous Bible passages disprove this idea, including passages in which Jesus readily accepts worship, which in the Jewish culture was due to God alone.

- *Shamanism* or *witchcraft*—various forms in which a person harnesses the powers of the spiritual dimension to affect life on earth.
- *Reincarnation* and past-life regression through *hypnosis.*
- *Auras* show one's inner spiritual nature through specialized photography or through occult powers.
- *Taoism* uses the terms *yin* and *yang* to explain the counterparts and opposites in nature, such as light and dark or male and female. Balancing the yin and yang is a fundamental goal in alternative medicine.
- *Yoga* as a means of spiritual enlightenment. In Hindu-based New Age theology, the serpent god's power, called kundalini, lives at the base of the spine and moves upward through yoga and meditation to power centers called chakras, eventually reaching the highest level located in the forehead, where the mystical third eye is located. Yoga means to yoke, referring to unity with Hindu gods, and is a spiritual practice incompatible with Christianity, despite the fact that many churches have unwisely begun yoga classes for exercise. Hindu leaders are offended that Christians would adopt yoga for use in Christian settings, stating that "Hinduism is at yoga's core."[12] Even Muslim leaders have forbidden their followers to practice yoga, stating that it is a Hindu religious practice.[13]
- *Crystals, charms, amulets, tokens,* or *fetishes.* Different colored crystals are said to bring courage, comfort, balance, self-esteem, and energy.
- *Neo-paganism* and *goddess worship* revive beliefs in the Norse and Celtic deities.
- *Portal or spiritual vortex* locations. There are special places where openings between worlds or dimensions exists. Major New Age centers in the US are found in New Mexico, Arizona, California, and Colorado.
- *Lost civilization legends.* Atlantis is the primary focus.
- *Astral projection, out-of-body experiences, levitation.*
- *Study of UFOs, extraterrestrial beings, and bizarre phenomena.*
- *Feng shui.* An application of eastern religious principles to architecture and interior decorating.
- *Meditation* on anything other than God and His Word. The meditative state is also encouraged through New Age music, which is designed for relaxation so that the listener can move into a higher state of consciousness.

NEW AGE BELIEFS ABOUT THE NATURE OF GOD AND MAN

The New Age movement uses the name *Jesus* and the word *Christ* but define both differently than Christians do.

Christ is defined as the divine nature that exists in all people. New Agers usually refer to "the Christ" or "the Christ spirit" rather than Christ (which means literally the Messiah or the Anointed One) or Jesus Christ. Rather than always being Christ, in New Age theology Jesus was an ordinary man who became the Christ, as did other avatars, and all people can do the same. This is a repeat of the Gnostic heresy from the first century. Occult books such as the Gospel of Thomas and the Aquarian Gospel tell of Jesus' early years and claim that Jesus studied mysticism in Egypt and India before beginning His public ministry. These books claim that by recognizing His divine nature, Jesus was able to live a perfect life. The New Age movement teaches that mankind's greatest problem is not realizing its individual divine nature.

The Human Potential Movement utilizes the New Age belief that we are all gods and stresses unlimited potential for achievement through development of the inner person. Major US corporations, including AT&T, General Foods, and Blue Cross, spend vast sums of money bringing New Age trainers to their employees.[14]

THE NEW AGE MOVEMENT AND OCCULTISM

Other New Age practices draw from aspects of occultism that have been followed throughout history. These include séances; hexes; spells and magic (common in some fantasy role-playing games, many of which draw their material from genuine witchcraft); occult books; and the mystical side of martial arts dealing with meditation and chi rather than physical conditioning, strength, and training. Divination is the use of supernatural power to foretell the future or find hidden knowledge through runes, tarot cards, crystal balls, astrology, biorhythms, handwriting analysis, numerology, palm reading, dowsing, Ouija boards, ESP, and I Ching.

The New Age movement differs from traditional hard-core occultism, such as Satan worship and magick (spelled this way to distinguish true occult power from sleight of hand, which means trickery involving distraction and skilled movement to simulate supernatural phenomena). The latter is consciously aware of its pursuit of evil and that it is siding against the God of the Bible, while the New Age movement, often rejecting belief in an evil entity such as the devil, ignores the Bible as archaic and irrelevant and puts its faith ultimately in man to make spiritual progress without his Creator.

NEW AGE IN THE CHURCH

New Age teaching is the basis for the Unity School of Christianity and its popular publication, *Daily Word*.[15] Unitarian or universalist churches have the appearance of Christianity but are completely unbiblical in doctrine and practice.

Liberal factions in some Protestant denominations (e.g., United Methodist, Lutheran [ELCA], and Presbyterians [PCUSA])[16] have opened the door to the New Age through radical feminist/lesbian organizations promoting goddess worship, materials allegedly channeled from Jesus (such as *A Course in Miracles* by Helen Schucman), and other New Age practices. However, many conservatives and genuine believers in these denominations have protested the false doctrines. Churches and individuals of any denomination may be involved in New Age practices.

Positive confession, visualization, and the "little gods" teachings in the Word of Faith movement echo New Age thought. As subjective experience is exalted over the objective truth of God's Word and Christians accept incidents and doctrines that have no basis in Scripture, the danger of deception increases. Ignorance of the Bible is the primary means by which deception can enter the church.

NEW AGE IN EDUCATION

Guided imagery, spirit guides, meditation, hypnosis, and progressive relaxation exercises have been incorporated into public schools since the 1970s. Values clarification exercises used in 85 percent of US schools teach kids to decide what they believe is right, echoing the New Age teaching that there are no absolutes or universally true moral values. An example of this is an exercise where students select which people will stay in an overcrowded bomb shelter during a nuclear war or be allowed to enter a lifeboat.

The object is to weigh the merits of one person over another, but the result is that the student learns to play God, believing that his or her personal opinion is the final word, even in life and death decisions.

NEW AGE IN MEDICINE

A key New Age medicinal term is *mind/body.* There is truth in the concept of holistic medicine. God has made us a three-part being: spirit, soul, and body (1 Thessalonians 5:23). What affects one part does affect the others, as seen in the Scriptures cited below. The danger is trying to change the body by methods that affect the mind or spirit through means outside the boundaries God has set for mankind: contact with other spirits, learning unscriptural philosophies, and relying on the mind to heal the body. Some of the pseudomedical practices are spiritually dangerous, and many people are innocently involved in them, unaware of the deeper philosophical basis of these practices.

Proverbs 18:14: The spirit of a man will sustain him in sickness, but who can bear a broken spirit?

Proverbs 17:22: A merry heart does good, like medicine, but a broken spirit dries the bones.

Common New Age practices and treatments include aromatherapy; acupuncture; acupressure; homeopathy; therapeutic touch; energy balancing; applied kinesiology; "medical" use of crystals; color therapy; polarity therapy; ayurveda; iridology; reflexology; biofeedback; hypnosis; certain types of massage (shiatsu, reiki, and rolfing, designed to balance energy and encourage chi flow); bioenergetics; guided imagery; macrobiotic diet; and diagnosis through pendulums, auras, and psychic powers.

Several significant qualifications distinguish New Age medical treatments from standard healthcare practices. Be aware of the following:

TRUE STORY

A youth group girl told me the following story.

A certain girl was known throughout her high school as a witch, with a carefully planned approach to intimidate others through a bizarre appearance. One day she had an argument with another student. The witch began to curse the other student and cast spells on her, then stormed out of the room. The shocked class looked to the victim of this verbal onslaught for her reaction, but the girl said, "I wasn't scared, because I'm wearing my crystals!"

Talk about putting your faith in the wrong object! Those crystals were no defense at all to a real spiritual attack. Many otherwise sophisticated Western people trust in charms, medallions, and icons in the same way that their counterparts in primitive jungles around the world believe in the fetishes given to them by their witch doctors.

- A treatment that will affect the energy flow in the body. Watch for key words like *prana, life force, chi,* and *cosmic* or *universal energy.*
- Any treatment requiring faith. This could be either psychological manipulation or occultic, but it is not purely natural (functioning according to the laws God has set into motion in creation, as genuine medicine does).

- Use of natural substances not recognized by the medical community. These could be valid treatments, or they could be harmful. Undiscovered therapies or herbal cures from primitive cultures may work, but if they do, it will be according to the laws of science that God set in place rather than by unexplainable mystical factors.
- Altered states of consciousness. Beware of non-Christian meditation, visualization (which uses mind power to control reality), and hypnosis.
- Therapeutic touch or laying on of hands without prayer in Jesus' name.

New Age medicine is full of quackery. One must ask the following questions about medical treatments: Is there a logical explanation? Is it a cure-all? (Anything that is supposed to cure everything probably cures nothing.) Is it an amazing discovery? (Wait and see the results. Sometimes desperate patients waste valuable time and money on fraudulent treatments, delaying genuine medical care until it is too late.)

KEY POINTS FOR EVANGELISM

1. Recognize that the make-it-up-as-you-go nature of the New Age movement means that not every New Ager will believe in all of these ideas, and some New Agers may even think some of these beliefs are ridiculous. Instead of assuming that a person believes in a particular New Age teaching, ask questions to find the specific beliefs he or she has and approach the person from that point.

2. Realize that New Agers are seeking truth and, although misled and deceived, may be sincere in their hunger for God. Never make fun of a person's beliefs, no matter how far out they may be, or you'll cause an offense that can close the door to future evangelism. Acknowledge things the person has gotten right. Avoid any trace of smugness in saying that you've found the truth and are no longer searching.

3. Find common ground by affirming that the person is seeking truth, and say that you are too. Say that we should all be interested in spiritual things and that too many people are caught up in materialism and don't think about the deeper issues of life.

4. Use your own testimony to show how your spiritual journey has brought you to faith in Jesus Christ and the Bible. Explain the peace and security that come from a relationship with your Creator. Talk about being freed from the power of sin and having a clear conscience in knowing that your sins are forgiven by Jesus' sacrifice.

5. Recognize the power of the argument that truth is relative, which New Agers can use as a shield to deflect your witness. New Agers echo the postmodern belief that there are no absolutes, although their absolute certainty of this is itself a contradiction. You can turn the tables by showing your absolute certainty that the universe runs on principles that are consistent, observable, dependable and reflect the nature of a Creator who has the right to call His creation to obedient faith. Point out the consistency of sunrise, sunset, tides, and gravity as examples of the unchanging nature of God. New Agers agree with the principle of moral relativism as long as it doesn't affect their own lives but do not agree with it when personal harm or loss could occur. Thus, they actually agree in their underlying belief with a universal code of ethics and morality that overrides each individual's reality. For example, in theory, child abuse, rape, and murder would all be permitted, since there is no right or wrong, but individual New Agers would say these things are wrong if they were to affect them personally.

6. Pray and fast. You are in a spiritual battle with demonic forces who blind and deceive New Agers.

7. Recognize that all false religions are full of contradictions and illogical views. Point some of these out, but realize that the New Ager, because of his or her unscriptural view of reality, may see such contradictions and views as both being true. Using reincarnation as an example, show that in addition to violating both the Bible and logic (as shown in the chapters on Hinduism and Buddhism), reincarnation violates our sense of justice. How can we learn the lessons needed to change if we can't remember our wrongs from our past lives? Won't we just repeat our errors? Doesn't history show that this is true of mankind? How can people who are supposedly suffering from their own errors through karma believe that this system is fair without knowing what they did wrong the last time around?

8. Show the desperation, misery, and suffering in nations with the religious beliefs that have been incorporated into the New Age and contrast them with the many beneficial aspects of life found in the West as a result of the Judeo-Christian basis in our culture: education, women's rights and roles, health care, lifespan, low infant mortality, high standards of living, social programs to benefit the weak, class-free society, freedom in government, respect for human life, stability, and safety. Would a New Ager really want to trade lives with the average farmer or beggar in India or Thailand?

CONCLUSION

Your New Age friend is on a quest for truth. Multitudes of spiritual pathways seem to offer enlightenment, but fulfillment is always just out of reach. Summing up New Age beliefs, the same lies that the serpent told Eve in the Garden of Eden (Genesis 3:4–5) still work for New Agers today: "You will not surely die" is reflected in the teaching of reincarnation, and "You will be like God" shows up in spiritual evolution, ascended masters, and spirit guides. Pray for God's mercy to help your friend realize that the New Age movement, while offering promises to its followers, has never kept any of them.

Scripture Study

Carefully read the beliefs in the left-hand column and ask yourself what is true, what is almost true, and what is completely wrong about them. In the right-hand column, write out Bible passages that correct or oppose each belief. Don't feel bad if you have a hard time finding biblical support to answer every belief. When you meet with your mentor or class, you'll find out what verses others have found and you can fill in what you lack.

New Age Beliefs

The Nature of Truth
"There is no room for absolute truth upon any subject whatsoever.... But there are relative truths, and we have to make the best we can of them."[1]

The Nature of God
"Key to the New Spirituality is a belief that God is not separate from anyone or anything—and neither are we."[2]

God is a force, not a Person: "Instead of constantly thinking, we become still and quiet, and we become conscious of being conscious. This is the realization of I AM, the realization of Being, our essence identity."[3]

Jesus
Jesus became the Christ.

Maitreya is the return of Christ.

Angels, Spirits, and the Dead
New Age angels and spirit guides receive prayer and give direction to their followers.

God's Word

_____
_____
_____
_____
_____
_____
_____
_____
_____
_____
_____
_____
_____
_____
_____
_____
_____
_____
_____
_____
_____
_____
_____
_____
_____
_____
_____
_____
_____
_____
_____
_____
_____

Humans can gain wisdom and knowledge of the future through supernatural means, including communicating with the dead.

"There is no need for help to enter Heaven for you have never left. . . . Helpers are given you in many forms. . . . Their names are legion."[4]

Humanity and Perfection
"If sin is real, both God and you are not."[5]

"God wants us to become Himself (or Herself or Itself). We are growing toward godhood. God is the goal of evolution."[6]

"You are God in a physical body. . . . You are a cosmic being. You are all power. . . . You are all intelligence. . . . You are perfection. You are magnificence. You are the creator and you are creating the creation of You on this planet."[7]

"Evolve or die: that is our only choice now. . . . The arising of space consciousness—a shift to vertical rather than horizontal awareness—is the next stage in the evolution of humanity, and it's happening more and more as our awareness remains in the now moment."[8]

The Earth and the Current Age
"The Age of Aquarius (c. 2000) starts at the dawn of Satya Yuga [the age of truth]. The beginning of this age was estimated by various calculations around the year 2000. Some astrologers believe that mankind will step out of the mystical age of Pisces right into the luminous age of Aquarius between 2000 and 2050, which means the end of superstitions and of dogmatic religions."[9]

"Even if we stopped immediately all further seizing of Gaia's land and water for food and fuel production, and stopped poisoning the air, it would take the Earth more than a thousand years to recover from the damage we have already done. . . . Like an old lady who has to share her house with a growing and destructive group of teenagers, Gaia grows angry, and if they do not mend their ways, she will evict them."[10]

_____

_____

_____

_____

_____

_____

_____

_____

_____

_____

PRAYER TIME

List the major prayer needs of people caught in the deceptions of the New Age movment and pray for them.

-

-

-

SCRIPTURE MEMORY

2 Timothy 4:2–5
Preach the word! Be ready in season and out of season. Convince, rebuke, exhort, with all longsuffering and teaching. For the time will come when they will not endure sound doctrine, but according to their own desires, because they have itching ears, they will heap up for themselves teachers; and they will turn their ears away from the truth, and be turned aside to fables. But you be watchful in all things, endure afflictions, do the work of an evangelist, fulfill your ministry.

FILL OUT EVALUATION 2 ON PAGE 159.

FILL OUT THE COURSE EVALUATION ON PAGE 160.

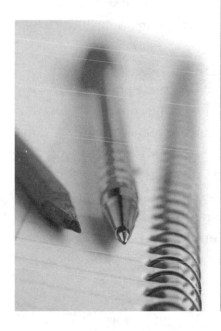

DAILY BIBLE READING

✓ Check when completed		
Sunday	Psalms 90–97	_____
Monday	Psalms 98–103	_____
Tuesday	Psalms 104–106	_____
Wednesday	Psalms 107–108	_____
Thursday	Psalms 109–110	_____
Friday	Psalms 111–118	_____
Saturday	Psalm 119	_____

BIBLE READING QUESTIONS/THOUGHTS

_____
_____
_____
_____
_____
_____
_____
_____
_____
_____

PRAYER NEEDS THIS WEEK

_____
_____
_____
_____
_____
_____
_____
_____

12

Lesson twelve

WITNESSING SCENARIOS FOR ROLE-PLAYING

Use this class session to see how much you have learned. If you are taking the course alone, use the following scenarios to role-play with your mentor. If you are part of a class, divide into groups to act out the scenarios, with one person as the person in the scenario and one person speaking as a Christian. Then have the rest of the group evaluate how effective you were in sharing the gospel, whether your attitude reflected the Lord, and what you could do to improve your witness. Be sure that when you are playing the part of those in false religions you do not blaspheme or misuse the name of the Lord. For example, you can say things like "Did you know that the New Age movement believes that Jesus discovered His divinity just as we can?" rather than saying that you believe you are a god or that you don't believe Jesus is God.

Scenario 1: You've noticed the signs in your coworker's life—the bumper sticker that says "Visualize World Peace," the crystals, the reference in conversations to astrology, contacting angels, and New Age authors. Finally you invite her to join you for lunch to discuss spirituality. Where will you begin?

Scenario 2: The new family on your street keeps to themselves, but they have a son your age. It's been a slow process getting to know him. The neighbors are whispering that they are Jehovah's Witnesses and hope that they won't intrude on people with their religious fanaticism. One day the son confides in you that he's not nearly as convinced of the teachings of his church as his parents are and asks what you believe.

Scenario 3: You're on the plane heading for a mission outreach in Bolivia. It's going to be a long flight. Seated next to you are two smiling young men on their way to a mission outreach that is very different from yours. They are talking excitedly about their plans for the next two years. One of them turns to you and introduces himself as Elder Johnson. You have an opportunity to reach two young Mormons before they deceive anyone else.

These scenarios provide the setting for your witnessing opportunity. Take these practices seriously and prepare for them as though they were real-life situations. Plan ahead for the conversation so that you can keep it aimed at the most significant points. While it is good to answer honest questions, don't let the other person direct the conversation. Otherwise, he or she may keep the conversation focused on points of lesser importance, attempt to convert you to his or her beliefs, or bring up points for which you are not prepared to give an answer. You can overcome these obstacles by firmly and repeatedly going back to the main focus: to exalt the Lord Jesus Christ and point the person to Him. Promise to answer difficult questions at a later time, and if you ever see that you are outnumbered and need backup in an actual evangelistic setting, reschedule the meeting and invite your mentor or a knowledgeable Christian leader to join you.

Answer the following questions to help you plan your approach to each scenario.

1. What points do you expect the other person to bring up?

Scenario 1:

_____

_____

_____

_____

Scenario 2:

_____

_____

_____

_____

Scenario 3:

_____

_____

_____

_____

2. What are the main points you will bring up?

Scenario 1:

_____

_____

_____

_____

Scenario 2:

_____

_____

_____

_____

Scenario 3:

_____

_____

_____

_____

3. What parts of your own testimony and personal walk with the Lord would relate to the person's life and beliefs?

Scenario 1:

_____

_____

_____

_____

Scenario 2:

_____

_____

_____

_____

Scenario 3:

_____

_____

_____

_____

EVALUATION 2: *What Did You Learn?*

Discuss your answers to the following questions with your mentor or class.

1. Which belief system was the most interesting to you? Why?
2. Have you heard God's call to reach out to people from a certain cult or religion?
3. Do you have friends, relatives, coworkers, or fellow students who are part of these belief systems? If so, will you approach them with the gospel? When?

Now update the questions you answered during week 1 of the course.

1. Have you ever seen someone come to the Lord through your witness?

2. Do you feel more equipped to speak about your faith?

3. What would you say in witnessing to the following people?

   • A Muslim:

   • A Hindu:

   • A Buddhist:

   • A Mormon:

   • A Jehovah's Witness:

   • A New Ager:

   • Someone from other cults and religions:

4. Have you had an opportunity to witness to any of the above? How did it go?

5. Have you put forth the time, energy, and work necessary to prepare yourself to reach a lost world?

6. What else do you need to be equipped to deal with false doctrine and opposing beliefs?

COURSE EVALUATION: *Reaching a Lost World*

Name _____ Age _____

Date _____

Please answer completely and honestly.

1. What has IDC done for your walk with the Lord?

2. What was the most beneficial part of the course?

3. What was the least beneficial part of the course?

4. What would you change about the course?

5. Were you disappointed in any aspect of the course? Explain.

6. Please comment about the following aspects of the course. How important and valuable were they to you?

   • The amount of reading and homework:

   • The teachings:

7. Please provide us with a quote we can use to advertise the course the next time it is offered.

Thanks for your help!
Please photocopy and mail to
Vinnie Carafano, 936 W Sunset Rd., El Paso, TX 79922

RESOURCES *Resources* ⇨

YOU'VE FINISHED twelve weeks of challenge. Here are some resources to help you continue growing and learning. Don't stop challenging yourself!

ALTERNATE DAILY BIBLE READING PLAN

If this is your first book in the Intensive Discipleship Course series, we recommend that you begin reading three to four chapters of the New Testament daily. After you have completed the New Testament, start the Old Testament. If you read the Bible for about fifteen minutes each day, you can finish it in one year. Just keep at it. If you miss a day or get behind, try to catch up but don't quit. Check off each day after you read the chapters, and start the next day where you left off.

	Sunday	Monday	Tuesday	Wednesday	Thursday	Friday	Saturday
Week 1	Matthew 1–4	5–7	8–11	12–15	16–19	20–23	24–25
Week 2	26–28	Mark 1–3	4–7	8–10	11–13	14–16	Luke 1–2
Week 3	3–6	7–9	10–12	13–15	16–18	19–21	22–24
Week 4	John 1–2	3–5	6–8	9–12	13–17	18–21	Acts 1–4
Week 5	5–7	8–9	10–12	13–15	16–18	19–23	24–26
Week 6	27–28	Romans 1–3	4–5	6–8	9–11	12–16	1 Corinthians 1–6
Week 7	7–11	12–14	15–16	2 Corinthians 1–6	7–9	10–13	Galatians 1–6
Week 8	Ephesians 1–6	Philippians 1–4	Colossians 1–4	1 Thessalonians 1–5	2 Thessalonians 1–3	1 Timothy 1–3	4–6
Week 9	2 Timothy 1–3	Titus 1–3	Philemon	Hebrews 1–2	3–4	5–7	8–10
Week 10	11–13	James 1–5	1 Peter 1–5	2 Peter 1–5	1 John 1–5	2 John, 3 John	Jude
Week 11	Revelation 1–3	4–6	7–9	10–13	14–16	17–19	20–22
Week 12	Catch up if you're behind.						

ANSWERS TO SCRIPTURE STUDIES

This section will provide you with useful Scripture passages relating to and refuting the beliefs of the cults and religions we have studied. The topics covered on the left-hand side of the fill-in pages in each chapter are answered in the same order they were found. In the event that a topic was covered in a previous chapter and repeated later, refer to the first instance for helpful scriptures. For example, salvation by works is a common false belief, so verses disproving this error are not listed under every cult and religion that holds to it. There are many verses in God's Word that disprove false doctrine—many that aren't listed here. Try to find verses on your own before referring to this list.

ISLAM

The Nature of God
Ezekiel 33:11
2 Peter 3:9
1 Peter 5:7
1 John 4:9–10
John 3:16
Romans 5:8
James 1:17
James 1:13–15
Luke 1:78–79
Psalm 119:105
Jeremiah 31:3
Matthew 18:14
John 10:28

Jesus, Mary, and the Trinity
Matthew 1:20
Luke 1:35
Matthew 3:11
Matthew 3:16–17
Matthew 11:4–6
1 Timothy 3:16
Luke 4:14–20
1 John 5:20
Revelation 21:6
Hebrews 1:1–4
Hebrews 2:8
1 John 5:10–11
Colossians 1:16–18
John 19:25–30
Matthew 27:3–5

2 Corinthians 13:14
Matthew 28:18–20
Genesis 1:26

Salvation
Ephesians 2:8–9
Titus 3:4–7
2 Timothy 1:8–9
Hebrews 4:15–16
Hebrews 7:25
1 Timothy 2:5–6
Job 9:33
2 Corinthians 5:21
Isaiah 53:5–6

The Law and the Gospel
2 Timothy 3:16
2 Peter 1:21
Isaiah 40:8
2 Peter 1:16
Luke 1:1–4
Matthew 5:17
Luke 24:44
2 Corinthians 11:4
Galatians 1:6–7

Treatment of Non-Muslims
Proverbs 25:21–22
Matthew 5:21–22
Matthew 5:38–48
2 Timothy 2:24–26
Colossians 3:8

HINDUISM

The Nature of God
John 14:30
1 Peter 5:8
John 10:10
1 Corinthians 10:20–21
Deuteronomy 6:4–6
Exodus 20:3–5
Isaiah 43:10
James 2:19
James 1:17
1 John 1:5
Revelation 15:3–4
1 Peter 1:16
Numbers 23:19
John 3:16
1 Corinthians 8:6
Romans 1:23
John 3:17
Matthew 18:14
Romans 5:6
Proverbs 8:13
Psalm 91:2
Judges 10:16
Song of Solomon 2:16
1 John 4:19
1 John 4:7–12
Isaiah 54:10
1 Peter 5:7

Jesus
Isaiah 9:6
Mark 1:11

Romans 5:17
Hebrews 4:14–16
Hebrews 7:26
Colossians 1:15

Salvation
Hebrews 9:12
Matthew 9:13
John 14:6
Romans 4:4–5

Life, Death, and Enlightenment
2 Corinthians 5:1
Hebrews 9:27
Philippians 1:21–23
Romans 9:11
Romans 2:16
Matthew 25:31–32
Acts 10:42
1 Peter 4:5
Acts 17:30–31

Roles in Society
1 Peter 3:7
Colossians 3:18–19
Galatians 3:28
Psalm 34:6

Astrology
Isaiah 47:12–14
Jeremiah 10:2

BUDDHISM

Scriptures
Luke 1:1–2
1 Corinthians 15:3–7
Matthew 28:1–3, 11–15
2 Peter 1:16–21

The Nature of God
Genesis 1:1
Jeremiah 27:5
Joshua 3:10
Psalm 42:2
Jeremiah 10:10
Judges 10:16
Jeremiah 31:3
1 Corinthians 6:17
Matthew 6:25–33
Job 38:1–4
Micah 6:8

The Way to Truth and Wisdom
Ecclesiastes 12:13
Psalm 119:130
John 14:6
Romans 9:16
Isaiah 64:6
Psalm 33:20
Matthew 11:28–29
Hebrews 4:9–10
Romans 10:4
Romans 7:18–25
Proverbs 20:9
Jeremiah 17:10
Galatians 6:7–8
Isaiah 53:6
Isaiah 1:4–6
Romans 3:10–18
Matthew 15:18–19
Psalm 119:105
Proverbs 3:5–6
Jeremiah 17:5

Jesus
2 Corinthians 5:15, 21

Hebrews 9:12
Hebrews 9:22

The Natural World
Genesis 1:1–2:1
Job 38:4–14
Genesis 8:21–22
Psalm 24:1

Life, Death, and Enlightenment
See section under Hinduism.

MORMONISM

Salvation and the Church
Matthew 7:15
Matthew 24:11
1 Peter 2:9–10
Hebrews 7:22–28
Revelation 1:4–6
Acts 4:12
John 1:12
1 Thessalonians 5:9
Titus 3:4–6
Matthew 16:18
Psalm 100:5
Galatians 1:6–9
Acts 14:15–17
Romans 10:3–4
1 John 1:7
Acts 16:31
2 Corinthians 6:16–18
2 Corinthians 7:1
1 Corinthians 15:29
1 Corinthians 1:14–17

Jesus
Isaiah 7:14
Matthew 1:18–20
Genesis 3:1
John 1:1–3
Hebrews 1:3

2 Corinthians 6:14–15
Revelation 12:9–10

God and Man
Deuteronomy 6:4–6
Numbers 23:19
Romans 1:22–23
Hosea 11:9
Isaiah 43:10
Isaiah 44:8
Isaiah 45:6
Isaiah 45:21–22
Isaiah 46:9
Malachi 3:6
Psalm 102:27
Colossians 1:16–17
1 Timothy 2:5
Deuteronomy 4:35
1 Corinthians 8:4–6
John 4:24
Luke 24:39
1 Kings 8:27
1 John 4:12

Knowing Truth
Proverbs 14:12
Jeremiah 17:9–10
Matthew 15:18–20
Ephesians 4:13–14
Titus 1:2
Isaiah 33:6
2 Peter 1:3
1 John 4:1

Revelation and Doctrine
1 Timothy 6:3–4
2 Corinthians 13:5
Revelation 2:2
1 John 4:1
1 Thessalonians 5:21
2 Peter 1:3
Matthew 24:11
Proverbs 30:6
Deuteronomy 4:2
Revelation 22:18–19

Marriage
Leviticus 18:18
Deuteronomy 17:17
Ephesians 5:31

Equality
Galatians 3:28
Colossians 3:11
Romans 10:12–13
Acts 10:34–35
Acts 17:26
Revelation 5:9
Revelation 7:9

JEHOVAH'S WITNESS

Jesus' Divinity
Hebrews 1:3
Colossians 1:16–17
Isaiah 44:24
Hebrews 1:10
John 8:58
Daniel 10:13
Hebrews 1:5–13
Colossians 2:9
John 10:30
1 John 5:20
Titus 2:13
Acts 2:36

Jesus' Resurrection
Luke 24:37–43
1 Corinthians 15:3–8, 44
John 2:19–22
John 20:15–18
Acts 1:11

Jesus as the Christ
Ephesians 1:4–5
1 Peter 1:20
John 5:8
Revelation 1:7
John 3:17
Luke 23:34
1 Corinthians 15:3

1 Timothy 1:15
2 Corinthians 5:15–21
Hebrews 1:3
Hebrews 9:26–28
Romans 3:23–24
1 John 2:2
John 1:29

Jesus' Return
1 Thessalonians 3:13
Matthew 24:14
Matthew 24:30
Revelation 19:11–16

The Holy Spirit
Acts 13:2
Ephesians 4:30
1 Corinthians 12:11
1 Corinthians 2:11
Matthew 12:32

The Trinity
Genesis 1:26–27
Isaiah 6:1–10
Luke 1:35
Luke 1:21–22
Matthew 28:19
1 Corinthians 12:4–6
2 Corinthians 13:14
John 1:33–34
John 4:16, 26
1 John 4:2

Salvation
See other "Salvation"
sections.

Heaven and Hell
Revelation 7:9
John 14:2
1 Timothy 2:5
Revelation 21:1–3
Revelation 20:10
Matthew 25:41
Jude 1:7
Luke 16:23

THE NEW AGE MOVEMENT

The Nature of Truth
Psalm 119:89
John 18:37
1 Timothy 2:3–7
Romans 1:25
Hebrews 10:26
John 14:6

The Nature of God
Genesis 2:4
Deuteronomy 3:24
Deuteronomy 4:29
2 Kings 19:15
Psalm 115:3
Ecclesiastes 5:2
Acts 17:24
Romans 1:25

Jesus
Luke 2:26
Luke 2:11
Matthew 24:4–5
Matthew 24:23–27
2 Thessalonians 2:1–12
1 John 2:18–27
Also see "Jesus' Return"
under Jehovah's Witness.

Angels, Spirits, and the Dead
Leviticus 20:6
Leviticus 20:27
Acts 16:16
Revelation 9:20–21
Deuteronomy 18:9–12
1 Corinthians 6:3
Galatians 1:6–9
2 Corinthians 11:14
Hebrews 1:14
Psalm 103:20
Matthew 25:41
Revelation 22:8–9

Mark 5:9
Psalm 54:4
Luke 16:22–26
Isaiah 8:19–20
Ecclesiastes 9:5–6

Humanity and Perfection
Romans 3:23
2 Timothy 3:1–5
2 Timothy 3:13
Jeremiah 17:9–10
Numbers 23:19
Ephesians 4:11–13
2 Peter 3:18

The Earth and the Current Age
1 Corinthians 1:20
2 Corinthians 4:4
Job 38:31–33
Daniel 2:20–21
Ephesians 1:7–10
Ephesians 1:20–21
Matthew 24:3–31
2 Peter 3:11–13
Revelation 22:12–13
Revelation 21:1–3

NOTES

LESSON 4: KEYS TO SHARING THE GOSPEL WITH PEOPLE FROM CULTS AND WORLD RELIGIONS

1. Laurence Singlehurst, *Sowing, Reaping, and Keeping* (Leicester, England: Crossway Books, 1995), 25.

LESSON 5: ISLAM

1. Patrick Johnstone and Jason Mandryk, *Operation World: 21st Century Edition,* updated and revised ed. (Tyrone, Ga.: Authentic Media, 2005), 255.

2. Population data is from Johnstone and Mandryk, *Operation World,* 658, 311, 255, 540, 160, 619.

3. Douglas Layton, *Deceiving a Nation: Islam in America* (Nashville: World Impact Press, 2002), 168.

4. Douglas Layton, "Answering Islam" (lecture, Church of St. Clement, El Paso, Texas, February 15, 2003).

5. "The Salah (Obligatory Prayer of the Muslims): Rakat 2," *Muttaqun Online: For Those Who Fear Allah,* December 12, 2008, http://muttaqun.com/salah.html#rakat2.

6. Isaac Adams, *Persia by a Persian: Personal Experiences, Manners, Customs, Habits, Religious and Social Life in Persia* (E. Stock Publications, 1906), 436.

7. Jack Kelley, "Devotion, Desire Drive Youth to 'Martyrdom,'" *USA Today,* June 26, 2001.

8. Layton, "Answering Islam."

9. Eric Pement, "Louis Farrakhan and the Nation of Islam, Part I," *Cornerstone Magazine* (1999), http://www.cornerstonemag.com/features/iss111/islam1.htm.

10. "Islam and Slavery," *Barnabas Fund* (March–April 2007): iii–iv.

11. Robert Spencer, "Sudanese Christian Slave 'Crucified' by Muslim Master," *Dhimmi Watch,* April 7, 2004, http://www.jihadwatch.org/dhimmiwatch/archives/001481.php.

12. "UNHCR Wants Muslim Countries to Help Refugees," Agence France Presse, October 14, 2006, http://www.arabnews.com/?page=4&section=0&article=88188&d=14&m=10&y=2006.

13. "Indonesians Jailed for Beheadings," *BBC News,* March 21, 2007, http://news.bbc.co.uk/2/hi/asia-pacific/6473897.stm.

14. "Sudan arrests UK teacher for teddy bear blasphemy," *CNN,* November 26, 2007, http://www.cnn.com/2007/WORLD/africa/11/26/sudan.bear/index.html.

15. "The rise of the female suicide bomber: Number of Iraq attacks involving women has doubled this year," *Associated Press,* June 7, 2008, http://www.msnbc.msn.com/id/25015072/.

16. "Muslim cartoon fury claims lives," *BBC News,* February 6, 2006, http://news.bbc.co.uk/2/hi/south_asia/4684652.stm.

17. Jon Dougherty, "Radical Islam blamed for French rioting," *WorldNetDaily,* November 5, 2005, http://www.wnd.com/index.php?pageId=33243.

18. Eric Lacitis, "National Publisher Kills Spokane Journalist's Book," *Seattle Times,* August 20, 2008, http://seattletimes.nwsource.com/html/localnews/2008125629_yankedbook20m.html.

19. Don Richardson, *Secrets of the Koran* (Ventura: Regal, 2003), 54.

20. Brigitte Gabriel, *Because They Hate* (New York: St. Martin's Press, 2006), 202. The Ayatollah's role as the leader of the Shiite world resulted in a devastating war with Sunni-dominated Iraq, in which Iranian children were sent into battle with a plastic key to paradise hung around their necks. The Ayatollah's teachings inspired the formation of the radical organization Hezbollah (see http://www.globalsecurity.org/military/world/para/hizballah.htm), which has been responsible for numerous suicide bombings and other terrorist attacks.

21. Peter Hammond, *Slavery, Terrorism and Islam: The Historical Roots and Contemporary Threat* (Cape Town, South Africa: Christian Liberty Books, 2005), 105.

22. Manabu Kitagawa, "Asia: For Abused And Bullied Afghan Women, Suicide Can Be The Only Way Out," *Asahi,* May 24, 2007, http://www.womenforafghanwomen.org/press/Asahi5_24_07.html.

23. Diane Moder, *Islam: Unveiling the System . . . Loving the People!* (Weirton, WV: ISA Publications, 2003), 13.4.

24. Lara Setrakian, "Yemen's 8-Year-Old Divorcee," *ABC News,* April 25, 2008, http://abcnews.go.com/International/story?id=4725577&page=1.

25. Shafika Mattar, "Father Kills Daughter; Doubted Virginity," *Free Republic,* January 25, 2007, http://www.freerepublic.com/focus/f-news/1773460/posts.

26. "Slain Over Hijab? Father Allegedly Strangles Daughter Over Head Scarf," *ABC News,* December 12, 2007. http://abcnews.go.com/GMA/story?id=3987812.

27. "Saudi Rape Victim Gets 200 Lashes and Jail," *Associated Press,* Riyadh, Saudi Arabia, November 21, 2007, http://www.cbsnews.com/stories/2007/11/16/world/main3511560.shtml?source=search_story.

28. Bruce Loudon, "Married at 9, slain by parents at 17," *The Australian,* September 6, 2008, http://www.news.com.au/story/0,23599,24302102–401,00.html.

29. "Muslim father burns Christian daughter alive," *WorldNetDaily,* August 13, 2008, http://www.wnd.com/index.php?fa=PAGE.view&pageId=72273.

30. "Somali rape victim, 13, stoned to death," *Associated Press,* November 1, 2008, http://abcnews.go.com/International/wireStory?id=6161141.

31. Noor Khan and Heidi Vogt, "Acid Attacks Keep Afghan Girls Away From Classes," *Associated Press*, Kandahar, Afghanistan, November 14, 2008, http://abcnews.go.com/International/wireStory?id=6251856.

32. Quoted in Robert Spencer, *Islam Unveiled: Disturbing Questions About the World's Fastest-Growing Faith* (San Francisco: Encounter Books, 2002), 48.

33. Moder, *Islam*, 13.9.

34. Hadeel Al-Shalchi, "8-Year-Old Saudi Girl Divorces 50-Year-Old Husband," *ABC News*, April 30, 2009, http://abcnews.com/International/wireStory?id=7471227.

35. Richardson, *Secrets of the Koran*, 69.

36. Jeffrey Goldberg, "Inside Jihad U.; The Education of a Holy Warrior," *New York Times*, June 25, 2000, http://query.nytimes.com/gst/fullpage.html?res=9501E0DA1531F936A15755C0A9669C8B63&scp=1&sq=Inside%20Jihad%20U.;%20The%20Education%200f%20a%20Holy%20Warrior&st=cse.

37. Gerard Chaliand and Arnaud Blin, eds., *The History of Terrorism: From Antiquity to al Qaeda* (Berkeley: University of California Press, 2007), 420.

38. Johnstone and Mandryk, *Operation World*, 662.

39. Ibid., 14.

LESSON 5: SCRIPTURE STUDY

1. Koranic quotations come from the Pickthall and Yusuf Ali editions.

LESSON 6: HINDUISM

1. Dean C. Halverson, *The Compact Guide to World Religions* (Minneapolis: Bethany House Publishers, 1996), 88.

2. Mary Pat Fisher, *Living Religions*, 5th ed. (Upper Saddle River, N.J.: Prentice-Hall, 2002), 118.

3. Ibid., 88.

4. Ibid., 87.

5. "The Code of Manu," *Truth Seekers International*, September 2008, New Delhi, India.

6. Satish Jacob, "Buddhism's Appeal for Low Caste Hindus," *BBC News*, November 5, 2001, http://news.bbc.co.uk/1/hi/world/south_asia/1639245.stm.

7. J. Lee Grady, "God's Moment for India," *Charisma Magazine* (February 2009): 27–33, 58–60.

8. "YOGA: Today's Lifestyle for Health," Let Us Reason Ministries, 2008, http://www.letusreason.org/NAM1.htm.

9. Fisher, *Living Religions*, 131.

10. Chandrika Mago, "Of Holy Cow and Designer Milk," *The Times of India*, August 29, 2004, http://timesofindia.indiatimes.com/articleshow/831673.cms.

11. Interview with Nagpur pastor, July 1998.

12. "BSI Print Products," Bible Society of India, http://www.bsind.org/print.htm (accessed January 21, 2009).

13. Patrick Johnstone and Jason Mandryk, *Operation World: 21ˢᵗ Century Edition*, updated and revised ed. (Tyrone, Ga.: Authentic Media, 2005), 311.

14. "Building Churches for Unreached Villages," Mission ONE Strategic Project, April 1, 2002.

15. Johnstone and Mandryk, *Operation World*, 316.

16. Avijit Ghosh, "Farmer Suicide in Prosperous Western UP," *The Times of India*, May 9, 2007, http://timesofindia.indiatimes.com/articleshow/2020078.cms.

17. Shefali Srinivas, "Low-Caste Women to Protest at UN Racism Meeting," *Women's E News*, August 17, 2001, http://www.womensenews.org/article.cfm/dyn/aid/448/context/archive.

18. "Legacy of the Devadasi System," Weaker Section Welfare Association, http://weswa.org/devadasi.htm.

19. Suchandana Gupta, "Woman's Death Sparks 'Sati' Row," *The Times of India*, August 23, 2006, http://timesofindia.indiatimes.com/articleshow/1917392.cms; Himanshi Dhawan, "Sati Law To Get Tougher," *The Times of India*, July 14, 2007, http://timesofindia.indiatimes.com/articleshow/2202409.cms.

20. Fisher, *Living Religions*, 88.

21. Ron Rhodes, *The Challenge of the Cults and New Religions* (Grand Rapids: Zondervan, 2001), 187.

22. Bobbie Kalman, *India: The Culture* (New York: Crabtree Publishing Company, 1990), 26.

LESSON 6: SCRIPTURE STUDY

1. Bhagavad Gita 10:34.

2. Bhagavad Gita 11:25.

3. Bhagavad Gita 4:8.

4. Bhagavad Gita 11:32.

5. Bhagavad Gita 18:45.

6. Bhagavad Gita 4:10.

7. Bhagavad Gita 8:16.

8. Code of Manu 5:148.

9. Bhagavad Gita 4:13.

LESSON 7: BUDDHISM

1. Fritz Ridenour, *So What's the Difference?* (Ventura, Calif.: Regal, 2001), 100.

2. Josh McDowell and Don Stewart, *Handbook of Today's Religions* (Nashville: Thomas Nelson, 1983), 310.

3. Mary Pat Fisher, *Living Religions*, 5th ed. (Upper Saddle River, N.J.: Prentice-Hall, 2002), 157.

4. Patrick Johnstone and Jason Mandryk, *Operation World: 21ˢᵗ Century Edition*, updated and revised ed. (Tyrone, Ga.: Authentic Media, 2005), 2.

5. Arthur Versluis, *American Transcendentalism and Asian Religions* (New York: Oxford University Press, 1993), 79.

6. "Buddhism in America: A New American Icon?" *Christian Research Report* 11, no. 2 (1998), http://www.equip.org/articles/buddhism-in-america.

7. John Weldon, "Nichiren Shoshu Buddhism: Mystical

Materialism for the Masses," *Christian Research Institute*, http://www.equip.org/articles/nichiren-shoshu-buddhism.

8. Binaj Gurubacharya, "Buddha Boy in Nepal Re-Emerges After a Year," *ABC News*, November 11, 2008, http://abcnews.go.com/International/wireStory?id=6227385.

9. Ridenour, *So What's the Difference?*, 101.

10. Geshe Dakpa Topgyal, "Introduction to Buddhism: Part 2," South Carolina Dharma Group, http://scdharma.org/portal/resources/intro2.htm.

11. Melford E. Spiro, *Buddhism and Society* (Berkeley: University of California Press, 1982), 292.

12. Bhikku Thick Minh Thanh, "Chronological Survey of the Nikayas," in *The Mind in Early Buddhism*, http://www.buddhanet.net/budsas/ebud/mind/02_chap2.htm.

13. Ven. Suvanno Mahathera, *The 31 Planes of Existence* (Penang, Malaysia: Inward Path, 2001), 18.

14. Dean C. Halverson, *The Compact Guide to World Religions* (Minneapolis: Bethany House Publishers, 1996), 56.

15. J. Isamu Yamamoto, "The Arrival of Theravada: Southeast Asians Bring Their School of Buddhism to America," *Christian Research Journal* 17, no. 2 (1994), http://www.equip.org/PDF/DB565-2.pdf.

16. Fisher, *Living Religions*, 165.

17. Ridenour, *So What's the Difference?*, 103.

18. McDowell and Stewart, *Handbook of Today's Religions*, 310.

19. J. Isamu Yamamoto, "Zest for Zen: North Americans Embrace a Contemplative School of Buddhism," *Christian Research Journal* 17, no. 3 (1995), http://www.equip.org/PDF/DB565-3.pdf

20. McDowell and Stewart, *Handbook of Today's Religions*, 318.

21. Yamamoto, "Zest for Zen."

22. Ridenour, *So What's the Difference?*, 103.

23. Weldon, "Nichiren Shoshu Buddhism."

24. McDowell and Stewart, *Handbook of Today's Religions*, 317.

25. Weldon, "Nichiren Shoshu Buddhism."

26. Keziah Scott, audio lecture.

LESSON 7: SCRIPTURE STUDY

1. Dhammapada 18:236.

2. Stanzas of the Dhammapada, selection 5, Mahindarama Sunday Pali School, http://www.mahindarama.com/mbt/stanza.htm.

3. Dhammapada 23:327.

4. Dhammapada 12:165.

5. Colonel H. S. Olcott, "A Buddhist Creed," quoted in Christmas Humphreys, *Buddhism* (London: Penguin Books, 1962), 72.

6. Yasuji Kirimura, *Fundamentals of Buddhism* (Tokyo: Nichiren Shoshu International Center, 1978), 161, quoted in John Weldon, "Nichiren Shoshu Buddhism Mystical Materialism for the Masses," *Christian Research Journal* (Fall 1992): 8.

7. Mahaparinibbana-sutta 2:33.

LESSON 9: MORMONISM

1. Joel B. Groat, "A Mormon General Authority's Doubts About the Authenticity of the Book of Mormon," Institute for Religious Research, http://www.irr.org/mit/studies-bom-br.html.

2. Allen Harrod, "Who Was Joseph Smith?" *The Watchman Expositor* 16, no. 1 (1999), http://www.watchman.org/lds/whoisjosephsmith.htm.

3. Harrod, "Who Was Joseph Smith?"

4. Chuck Sackett, *What's Going On In There? The Verbatim Text of the Mormon Temple Rituals Annotated and Explained by a Former Temple Worker* (Ministry to Mormons, 1982), 13–14.

5. Bill McKeever, "The Nauvoo Pentagrams," Mormonism Research Ministry, http://www.mrm.org/topics/the-mormon-temple/the-nauvoo-pentagrams.

6. *Journal of Discourses*, vol. 2, 47.

7. Fawn M. Brodie, *No Man Knows My History: The Life of Joseph Smith* (New York: Vintage Books, 1995), xii.

8. "Helen Mar Kimball," Remembering the Wives of Joseph Smith, http://www.wivesofjosephsmith.org/26-HelenMarKimball.htm.

9. Fritz Ridenour, *So What's the Difference?* (Ventura, Calif.: Regal, 2001), 134.

10. George A. Mather and Larry A. Nichols, *Dictionary of Cults, Sects, Religions and the Occult* (Grand Rapids: Zondervan, 1993), 191.

11. Peggy Fletcher Stack, "Mormon milestone: Missionary army has enlisted 1 million since church's 1830 founding," *The Salt Lake Tribune, USA*, June 26, 2007, under The Ross Institute Internet Archives, http://www.rickross.com/reference/mormon/mormon405.html.

12. Ron Rhodes and Marian Bodine, *Reasoning from the Scriptures with the Mormons* (Eugene: Harvest House Publishers, 1995), 32.

13. *Journal of Discourses*, vol. 9, 37.

14. Stanley B. Kimball, *Heber C. Kimball: Mormon Patriarch and Pioneer* (Champaign, Ill.: University of Illinois Press, 1981), 228; Jill Martin Rische, "The Pain of Polygamy," *The Watchman Expositor* 18, no. 1 (2001), http://www.watchman.org/lds/painpolygamy.htm.

15. "Rape in Utah," *Utah Commission on Criminal and Juvenile Justice* (2001): 3, http://www.justice.utah.gov/research/sexoffender/rapeinutah.pdf.

16. Ned Searle and Julie Christenson, "Domestic Violence in Utah 2007," Governor's Violence Against Women and Families Cabinet Council (2007), http://www.nomoresecrets.utah.gov/DVReports/2007DVReport.pdf.

17. Shelley Osterloh, "Teen Suicide," *KSL-TV,* June 9, 2000, http://web.ksl.com/dump/news/cc/suic0609.htm#more.
18. Russell Goldman, "Two Studies Find Depression Widespread in Utah," *ABC News,* March 7, 2008, http://abcnews.go.com/Health/MindMoodNews/story?id=4403731&page=1.
19. "Can I Get a Witness to the Book of Mormon Translated?" Let Us Reason Ministries, http://www.letusreason.org/LDS14.htm.
20. Walter R. Martin, *The Kingdom of the Cults* (Minneapolis: Bethany Fellowship Publishers, 1974), 163.
21. Ibid., 170. Also Groat, "A Mormon General Authority's."
22. Martin, *The Kingdom of the Cults,* 165.
23. James Walker, "The Book of Abraham Translation," *The Watchman Expositor* 9, no. 4 (1992), http:/watchman.org/lds/abraham2.htm.
24. *History of the Church,* vol. 4, 461. (See also *Doctrine and Covenants* 42:12 and 135:3.)
25. Milton R. Hunter of the First Council of Seventy, *The Gospel Through the Ages,* quoted in Rob Phillips, "A Side-by-Side Comparison," *Christian Post Contributor,* November 25, 2007, http://www.rickross.com/reference/mormon/mormon458.html.
26. Alan W. Gomes, *Truth and Error: Comparative Charts of Cults and Christianity* (Grand Rapids: Zondervan, 1998), 15.
27. Rhodes and Bodine, *Reasoning from the Scriptures,* 372.
28. *Doctrines of Salvation,* vol. 2, 133, quoted in Rick Branch, "Hell, Paradise and Spirit Missionaries," *The Watchman Expositor* 8, no. 4 (1991), http:/watchman.org/lds/hell.htm.
29. Josh McDowell and Don Stewart, *Handbook of Today's Religions* (Nashville: Thomas Nelson, 1983), 71.
30. Sackett, *What's Going On In There?,* 53.
31. *Doctrine and Covenants* 132:63.
32. *Journal of Discourses,* vol. 8, 178–179.
33. Sackett, *What's Going On In There?,* 20.
34. Ridenour, *So What's the Difference?,* 134.
35. Jill Martin Rische, "The Pain of Polygamy," *The Watchman Expositor* 18, no. 1 (2001), http://www.watchman.org/lds/painpolygamy.htm.
36. Melvin Joseph Ballard, *Three Degrees of Glory,* quoted in Bill McKeever, "Black Skin and the Seed of Cain," Mormonism Research Ministry, http://mrm.org/topics/miscellaneous/black-skin-and-seed-cain.
37. Matthew J. Slick, "Some of the Many Changes in the Book of Mormon," *Christian Apologetics & Research Ministry,* http://www.carm.org/lds/bom_changes.htm.
38. Bill McKeever, "Aliens? LDS Leaders Insist 'We Are Not Alone,'" Mormonism Research Ministry, http://mrm.org/topics/miscellaneous/aliens-lds-leaders-insist-we-are-not-alone; Also Rick Branch, "Mormonism Explains: God's Grace is Inadequate for Salvation,"
The Watchman Expositor 6, no.10 (1989), http://www.watchman.org/lds/grace.htm.
39. The National Museum of Natural History, Department of Anthropology at the Smithsonian Institute, Washington, D.C., quoted in Jeff Dannemiller, "It's Your Choice: Believe the Heart, Believe the Facts," *The Watchman Expositor* 7, no. 9 (1990), http://www.watchman.org/lds/heart.htm.
40. Martin, *The Kingdom of the Cults,* 162–163.
41. Thomas Key, "A Biologist Examines the Book of Mormon," *Journal of The American Scientific Affiliation* XXXVII, no. 2 (1985).
42. Martin, *The Kingdom of the Cults,* 163.
43. Rhodes and Bodine, *Reasoning from the Scriptures,* 126.
44. Marvin W. Cowan, *Mormon Claims Answered* (n.p.: Utah Christian Publications, 1984), 48. Text available online at Utah Lighthouse Ministry, http://www.utlm.org/onlinebooks/mclaimscontents.htm.
45. Ibid., 48.

SIMILARITIES BETWEEN ISLAM AND MORMONISM
1. Joseph Smith, quoted in Timothy Marr, *The Cultural Roots of American Islamicism* (New York: Cambridge University Press, 2006), 199.

THEOLOGY 101: CAN WE TRUST THE BIBLE?
1. "Manuscript Evidence for Superior New Testament Reliability," Christian Apologetics & Research Ministry, http://www.carm.org/questions/about-bible/manuscript-evidence-superior-new-testament-reliability.
2. Joseph P. Gudel, "To Every Muslim an Answer," Christian Research Institute, http://www.equip.org/articles/to-every-muslim-an-answer-.
3. "Manuscript Evidence for Superior New Testament Reliability."
4. Greg Garrison, "Unscrolling the Commandments," Religion News Blog, under *The Birmingham News, USA,* January 6, 2005, http://www.religionnewsblog.com/9828/unscrolling-the-commandments.

LESSON 9: SCRIPTURE STUDY
1. *Doctrines of Salvation,* vol. 1, 188, cited in "What Does Mormonism Teach," Christian Apologetics & Research Ministry, http://www.carm.org/religious-movements/mormonism/what-does-mormonism-teach.
2. *Journal of Discourses,* vol. 7, 289.
3. *Doctrine and Covenants* 1:30.
4. Lowell L. Bennion, *The Religion of the Latter-day Saints,* 160, quoted in "I Bear You My Testimony," Let Us Reason Ministries, http://www.letusreason.org/LDS23.htm.
5. *Journal of Discourses,* vol. 8, 115.
6. *Doctrines of Salvation,* vol. 2, 48.
7. *Ensign,* February 1982, 39–40, quoted in Rick Branch, "The Church of Jesus Christ of Latter-day Saints,"

Watchman Fellowship Profile 10, no. 2 (1993), http://www.watchman.org/profile/ldspro.htm.

8. Joseph Smith, *Teachings of the Prophet Joseph Smith,* 345–346.

9. *Doctrine and Covenants* 130:22.

10. *Journal of Discourses,* vol. 11, 269.

11. *Journal of Discourses,* vol. 7, 290.

12. *Ensign,* June 1988, 59, quoted in Timothy Oliver, Rick Branch, and James Walker, "Historical Events, Notable Doctrines: Mormonism Overview," *The Watchman Expositor* 13, no. 4 (1996).

LESSON 10: JEHOVAH'S WITNESS

1. Ralph F. Wilson, "Correct Spelling and Pronunciation of Yahweh vs. Jehovah," Jesus Walk, http://www.jesuswalk.com/names-god/yahweh_jehovah.htm.

2. David A. Reed, "Michael Jackson Leaves Jehovah's Witnesses," Christian Research Institute, http://www.equip.org/articles/michael-jackson-leaves-jehovah-s-witnesses.

3. Edna Gundersen, "Prince Shows Off a Different Side for '21 Nights,'" *USA Today,* September 27, 2008, http://www.usatoday.com/life/books/news/2008-09-25-prince-21-nights_N.htm.

4. "Statistics: 2008 Report of Jehovah's Witnesses Worldwide," Watch Tower Bible and Tract Society of Pennsylvania, http://www.watchtower.org/e/statistics/wholereport.htm.

5. Craig Branch, "Watchtower Dodges," *The Watchman Expositor* 8, no. 9 (1991), http://www.watchman.org/jw/dodges.htm.

6. Jerry Bergman, "Paradise Postponed…and Postponed: Why Jehovah's Witnesses Have a High Mental Illness Level," *Christian Research Journal* 19, no. 1 (1996), http://www.equip.org/articles/paradise-postponed-and-postponed.

7. "Statistics: 2008 Report of Jehovah's Witnesses Worldwide," Watch Tower Bible and Tract Society of Pennsylvania, http://www.watchtower.org/e/statistics/worldwide_report.htm.

8. Jason Barker, "For Ever, O Lord, Thy Word is Settled in Heaven," *The Watchman Expositor* 16, no. 2 (1998), http://www.watchman.org/cults/wordforever.htm.

9. Ron Rhodes, *Reasoning from the Scriptures with the Jehovah's Witnesses* (Eugene: Harvest House Publishers, 1993), 97–98.

10. Jason Barker, "For Ever, O Lord, Thy Word is Settled in Heaven."

11. Ron Rhodes, *Challenge of the Cults and New Religions* (Grand Rapids: Zondervan, 2001), 77.

12. "Current Topics," Watch Tower Bible and Tract Society of Pennsylvania, http://www.watchtower.org/e/current_topics.htm.

13. "Statistics: 2008 Report of Jehovah's Witnesses Worldwide."

14. Ibid.

15. Fritz Ridenour, *So What's the Difference?* (Ventura, Calif.: Regal, 2001), 122.

16. Ibid., 128.

17. Mary Pat Fisher, *Living Religions,* 5th ed. (Upper Saddle River, N.J.: Prentice-Hall, 2002), 437.

18. Rick Branch, James Walker, and Timothy Oliver, "An Overview of Important Events and Doctrines: New Light on Watchtower History," *The Watchman Expositor* 14, no. 4 (1997), http://www.watchman.org/jw/1404-2.htm.

19. "Statistics: 2008 Report of Jehovah's Witnesses Worldwide."

20. Walter R. Martin, *The Kingdom of the Cults* (Minneapolis: Bethany Fellowship, 1974), 46, 108.

21. Alan W. Gomes, *Truth and Error: Comparative Charts of Cults and Christianity* (Grand Rapids: Zondervan, 1998), 7.

22. Bergman, "Paradise Postponed…and Postponed."

23. Ibid.

24. Ibid.

25. Gomes, *Truth and Error,* 8.

26. Branch, Walker, and Oliver, "An Overview of Important Events and Doctrines."

27. Ibid.

28. Rhodes, *Reasoning from the Scriptures with the Jehovah's Witnesses,* 346–348.

29. Branch, Walker, and Oliver, "An Overview of Important Events and Doctrines."

30. Rhodes, *Reasoning from the Scriptures with the Jehovah's Witnesses,* 350.

31. Scripture references from Everett Shropshire, "Should You Believe in the Watchtower," *The Watchman Expositor* 18, no. 2 (2001).

32. "Have No Dealings with Apostates," *Watchtower* (March 15, 1986): 12–14, reprinted at Christian Apologetics & Research Ministry, http://www.carm.org/religious-movements/jehovahs-witnesses/have-no-dealings-apostates.

LESSON 10: SCRIPTURE STUDY

1. *Should You Believe in the Trinity* (Watch Tower Bible and Tract Society of Pennsylvania, 1989), 14, 20, quoted in Alan W. Gomes, *Truth and Error* (Grand Rapids: Zondervan, 1998), 9.

2. *Survival into a New Earth* (Watch Tower Bible and Tract Society of Pennsylvania), quoted in Timothy Oliver, "Jehovah's Witnesses: Is Jesus Christ Your Mediator," *The Watchman Expositor* 12, no. 3 (1995).

3. *Reasoning from the Scriptures* (Watch Tower Bible and Tract Society of Pennsylvania, 1985), 381, quoted in Alan W. Gomes, *Truth and Error* (Grand Rapids: Zondervan, 1998), 9.

4. *Let God Be True* (Watchtower Bible and Tract Society), 100, quoted in George A. Mather and Larry A. Nichols, *Dictionary of Cults, Sects, Religions and the Occult*

(Grand Rapids: Zondervan, 1993), 151.

5. *The Watchtower,* April 1, 1974, 204, quoted in Rhodes, *Reasoning from the Scriptures with the Jehovah's Witness,* 284.

6. *The Watchtower,* November 15, 1981, 21, quoted in Rhodes, *Reasoning from the Scriptures with the Jehovah's Witness,* 283.

LESSON 11: THE NEW AGE MOVEMENT

1. George A. Mather and Larry A. Nichols, *Dictionary of Cults, Sects, Religions and the Occult* (Grand Rapids: Zondervan, 1993), 202.

2. Dean C. Halverson, *The Compact Guide to World Religions* (Minneapolis: Bethany House Publishers, 1996), 160.

3. Fritz Ridenour, *So What's the Difference?* (Ventura, Calif.: Regal, 2001), 150.

4. James Lovelock, *The Revenge of Gaia: Earth's Climate Crisis & The Fate of Humanity* (New York: Basic Books, 2006), 6, 47.

5. "Maitreya's worldwide appearances," Share International, http://www.share-international.org/maitreya/Ma_wwa.htm.

6. "Oprah Talks to Eckhart Tolle," *O Magazine,* May 2008, http://www.oprah.com/article/omagazine/200805_omag_eckhart_tolle.

7. Susan Wilson, "Heaven on Earth: All Good Everywhere and Non-Good Nowhere," *Transcendental Consciousness* (2009), http://www.transcendentalconsciousness.com/heaven_on_earth.htm.

8. Gail M. Harley, "From Atlantis to America: JZ Knight Encounters Ramtha," in *Controversial New Religions,* ed. James R. Lewis and Jesper Aagaard Petersen (Oxford: Oxford University Press, 2005), 323.

9. Halverson, *The Compact Guide to World Religions,* 163.

10. Craig Branch, "Conversations with the Counterfeit," *Watchman Expositor* 15, no. 3 (1998), http://www.watchman.org/na/conversationswithgod.htm.

11. "Judaism Lexicon: Sorcery," *Israel Today,* January 24, 2006, http://www.israeltoday.co.il/default.aspx?tabid=139&view=item&idx=884.

12. "Can Yoga Be Christianized?" *The Berean Call,* http://www.thebereancall.org/node/5789.

13. "Islamic Leaders in Malaysia Ban Yoga for Muslims," *FOX News,* November 21, 2008, http://www.foxnews.com/story/0,2933,456367,00.html.

14. Jason Barker, "Are We Living in a New Age?" *Watchman Expositor* 16, no. 4 (1999), http://www.watchman.org/na/livinginnewage.htm.

15. "A Brief Timeline of the New Age Movement," *Watchman Expositor* 16, no. 4 (1999), http://www.watchman.org/na/natimeline.htm.

16. Craig Branch, "Re-imagining God: Sophia Worship," *Watchman Expositor* 11, no. 5 (1994), 6.

LESSON 11: SCRIPTURE STUDY

1. H. P. Blavatsky, "What Is Truth?" *Lucifer Magazine* 1, no. 6 (February 15, 1888), quoted in Tamara Hartzell, "Are You 'Being Led Away with the Error of the Wicked' to the New Age Ark of Oneness?" (February 2008, http://www.inthenameofpurpose.org/arkofoneness.pdf), 8.

2. "About Humanity's Team," Humanity's Team: Awakening the World to Oneness, http://humanitysteam.org/about, quoted in Tamara Hartzell, "Are You 'Being Led Away with the Error of the Wicked' to the New Age Ark of Oneness?" (February 2008, http://www.inthenameofpurpose.org/arkofoneness.pdf), 12.

3. Kathy Juline, "Awakening to Your Life's Purpose," *Science of Mind Magazine* (October 2006), reprinted at http://eckharttolle.com/interviews_68.

4. Helen Schucman, *A Course in Miracles,* quoted in Linda Woodhead and Paul Heelas, *Religion in Modern Times: An Interpretive Anthology* (Malden, Mass.: Blackwell, 2000), 161.

5. Helen Schucman, *A Course in Miracles: Combined Volume,* 3rd ed. (Mill Valley, Calif.: Foundation for Inner Peace, 2007), 556.

6. M. Scott Peck, *The Road Less Traveled, 25th Anniversary Edition: A New Psychology of Love, Traditional Values, and Spiritual Growth* (New York: Touchstone, 2003), 270.

7. Rhonda Byrne, *The Secret* (New York: Atria Books, 2006), 164.

8. Juline, "Awakening to Your Life's Purpose."

9. Shri Mataji, "Age of Aquarius," Divine Feminine Adi Shakti, http://www.adishakti.org/age_of_aquarius.htm.

10. James Lovelock, *The Revenge of Gaia: Earth's Climate Crisis & The Fate of Humanity* (New York: Basic Books, 2006), 6 and 47.

NEW AGE IN WESTERN CULTURE

1. Statistics are from the following sources: David W. Moore, "Three in Four Americans Believe in Paranormal," *Gallup News Service,* June 16, 2005, http://www.gallup.com/poll/16915/Three-Four-Americans-Believe-Paranormal.aspx; Dana Blanton, "More Believe in God Than Heaven," *Fox News,* June 18, 2004, http://www.foxnews.com/story/0,2933,99945,00.html; "Barna Survey Examines Changes in Worldview Among Christians in the Past 13 Years," *Barna Group,* March 6, 2009, http://www.barna.org/barna-update/article/21-transformation/252-barna-survey-examines-changes-in-worldview-among-christians-over-the-past-13-years.

2. Statistics from "New Research Explores Teenage Views and Behavior Regarding the Supernatural," Barna Group, January 23, 2006, http://www.barna.org/barna-update/article/5-barna-update/164-new-research-explores-teenage-views-and-behavior-regarding-the-supernatural.

Selected Bibliography and Resources

Most of the books listed here are Christian or secular evaluations of cults, world religions, or cultures. However, four of the books about the New Age movement are primary sources from New Age authors. They are *A Course in Miracles*, *The Road Less Traveled*, *The Secret*, and *The Revenge of Gaia*.

General

Brumback, Carl. *God in Three Persons.* Cleveland, Tenn.: Pathway Press, 1959.

Fisher, Mary Pat. *Living Religions.* Fifth edition. Upper Saddle River, N.J.: Prentice-Hall, 2002. (A seventh edition is now available.)

Freeman, Hobart E. *Every Wind of Doctrine.* Warsaw, Ind.: Faith Ministries & Publications, 1975.

Gomes, Alan W. *Truth and Error: Comparative Charts of Cults and Christianity.* Grand Rapids: Zondervan, 1998.

Halverson, Dean C. *The Compact Guide to World Religions.* Minneapolis: Bethany House, 1996.

Johnstone, Patrick, and Jason Mandryk. *Operation World: 21st Century Edition.* Updated and revised edition. Tyrone, Ga.: Authentic Media, 2005.

Larson, Bob. *Larson's New Book of Cults.* Wheaton: Tyndale House, 1982.

Martin, Walter R. *The Kingdom of the Cults.* Minneapolis: Bethany Fellowship, 1974.

Mather, George A., and Larry A. Nichols. *Dictionary of Cults, Sects, Religions and the Occult.* Grand Rapids: Zondervan, 1993.

McDowell, Josh, and Don Stewart. *Handbook of Today's Religions.* Nashville: Thomas Nelson, 1983.

Rhodes, Ron. *The Challenge of the Cults and New Religions.* Grand Rapids: Zondervan, 2001.

Ridenour, Fritz. *So What's the Difference?* Ventura: Regal, 2001.

Sire, James W. *Scripture Twisting.* Downers Grove, Ill.: InterVarsity Press, 1980.

Woodhead, Linda, and Paul Heelas. *Religion in Modern Times: An Interpretive Anthology.* Malden, Mass.: Blackwell, 2000.

Islam

Abdul-Haqq, Abdiyah Akbar. *Sharing Your Faith with a Muslim.* Minneapolis: Bethany House Publications, 1980.

Al-Araby, Abdullah. *Islam Unveiled.* Los Angeles: The Pen vs. The Sword, 1994.

Al-Araby, Abdullah. *The Islamization of America: The Islamic Strategies and The Christian Response.* Los Angeles: The Pen vs. The Sword, 2003.

Bradley, Mark. *Iran: Open Hearts in a Closed Land.* Colorado Springs: Authentic Media, 2007.

Budd, Jack. *The Heart and Mind of the Muslims: Studies on Islam.* Metro Manila, Philippines: Global Challenge, n.d.

Cati, W. L. *Married to Muhammed.* Lake Mary, Fla.: Creation House, 2001.

Layton, Douglas. *Deceiving a Nation: Islam in America.* Nashville: World Impact Press, 2002.

Moder, Diane. *Islam: Unveiling the System…Loving the People!* Weirton, W.Va.: ISA Publications, 2002.

Otis, George Jr. *The Last of the Giants: Lifting the Veil on Islam and the End Times.* Grand Rapids: Baker Books, 1999.

Parshall, Phil. *Bridges to Islam: A Christian Perspective on Folk Islam.* Grand Rapids: Baker Book House, 1985.

Richardson, Don. *Secrets of the Koran.* Ventura: Regal, 2003.

Spencer, Robert. *Islam Unveiled: Disturbing Questions about the World's Fastest-Growing Faith.* San Francisco: Encounter Books, 2002.

Zacharias, Ravi. *Light in the Shadow of Jihad: The Struggle for Truth.* Sisters, Ore.: Multnomah Publishers, 2002.

HINDUISM

Kalman, Bobbie. *India: The Culture.* New York: Crabtree, 1990.

Thirumalai, Madasamy. *Sharing Your Faith with a Hindu.* Minneapolis: Bethany House, 2002.

BUDDHISM

Spiro, Melford E. *Buddhism and Society.* Berkeley: University of California Press, 1982.

Versluis, Arthur. *American Transcendentalism and Asian Religions.* New York: Oxford University Press, 1993.

MORMONISM

Cowan, Marvin W. *Mormon Claims Answered.* Salt Lake City: Utah Lighthouse Ministries, 1997. Text available online at http://www.utlm.org/onlinebooks/mclaimscontents.htm.

Gruss, Edmond C. *What Every Mormon Should Know.* Accent Books, 1976.

Rhodes, Ron, and Marian Bodine. *Reasoning from the Scriptures with the Mormons.* Eugene: Harvest House, 1995.

Sackett, Chuck. *What's Going On in There? The Verbatim Text of the Mormon Temple Rituals Annotated and Explained by a Former Temple Worker.* Thousand Oaks, Calif.: Sword of the Shepherd Ministries, 1982.

JEHOVAH'S WITNESS

McKinney, George D. *The Theology of Jehovah's Witnesses.* San Diego: Production House, 1975.

Rhodes, Ron. *Reasoning from the Scriptures with the Jehovah's Witnesses.* Eugene: Harvest House, 1993.

NEW AGE MOVEMENT

Ankerberg, John, and John Weldon. *The Facts on the New Age Movement.* Eugene: Harvest House, 1988.

Byrne, Rhonda. *The Secret.* New York: Atria Books, 2006.

Hartzell, Tamara. "Are You 'Being Led Away with the Error of the Wicked' to the New Age Ark of One-ness?" February 2008. http://www.inthenameofpurpose.org/arkofoneness.pdf.

Jones, Peter. *The Gnostic Empire Strikes Back.* Phillipsburg, N.J.: Presbyterian and Reformed Publishing, 1992.

Lovelock, James. *The Revenge of Gaia: Earth's Climate Crisis & The Fate of Humanity.* New York: Basic Books, 2006.

Peck, M. Scott. *The Road Less Traveled: A New Psychology of Love, Traditional Values, and Spiritual Growth.* 25th anniversary edition. New York: Touchstone, 2003.

Schucman, Helen. *A Course in Miracles: Combined Volume.* Third edition. Mill Valley, Calif.: Foundation for Inner Peace, 2007.

USEFUL WEBSITES

The 30-Days Prayer Network, www.30-days.net

Ankerberg Theological Research Institute, www.ankerberg.com/articles.html

Apologetics Index, www.apologeticsindex.org

The Berean Call, www.thebereancall.org

Christian Research Institute, www.equip.org

Cult News from Rick Ross, www.cultnews.com

Kjos Ministries, www.crossroad.to

Operation World, www.operationworld.org/index.html

Spiritual Counterfeits Project, www.scp-inc.org

US Center for World Mission, www.uscwm.org

Walter Martin's Religious InfoNet, www.waltermartin.org

Watchman Fellowship, www.watchman.org

World Religions Index, http://wri.leaderu.com

ABOUT THE AUTHORS

This father/daughter writing team has enjoyed developing this book. Vinnie wrote the original book, and Kimberly updated all its statistics, extensively researched background information, and helped develop the teachings.

Vinnie Carafano lives in El Paso, Texas. He and his wife, Jodie, have four children: Vincent, Kimberly, Kristin, and Julie. Vinnie was the youth pastor of Jesus Chapel East for fourteen years until God called his family into Youth With A Mission's King's Kids ministry in December of 1993. His lifetime commitment is to see young people come into a living relationship with Jesus Christ and affect the world around them.

The Carafano family's missionary travels have taken them to India, the Philippines, Korea, Paraguay, Panama, Nicaragua, Mexico, Canada, Haiti, St. Croix, Barbados, Grenada, Jamaica, Russia, Ethiopia, Ecuador, Taiwan, Thailand, China, and throughout the United States.

Kimberly Arnold and her husband, David, live in El Paso, where they own a Web development and information technology company. Kimberly grew up homeschooled and traveled extensively with the family around the world. She has a BA in English from New Mexico State University.

More volumes in the
Intensive Discipleship Course

You did it! After three months of studying the Word and seeking the Lord, you are not the same person you were when you started. We hope your hunger for God continues. Here are other steps in the Intensive Discipleship Course for continued learning and growth.

Developing Godly Character
This is the foundation of the Intensive Discipleship Course—an intense twelve weeks of spiritual growth, with twelve powerful messages on how you can become who God wants you to be. You'll learn how to study the Bible effectively, develop a strong prayer life, serve in humility, overcome sin, and grow spiritually.
ISBN 978-1-57658-410-1

Being Useful to God Now
Ready to put your faith into action? This volume is all about serving God and others—right now, right where you're at in life. You'll learn how to be an active, effective disciple of Christ by modeling God's love and compassion, studying evangelism techniques, preparing Bible studies, counseling peers through life-controlling problems, and hearing God's call on your life.
ISBN 978-1-57658-470-5

Knowing God's Heart: Missions and Evangelism
Here are twelve weeks of outward thinking. You'll dive into the Word and discover the Lord's perspectives on the poor, the suffering, and the lost. You'll learn about God's grand, unfolding plan for the world, discover where you fit into this plan, and gain the tools you'll need to accomplish God's purposes in your life.
ISBN 978-1-57658-520-7 (forthcoming)

Available at your local Christian bookstore or through YWAM Publishing
www.ywampublishing.com
1-800-922-2143